Retirement In Canada

by

P. Lynn McDonald

Faculty of Social Work
The University of Calgary

and

Richard A. Wanner

Department of Sociology
The University of Calgary

Butterworths
Toronto and Vancouver

Retirement In Canada
© 1990 Butterworths Canada Ltd.

Printed and bound in Canada

The Butterworth Group of Companies

Canada:	Butterworths Canada Ltd., Toronto and Vancouver, 75 Clegg Road, Markham, Ontario, L6G 1A1 and 409 Granville St., Ste. 1455, Vancouver, B.C., V6C 1T2
Australia	Butterworths Pty Ltd., Sydney, Melbourne, Brisbane, Adelaide, Perth, Canberra and Hobart
Ireland	Butterworths (Ireland) Ltd., Dublin
New Zealand	Butterworths of New Zealand Ltd., Wellington and Auckland
Puerto Rico	Equity de Puerto Rico, Inc., Hato Rey
Singapore	Malayan Law Journal Pte. Ltd., Singapore
United Kingdom	Butterworth & Co. (Publishers) Ltd., London and Edinburgh
United States	Butterworth Legal Publishers, Austin, Texas; Boston, Massachusetts; Clearwater, Florida (D & S Publishers); Orford, New Hampshire (Equity Publishing); St. Paul, Minnesota; and Seattle, Washington

Canadian Cataloguing in Publication Data

McDonald, P. Lynn
   Retirement in Canada

(Perspectives on individual and population aging; 9) Includes bibliographical references.
ISBN 0-409-80518-1

1. Retirement - Canada.   I. Wanner, Richard A.
II. Title.   III. Series.

HQ1062.M23 1989   306'.38'0971   C89-090567-3

Sponsoring Editor – Gloria Vitale
Editor – Anne Butler
Freelance Coordinator – Catherine Haskell
Cover Design – Patrick Ng
Production – Nancy Harding

To the memory of Barbara, who always cared.
R.A.W.

To Geoff
P.L.M.

BUTTERWORTHS PERSPECTIVES ON INDIVIDUAL AND POPULATION AGING SERIES

This Series represents an exciting and significant development for the field of gerontology in Canada. The production of Canadian-based knowledge about individual and population aging is expanding rapidly, and students, scholars and practitioners are seeking comprehensive yet succinct summaries of the literature on specific topics. Recognizing the common need of this diverse community of gerontologists, Janet Turner, while she was Sponsoring Editor at Butterworths, conceived the idea of a series of specialized monographs that could be used in gerontology courses to complement existing texts and, at the same time, to serve as a valuable reference for those initiating research, developing policies, or providing services to elderly Canadians.

Each monograph includes a state-of-the-art review and analysis of the Canadian-based scientific and professional knowledge on the topic. Where appropriate for comparative purposes, information from other countries is introduced. In addition, some important policy and program implications of the current knowledge base are discussed, and unanswered policy and research questions are raised to stimulate further work in the area. The monographs are written for a wide audience: undergraduate students in a variety of gerontology courses; graduate students and research personnel who need a summary and analysis of the Canadian literature prior to initiating research projects; practitioners who are involved in the daily planning and delivery of services to aging adults; and policy-makers who require current and reliable information in order to design, implement and evaluate policies and legislation for an aging population.

The decision to publish a monograph on a specific topic is based in part on the relevance of the topic for the academic and professional community, as well as on the amount of information available at the time an author is signed to a contract. Because gerontology in Canada is attracting large numbers of highly qualified graduate students as well as increasingly active research personnel in academic, public and private settings, new areas of concentrated research are evolving. Future monographs will reflect this evolution of knowledge pertaining to individual or population aging in Canada.

Before introducing the ninth monograph in the Series, I would like, on behalf of the Series' authors and the gerontology community, to acknowledge the following members of the Butterworths "team" and their respective staff for their unique and sincere contribution to gerontology in Canada: Andrew Martin, President, for his continuing support of the Series; Gloria Vitale, Managing Academic Editor: Acquisitions, for her enthusiastic commitment to the promotion and expansion of the Series; and Linda Kee, Executive Editor, for her co-ordination of the production, especially her constant reminders to authors (and the Series Editor) that the hands of the clock continue to move in spite of our perceptions that manuscript deadlines were still months or years away. For each of you, we hope the knowledge provided in this Series will have personal value - but not until well into the next century!

Barry D. McPherson
Series Editor

FOREWORD

As a social invention, retirement has become an institutionalized social process and social event that has profound effects on both an individual and a society. Regardless of whether retirement is early or late, voluntary or involuntary, the process represents a major role transition that can have a considerable impact on the individual, his or her family, the peer group, the employer and numerous sectors of a society, including the social welfare, health care, labour force, housing, transportation, and immigration systems.

Moreso than any other age-related event, the process of retirement aptly illustrates the interplay between individual and population aging. Yet, to date, most research has focused on the outcomes of being retired for the individual, rather than on the individual and social structural factors that influence the process, or on the outcomes for a society. Moreover, most research has been limited to describing the consequences of retirement for white, middle-class anglophone males.

As we enter the 1990s, the act, process and meaning of retirement may undergo significant changes. Given the onset of declining birth rates, changing immigration policies, variable rates of unemployment, increased entry and retention of women in the labour force, and new interpretations and meanings of human rights, the meaning, regulations, onset and adjustments of retirement could change dramatically. Indeed, we can ask such questions as: Will retirement remain as a universal right or requirement? When will future workers retire, if at all? and Why will individuals retire if not required by law to do so? While not providing definitive answers to these specific questions, the authors of this monograph do provide the background information necessary to raise and address the needed theoretical, research and policy questions about retirement that will emerge in the next decade.

Professors McDonald and Wanner are recognized experts in the area of retirement research, having conducted extensive secondary analyses of retirement issues using Canadian data sets. In this monograph they provide a composite picture of retired Canadians, and a thorough analysis of both the antecedent individual and societal factors leading to retirement, and of the individual and societal consequences of retirement. Moreover, they present and discuss the findings within a variety of theoretical perspectives, and constantly raise new research and policy questions and issues that should stimulate further inquiry and analysis in this rapidly evolving area of gerontology.

In Chapter One the reader is introduced to the myriad of conceptual, analytical and operational definitions that have both clarified and clouded our understanding of retirement. These definitions are linked to the major micro and macro theories of aging. Above all, this chapter stresses that retirement is a complex process that involves a variety of interacting individual, political, economic and social structural factors. Chapter Two represents an original and unique contribution to the retirement literature in Canada. Here, the authors discuss the history of retirement in Canada, including the onset of issues arising from the introduction of varying human rights legislation, the passage of the Charter of Rights and Freedoms, and the unique needs and situation of the indigenous peoples of Canada.

Chapter Three focuses on how political, social and economic changes in Canada following World War II have had an influence on retirement. Here, a demographic analysis of the retirement patterns for males *and* females is presented and interpreted in terms of existing theories. In addition, the trends in Canada are compared with those in other industrialized nations. In Chapter Four, the differing antecedent factors leading to a decision to retire "early", "on-time", or "late" are discussed, along with the outcomes of the decision for the individual and the family. Here, we learn that the transition from work to retirement is not, in most situations, characterized as a crisis, even in the absence of little pre-retirement planning.

Chapters Five and Six focus on the individual and societal consequences of retirement, respectively. At the micro level of analysis, the authors discuss the outcome of retirement for an individual's health, income adequacy and well-being, while at the macro level of analysis the concern is with the impact of the retirement process for the pension system, the labour market, the distribution of income, and public policy. These chapters include an important and interesting discussion of the often neglected issue of women and retirement. The concluding chapter creatively considers possible future scenarios for retirement in Canada, especially with respect to the possible implications for the practitioner and for public policy.

In summary, this monograph has been written for students, practitioners, policymakers and gerontology scholars in a variety of disciplines. By presenting and analyzing the existing evidence within a conceptual linkage that includes both individual and structural factors, the authors achieve their goal of providing "an integrated overview of retirement in Canada so that we can thoughtfully anticipate the next shift in the retirement kaleidoscope over the next several decades". A careful and thoughtful reading of this monograph should enable you to contribute to the next wave of retirement research, policy analysis, and practice in this important, but often understudied, area of gerontology in Canada. To conclude, I urge you to give special attention to retirement issues, on both an individual and societal level, as they pertain to women, ethnic and racial groups, the unemployable, those from low income groups, and those who refuse to, or can not retire. As with other areas of study within gerontology, retirement can no longer be viewed as an automatic process, nor as a homogeneous process. Just as there is considerable diversity across the population in work and leisure matters, so too is there diversity in when, how and if Canadians retire.

Barry D. McPherson, Ph.D.
Series Editor
Wilfrid Laurier University
Waterloo, Ontario, Canada
August, 1989

PREFACE

Retirement has become an important political and scholarly issue in recent years and will undoubtedly attract even more attention over the next several decades as the Canadian population continues to age. Although researchers have attempted seriously to account for the plummeting labour force participation rates of older workers and their tendency to retire ever earlier, a full explanation remains elusive.

Retirement, as a social institution, has only recently emerged in human societies, and then only in those characterized by industrial economies. Investigations into the phenomenon were only begun in earnest in the late 1940s and early 1950s. Because of the recency of the emergence of large scale retirement and its subsequent rapid development, there is limited empirical evidence available about the process and some doubt about the relevance to the current situation of research conducted in earlier time periods. As social scientists make progress, the retirement kaleidoscope shifts yet again, presenting new configurations of policies, preferences, and economic conditions that require explanation. While gains have been made in explaining the impact of retirement on the individual, it has become apparent that the impact on society must be considered and, no less so, the dynamic interplay between the individual and the society.

During a time which has witnessed the advent of human rights legislation, the return of women to the labour force in increasingly large numbers, and a rapidly shifting economy plagued by high unemployment and inflation, older persons are comprising an increasingly large proportion of Canada's population. In light of new provincial human rights legislation and the introduction of the Canadian Charter of Rights and Freedoms (1981), the whole practice of mandatory retirement has come under national scrutiny. The question of whether to retire early or not may be replaced by the question of whether one retires at all, setting into motion a whole new set of conditions that will have to be confronted by both society and the individual. Indeed, the retirement process grows ever more complex and requires our close attention, perhaps more so than at any other time in history. Labour force withdrawal clearly has serious ramifications not only for the welfare of the individuals and families involved and for professionals who serve them, but also for determining the actuarial requirements of public and private pensions, the size and composition of the future labour force, and the overall formulation of Canadian social policy.

The intent of this monograph is to provide a composite picture of Canadians who retire and the social and individual forces impelling them to retirement. We will accomplish this by means of a review and interpretation of the most current empirical research on the retirement process as well as the presentation of original analyses of data collected by Statistics Canada and other agencies.

Our approach will be guided by three considerations. An explanation of retirement is far too complex not to include both individual and social structural factors, so we consider both. At the individual level we focus on the link between people, their work and retirement, peoples' attitudes toward retirement, the timing of their retirement, the events they experience when they do retire, and their adjustment to retirement. At the societal level we consider the conditions that led to the institutionalization of retirement in Canada and the demographic social, political, and economic structures presently influencing retirement patterns.

Our second consideration is derived from what we consider to be a serious flaw in the retirement literature. Few researchers declare the theoretical position or the paradigm of aging that has informed their investigations. Different paradigms of aging imply different perspectives on the retirement process. While some paradigms actually assume retirement to be a normal, inevitable process, others do not accept that view as a given. To understand the implications of the existing research on retirement, we believe it is vital to identify the links between theory and the resulting research. We attempt to specify these links throughout the monograph.

Our third aim is to underscore those areas that require further research. Retirement is one of the more heavily researched areas in gerontology, so it is sometimes surprising when serious gaps in knowledge are uncovered. Therefore, special efforts are made in each chapter to identify avenues for further research.

With these considerations in mind, Chapter 1 provides an introduction to the study of retirement, examining the various definitions of retirement that have been proposed and linking them to the leading theories of aging in gerontology. Chapter 2 traces the institutionalization and evolution of retirement in Canada, culminating in the most recent developments stemming from the new Canadian Charter of Rights and Freedoms and recent provincial human rights legislation. Chapter 3 provides a demographic description of retirement patterns in Canada with comparisons made between men and women in recognition of the very different labour force experiences of the latter. Chapter 4 uses the most up-to-date empirical research to examine the antecedents of retirement at the individual level of analysis. Here, we examine individuals and their families as they leave the labour force and move through the retirement process. Chapter 5 examines the consequences of retirement in terms of peoples' health, wealth, and well-being. In Chapter 6 we turn to a consideration of the impact of social, political and economic structures on the retirement process. We conclude, in Chapter 7, with an exploration of possible future scenarios for retirement in Canada and assess the implications of existing retirement research for both public policy and professional practice.

Retirement in Canada is designed to serve the needs of undergraduate and graduate students in the areas of gerontology and public policy and of those practitioners facing an aging society. It may be used in courses in gerontology taught in departments of sociology or psychology, public policy courses taught in departments of political science, and courses on care and counselling of the elderly taught in faculties of social welfare, nursing, or medicine. Our goal is to provide an integrated overview of retirement in Canada so that we can thoughtfully anticipate the next shift in the retirement kaleidoscope over the next several decades.

A large number of people have assisted us in completing this monograph and the research on which it is based. We are especially grateful for the support and advice of Barry McPherson. As series editor, he encouraged us to tackle the imposing topic of retirement and provided helpful editorial suggestions throughout the writing process. The Research Grants Committee of The University of Calgary provided crucial financial support for the project. We also wish to thank Gloria Vitale and the staff at Butterworths for their assistance and patience when personal troubles made it difficult to carry on. We are especially grateful to Doreen Neville who patiently and cheerfully produced one draft after another with skill and commitment to the task. We appreciate the many hours of research assistance provided by Jane Gatt and Brian Hoffert. Norah Keating reviewed the entire manuscript, offering many helpful suggestions. Finally, we would like to thank our families who tolerated, with good cheer, the many hours of abandonment this project required. We will never forget writing the last paragraphs at sea amidst the beer bobbing crew.

CONTENTS

TABLES

CHAPTER 1

THE RETIREMENT SPECTRUM: CONCEPTS AND THEORIES

INTRODUCTION

As inevitably old age is in everyone's future, all adult Canadians have some stake in the individual and societal issues surrounding retirement. During a period in our history that has witnessed a surge in the older Canadian population, a rapidly shifting economy plagued by high unemployment and inflation, the increased labour force participation of women, and the advent of human rights legislation, the effects of retirement are pervasive. Retirement reaches into the pocketbooks of most Canadians, it shapes experiences in the workplace for all age groups, and touches the family life of young and old Canadians alike.

Faced with a burgeoning older population, workers and employers may have concerns about the possible tax burden created by increasing numbers of older Canadians receiving public pensions. In view of their increased labour force participation, Canadian women may be concerned about their retirement income, given the cumulative effects of wage discrimination over a lifetime and continuing inequities in the Canadian pension system. New families search for ways to provide retirement incomes for members of the family who decide to remain at home and fulfill the responsibilities of child care and housework. Dual-worker families must give serious consideration to who will retire first, because an age differential between partners can affect the level of pension benefits. Some older workers worry about being terminated from employment before they become eligible for pensions. Many new Canadians have concerns about meeting residency requirements for public pensions or whether the reciprocal pension agreement with their country of origin is adequate to meet their needs.

While economic matters are of considerable import to most Canadians, work is no less significant. Younger workers and the unemployed may be concerned about securing jobs that could be made available through the retirement of older workers, while middle-aged workers may wonder if they will ever advance to positions held by older workers. With the elimination of mandatory retirement in Canada imminent, many workers of all ages may question why they should retire at all. Almost everyone will have difficulty deciding whether the pleasures and benefits of retirement outweigh the loss of status, social contact, and purpose that retirement may temporarily bring about.

Retirement not only affects Canadians individually, but it also influences the society as a whole. Periodically, Canadians have expressed concerns about the solvency of old age pension programs, the consequences of abolishing mandatory retirement and the effects of retirement rates on the economy, taxes, and our health and welfare systems. Canadian planners struggle with the development of retirement policies that take account of such factors as the changing demographic structure of Canada, shifts in the state of the economy, the size, composition and requirements of the Canadian labour force and the balance of pension responsibilities between the public and private sectors. In the final analysis, all of these deliberations must consider the desires, needs, and behaviours of individual Canadians, both within the present historical context and in an uncertain future.

Retirement, then, covers a very broad spectrum that involves not only the interests of most individuals but the interests of society and the reciprocal relation between the two. Political, social, and economic structures will have some bearing on how Canadians approach retirement, and at the same time, how the individual goes about retiring will influence the political, social, and economic structures of Canadian society. In times of labour shortages, individual decisions about retirement, such as leaving the labour force early, can, in aggregate, create a trend necessitating adjustments in public policy to ensure an adequate labour supply. At the same time, a change in public policy, such as raising the normal age of retirement, may encourage individuals to stay in the labour force longer to ensure this supply. Whether Canada is at war or in a recession will colour these decisions. In times of war, early retirement may not be feasible, given an already depleted work force, while in a recession early retirement could help ease unemployment.

Seen in this light, retirement is a complex and challenging phenomenon that is important to all Canadians. This chapter attempts to untangle the ways in which retirement has been and can be studied. As a precursor to interpreting the existing retirement research, it reviews the various definitions of retirement and their implications, the dimensions of retirement that have captured the interest of researchers, and the theoretical perspectives that inform the study of retirement.

WHAT IS RETIREMENT?

In spite of its common usage, defining the term *retirement* is neither simple nor straightforward. Defining *retirement* involves at least three considerations: how is it conceptually defined, what is the concomitant operational definition, and how is it used analytically (see McPherson, 1983: 107-14). A conceptual definition is stated at the theoretical level and involves identifying a dimension along which units of analysis (e.g., individuals, societies) vary either in quantity or in quality. Thus, to define *retirement* as "withdrawal from the paid labour force" is to qualitatively distinguish those individuals who are members of the labour force from those who are not. An operational definition specifies an "operation" that allows us to measure the theoretical concept by assigning numbers to observed units of analysis that reflect category membership, ranking on the theoretical dimension, or the specific location on the dimension of a unit of analysis. In the case of our conceptual definition above, this might mean operationally defining retirement in terms of a person's response to a survey item, such as, "Last week, how many hours did you work for wages, salaries or tips or in your own business?" The number of hours worked becomes the operational definition of the degree of retirement for that respondent. In the sections that follow, a number of conceptual and operational definitions of *retirement* that have been used in the research literature will be described.

The analytical use of a concept refers to its role in a theoretical statement or hypothesis as either an independent variable (a "cause"), a dependent variable (an "effect") or a variable intervening between independent and dependent variables. Examples of these three roles are provided below. Because studies of retirement span a wide number of disciplines and represent a variety of theoretical approaches and research designs, it is crucial that these approaches to a definition of *retirement* be thoroughly understood. Indeed, different operational definitions of *retirement* can produce conflicting answers to the same research question!

Conceptual Definitions

There is no single agreed-upon definition of *retirement* that is used by all researchers. Conceptually, retirement has been thought of as a social institution, an event, a social role, a process, or a phase of life (Atchley, 1976a, 1980). All of these conceptualizations have been used in retirement research.

A social institution is a set of beliefs, values and norms that define how people, groups and organizations resolve central problems faced by all societies. Retirement, as an institution, is primarily concerned with the problem of moving older workers out of the labour force in an orderly fashion without causing undue financial hardship, given their previous contributions (Atchley, 1980: 264). The institutionalized form of retirement that Canadian society has adopted is a function of numerous factors, such as population aging, the state of the economy, technology, historical events, and pressures from various interest groups, as retirement has evolved over the past 75 years. Part of the institutionalization of retirement has been the growing acceptance of the belief that the older worker has the right to retire by virtue of many years of service at a job. Those who study retirement as an institution are usually interested in macro-level issues, such as the historical development of retirement (Atchley, 1976a; Fischer, 1978; Achenbaum, 1978; Graebner, 1980) the social and economic conditions that lead to retirement policies (Guillemard, 1983; Myles, 1983, 1984a), and outcomes of the institutionalization of retirement (Estes, 1979; Walker, 1983).

Retirement as an event involves the formal end of employment and the beginning of life without a job. This fleeting occasion may involve a ceremony, such as a dinner or party, and the presentation of a commemorative gift, such as the proverbial gold watch. It may be as simple as cleaning out a desk and the handing in of keys or completing the paperwork for receiving a retirement pension. Although retirement as an event is duly mentioned in all definitive lists of conceptual definitions of *retirement*, it has not garnered much attention from social gerontologists. It can only be speculated that either it is so obvious that it has been overlooked, that it may only now be emerging as a rite of passage and, hence, worthy of study, or that the concept may have little utility in the understanding of retirement, since it signifies little more than a simple one-time occasion having little influence on the subsequent life course.

Retirement as a social role consists of the general norms regarding the rights and duties of the social position "..retiree" (Atchley, 1976, 1980; George, 1980; Palmore, 1985). The rights of the retired person usually include the right to economic support without holding a job and without the stigma attached to being unemployed, the right to use one's time as one sees fit, and sometimes specific rights to use services or facilities associated with the former employer, union, or professional organization. The duties of the retired person usually include the duty to assume responsibility for oneself and avoid physical and financial dependence on the family or the state and the duty to avoid full-time employment. Social gerontologists who consider retirement to be a social role generally study the phenomenon at a micro level of analysis, exploring such factors as how individuals adjust to the retirement role, their attitudes to the role, how they perform the role and their satisfaction with it (Skoglund, 1980; O'Brien, 1981a; Blank and Ritchie, 1983; MacLean, 1983; Howard and Marshall, 1983).

Related to the idea of retirement as a role is the concept of retirement as a process, which includes the preparation for retirement, the decision to retire, the actual retirement event and the stages the individual might experience in retiring (Atchley, 1980; George, 1980; Palmore, 1985). Essentially, the study of retirement as a process has to do with how the retirement role is approached, taken, and relinquished by the individual retiree (McPherson, 1980; Martin Matthews, Tindale and Norris, 1984).

Finally, retirement as a phase of life generally occurs later in the life cycle, at or near the end of the occupational life cycle and usually in the family life cycle at a point when the last child has left home. In terms of the individual life cycle, retirement is usually included as one of several events happening to people in their sixties (Stull and Hatch, 1984). When the occupational life cycle is the focus, career shifts and changes, abilities of the older worker, and pre-retirement planning are frequently highlighted (Keating and Jeffrey, 1983; Connidis, 1982; Behling, Kilty and Foster, 1983; Doering, Rhodes and Schuster, 1983; Dobson and Morrow, 1984). Other investigators have focused on the effect of retirement on the family (Keating and Cole, 1980; Lupri and Frideres, 1981; Atchley and Miller, 1983; McConnel and Deljavan, 1983; Keith et al., 1984) and, to a lesser extent, the effect of the family on retirement (Henretta and O'Rand, 1983; O'Rand and Landerman, 1984). The study of retirement as a phase of life generally involves using a micro perspective.

The most noticeable aspect of the various conceptual definitions of *retirement* is the distinction between the micro and macro perspective and the over-representation of micro-level definitions. As will be evident in subsequent chapters, retirement is more likely to be viewed as an individual issue, while the societal implications of retirement receive short shrift. In fact, since the inception of the study of retirement in the 1940s and early 1950s, researchers have been fascinated with how individuals plan for retirement, how they arrive at the retirement decision, whether they will retire early, on time (age 65) or late, what kinds of leisure or voluntary activities they will pursue, how they will manage their reduced incomes, their health, their marriages, and their grandchildren, how many times they will move, how they will fare in retirement communities, and whether they are happy, enjoying themselves, experiencing high levels of morale, self-esteem or life satisfaction. It is only within the last decade that the societal dimensions of retirement have received serious notice, specifically in the policy arena and in reference to population aging.

Operational Definitions Of Retirement

Operational definitions of retirement abound. Among the definitions that have been used are: number of hours or weeks worked in the past year (Palmore et al., 1985; McDonald and Wanner, 1983; Hardy, 1982a); the rate of retirement (Tracy, 1982); nonparticipation in the labour force (Sharon and Argov, 1983); a reduction in work responsibilities (Gustman and Steimer, 1984); age at which the individual left his or her last main employer (Fields and Mitchell, 1984); receipt of social security benefits (Reno, 1971; Bixby, 1976; Wanner and McDonald, 1986); receipt of private pensions (McGoldrick, 1983; Fields and Mitchell, 1984); a definition of oneself as retired (Roadburg, 1985); and any combination of the preceding (George,

Fillenbaum and Palmore, 1984; Hooker and Ventis, 1984; Palmore, 1985). As Palmore (1985) has noted as a result of years of retirement research, different measures of retirement can produce different findings. To illustrate, armed forces personnel, police, and university professors might retire from their duties and receive their pensions but then go on to other jobs. If the definition of retirement is receipt of a pension, they are retired. If the definition of nonparticipation in the labour force is used, many of them would not be retired. Whether a particular person is considered retired varies with the operational definition and will shade the research findings.

Those measures of retirement that are continuous in nature - any version of the amount of employment or, conversely, the amount or degree of retirement - more closely resemble the retirement process, since total withdrawal from the labour force is by no means universal among older workers (Atchley, 1976a). This type of definition is also more objective insofar as it represents what people actually *do* rather than what they say they do in terms of retirement behaviour. Nevertheless, there are problems with these definitions. Often they do not distinguish between full- and part-time work or between permanent and temporary employment, even when a pension requirement is added to the definition. As well, the more objective definitions of retirement do not capture peoples' own perception of their retirement status.

Those definitions of retirement that are dichotomous - retired versus not retired - are frequently subjective in nature and therefore directly tap peoples' perceptions of their retirement status. In fact, this is the only type of definition that can be used when studying those people who have never entered the Canadian paid labour force, such as homemakers, recently arrived new Canadians, and some of the handicapped. Although Irelan and Bell (1972), in their analysis of data from the United States, found some evidence that labour force status and self-defined retirement are closely linked, other researchers have found self-definitions to be not entirely reliable (McDonald, 1983; McDonald and Wanner, 1984). Most recently, Palmore et al. (1985) have demonstrated that different findings can result if retirement is defined continuously (number of hours worked in the past year) or dichotomously (self-perceptions of retired or not retired) using several data sets from the United States. The strongest predictors of retirement defined dichotomously are factors such as socioeconomic status and job characteristics, while the strongest predictors of retirement defined continuously are job characteristics alone.

Operational definitions are important, then, because they determine who will be included and who will be excluded in retirement investigations, whose perception of retirement matters, and why contrary answers to the same research question might be produced.

Analytical Definitions of Retirement

Analytically, retirement can be seen as an independent variable, an intervening variable, or a dependent variable (see McPherson, 1983: 107). When retirement is used as an independent variable, the goal is to understand what effect it has on the individual or society. Most gerontologists have assumed that retirement constitutes a major life transition for the individual and therefore must have some impact on the individual's physiological, psychological, social, and economic circumstances, and, not surprisingly, a majority of existing research studies reflect this interest. Because of the aging of populations, retirement is only now being studied in terms of its impact on the rest of Canadian society, but studies of this nature are less in evidence in the literature. Retirement as an intervening variable usually appears in investigations in which retirement is not the central variable of interest but is part of a larger analytical model. For example, social policies have had an impact on retirement conditions, which in turn have spawned the dependency and domination of the aged (Walker, 1983). When retirement is used as a dependent variable, the purpose is to discover what factors "cause" retirement or influence retirement both at the individual and societal level. Again, most existing research has been at the individual level, involving attempts to explain retirement behaviour. Here researchers have focused on the characteristics of the individual (occupation, marital status, gender, level of income, attitudes, health, etc.) that lead to retirement. At the societal level such factors as social policies, population structure, the economy, and historical events have been studied as antecedents of retirement rates and patterns. In this research, either societies are studied at several points in time or a number of societies are compared (Myles, 1984a).

An understanding of the analytical use of the retirement concept tells us something significant about retirement research. As will be seen in Chapters 4, 5 and 6, retirement has been most frequently used as an independent or intervening variable. This suggests that less effort has been devoted to explaining the causes of retirement than to the outcomes of retirement. It was only when early retirement became a trend in industrial societies in the late 1960s that researchers engaged in a flurry of studies aimed at explaining this development.

Up to this point, the various definitions of *retirement* have been described in isolation. Obviously, conceptual, operational and analytical definitions must be linked in all studies of retirement. For example, if psychological adjustment to retirement is the issue at hand, then the conceptualization of retirement as a process (how the individual performs the retiree role) would be a likely choice. It also makes more sense to use a self-definition of retirement than the number of hours worked in the last year, since people have to consider themselves retired in order to adjust.

Likewise, retirement must precede adjustment in the causal ordering, so analytically it would be treated as an independent variable. If the impact of retirement on the solvency of our social security programs is being studied, retirement would most likely be conceptualized as a social institution, measured according to labour force participation rate and receipt of a public pension, and analytically treated as an independent variable.

This section has attempted to demonstrate that, when studying retirement, the definitions chosen are of central importance. The definitions indicate whether the issue of concern is individual or societal, who is included or excluded from the analysis, and whose view is of consequence. They also help us understand why the results of retirement research can sometimes be contradictory. Typically, these observations would be made about theoretical perspectives used to explain retirement rather than about the definitions of retirement that generally are embedded in some theoretical perspective. Regrettably, the level of theoretical development pertaining to retirement is meager at best. There are very few, if any, theories that explain retirement (Calasanti, 1981), and until very recently, retirement has been subsumed under most of the conventional gerontological perspectives used to explain some aspect of social aging. It is to this matter we now turn.

PERSPECTIVES ON AGING AND RETIREMENT

As already mentioned, there is a profusion of research on retirement at the individual (micro) level, but few studies at the societal (macro) level. Why is this so? This bias toward individualistic conceptualizations of retirement can, more often than not, be traced to the perspectives on aging that have served as a backdrop to the study of retirement. In this section retirement is placed within the context of the well-known theories on aging that have dominated the gerontological enterprise since the 1940s. We will argue that the perspectives represent an over-individualized conception of aging, and hence of retirement, which can be attributed to the reliance of both micro and macro theories on structural-functional assumptions derived from the sociological theory of the 1940s and 1950s (see McPherson, 1983: 141). The implications of these assumptions for the study of retirement will be detailed, and we will conclude with an examination of newer, alternative perspectives that could redress the theoretical imbalance.

The Micro Theories

Disengagement, activity, and continuity theories have been the progenitors of social gerontological thought on retirement, as in most other areas of gerontology. In turn, these theories have all been influenced by a functional model of social structure and human development (Dowd, 1980; Marshall,

1980a; Townsend, 1981). Transposing the guiding assumptions of structural functionalism into any of these theories on aging results in a strong emphasis on the inevitability of the social, psychological and physical aspects of the aging process, an emphasis on clearly scripted roles, the characteristics brought to these roles, and adjustment to them. In short, the social position of the older person is ultimately explained in terms of the individual and his or her own lifetime behaviour patterns played out within a given social, political and economic order.

In applying the three theories to retirement, one can detect these underlying assumptions. The disengagement theorist would argue that retirement is part of the normal, mutual, and beneficial withdrawal of the individual and society from each other. The activity theorist would view retirement as a withdrawal from an occupation that must be replaced with other forms of social involvement. The continuity theorist would see retirement as a discontinuity to be corrected through the expansion of roles played prior to retirement. Retirement, as a form of reduced activity, is functional for both the individual and society in the eyes of the disengagement theorist. But for the activity theorist, decreased activity through retirement can culminate in low morale unless it is replaced with some other functional activity. For the continuity theorist, time spent in roles prior to retirement should be increased during retirement if the person is to adjust.

Although these are seemingly different perspectives, there are commonalities underlying them. They all assume that social interaction will be reduced; they direct attention to the individual by emphasizing the quality and amount of activity; they ignore the autonomy of the individual (everyone is a script-reading occupant of a role); and they assume that the transition to retirement is potentially traumatic, since they offer prescriptions for the best way to adjust to retirement.

The implications of these perspectives for the study of retirement are far-reaching. None of the theories considers whether the decreased interaction that comes with aging could actually be caused by something other than obvious biologically related losses (Dowd, 1980: 4-7). The implication is that retirement is a normal, inevitable process. There is no acknowledgement of the possibility that social, economic or political structures could influence retirement behaviour. There is also the suggestion that individuals have little power to influence socioeconomic structures. Most importantly, retirement is viewed as a problem caused and solved by individual behaviour. Translated into social policies, disengagement theory would legitimize mandatory retirement, while the assumptions of activity theory would promote policies that assist in the social integration of the older person. Continuity theory would foster policies falling somewhere in between (Minkler, 1984). Whichever scenario is chosen, individuals are expected to accept the conditions and adjust accordingly; if they do not, they are held individually responsible (Guillemard, 1977, 1980, 1983). Society is held above reproach.

Some of the more recent versions of adjustment to retirement (see Eisdorfer, 1972; Shanas, 1972; Sussman, 1972; Atchley, 1976a) may have added structural components to their explanations of adjustment, but only to acknowledge that the individual has to change to accommodate social structures (Covey, 1981). For example, Atchley (1976a: 116-18) proposes his own theory of adjustment based on all three perspectives. It involves internal compromise and interpersonal negotiation. Basically, the individual must make some type of decision in order to alter his or her personal goals to suit the reality of the situation. The condition of retirement is a given not subject to change.

Notwithstanding the host of other criticisms that have been levelled at these micro perspectives (see McPherson, 1983: 136, 139, 140), they still appear in the retirement literature (Bond, 1982; Kafer and Davies, 1984; Palmore, Fillenbaum and George, 1984). Although they have provided a wealth of information about what individual retirement experiences are, or perhaps more accurately, what they are not, the picture is still incomplete. The only definitive conclusion that has been reached about retirement and adjustment is that retirement does not result in personal crisis for a majority of the retired (Beck, 1982).

The Macro Theories

A brief review of the macro theories of aging - modernization theory, age stratification theory and life cycle theory - is equally illustrative of our position. None of these theories deals directly with retirement, but they have all at least touched on the subject and are represented in the research literature on retirement.

Modernization theory (Cowgill, 1974) focuses on the decline in the status of the aged. Retirement is viewed as an intervening variable in the process. Increased longevity and declining birth rates create an aging population, which in turn produces intergenerational competition for jobs. At the same time, modern technology creates new jobs suitable to younger workers and fewer jobs to which older workers are suited. The conjunction of these two developments creates retirement; retirement inevitably leads to lower incomes, and lower incomes produce lower social status for the aged. Retirement, then, is seen as an inevitable result of the unidirectional and evolutionary march of society on its journey to full modernization (Marshall, 1980a). Retirement is assumed to be a normal part of the evolutionary process, precluding any consideration of social class, public policy, ethnicity, gender, and so forth, as possible mediating factors.

Role incumbency and associated norms are the basis of age stratification theory first proposed by Riley, Johnson and Foner (1972). The life course is seen as a series of related roles linked together on the basis of age, and behaviour is explained in terms of role occupancy of a group of people who were born at about the same time and who share the same experiences. Retirement, then, is explained in terms of the age criteria for entering and exiting roles for a cohort of people. Again, there is an over-emphasis on roles, to the extent that those who do not carry out their roles well, such as the retired, are deemed age deviants (Nelsen and Nelsen, 1972; Dowd, 1980). The fact that mandatory retirement has aroused little empirical attention, while early retirement and late retirement have kindled so much interest, can be seen as a direct outcome of studying behaviour outside the norm of retirement at age 65.

Age stratification theory has provided a social structural component to the life cycle perspective, which has been heralded as the pinnacle of theorizing in social gerontology (Marshall, 1980a: 121). The life cycle perspective attempts to link the macro and micro theories of aging, simultaneously considering the individual and society as the unit of study. The individual ages in chronological years or developmental stages and at the same time he or she moves through a social timetable of the life course defined by social norms and roles specific to age. This rhythm of age-related changes in social roles occurs within the context of social change over time (Elder, 1974). Because age stratification theory has been appended to the life cycle perspective, it comes as no surprise that retirement is seen as a stage in the life course through which each cohort must eventually move.

Although the macro theories attend to social structure via the notions of technology, population composition, age cohort and social change over time, the individual is still scripted to play out the inevitable role of retirement, a normative part of the life course. Like the micro perspectives, these theories have also been criticized on other grounds (see Atchley, 1980: 276-81), yet they, too, continue to appear in the literature (Cohn, 1982; Dowd, 1975; Stull and Hatch, 1984).

We now have at least a partial explanation of why individualistic conceptualizations of retirement predominate. Historically, the development of the major social gerontological theories, through their exposure to mainstream structural-functionalism, have promoted a singular interest in the individual. We can also understand why there is a paucity of theories explaining retirement itself. If it is assumed that retirement is a natural, inevitable process, it is not necessary to develop an explanation to account for it. Historical constants require no explanation.

This is not to suggest that individual retirement is not important. It is extremely important. It is so important that we must be aware of some of the unconscious assumptions about the individual and his or her retirement that are embedded in these theories, research based upon them, and policies derived from the research. An over-individualized perspective of retirement places the onus on the individual for his or her retirement behaviour, with no consideration of what economic, social, or political conditions might constrain that behaviour (Estes, 1979, 1983; Guillemard, 1983; Townsend, 1981). Rather than asking how society impacts on individual retirement behaviour, these theories direct attention to the problem of adjustment to retirement and elucidate ways to "soften the blow," while indirectly legitimizing possible flaws in the socioeconomic structure of society. Furthermore, there are no avenues available to study the effects of retirement behaviour on society or the interplay between individual behaviour and structural constraints within the context of these theories.

Alternative Perspectives

There are three alternative perspectives that have been applied to retirement that offer quite different views of the retirement process: exchange theory (Dowd, 1975, 1980), systems theory (Walker and Price, 1974; Kimmel, Price and Walker, 1978; Atchley, 1982), and political economy theory (Townsend, 1981; Estes, 1983; Guillemard, 1983; Walker, 1983; Myles, 1984a).

Dowd (1975, 1980) has applied exchange theory, a perspective with a long history in sociology, directly to retirement. Exchange theory begins with the assumption that interaction between people and groups is characterized by attempts to maximize rewards and reduce costs, whether these exchanges be material or non-material in nature. The ability to profit from social exchange depends on the resources available to the individual. These could include money, respect, knowledge, skill, or social position. From an exchange theory perspective, the problems of aging are primarily problems of decreasing power resources, with retirement being one case in point. Retirement is viewed as a series of exchange relations in which the power advantage favours the employer. The older worker can no longer exchange expertise for wages (the education and skills of the worker have become obsolete), and can only comply with mandatory retirement in exchange for financial support in retirement (Dowd, 1975: 587-90). Mandatory retirement is, therefore, seen as an example of an unfair exchange rate that became "fair," or institutionalized, over time on the basis of where the power resources lay at the time–namely, with the employers (Dowd, 1980: 50).

Atchley (1982: 280) argues that Dowd's theory is no longer valid because it describes conditions that applied only at the turn of the century when workers were quite powerless in exchanges with their employers. Today, workers have a new exchange resource in the form of earned pension credits. But more importantly, they have powerful groups of retired persons, along with unions, lobbying on their behalf for better pension deals. For Atchley, the relative power of the collective advocates of retirement is more crucial than the distribution of individual resources. Rather than being invalid, Dowd's position is, we think, even more relevant in light of these developments. If the significant power resources have shifted from individual to group exchanges, then the level of analysis can be adjusted from the micro to the macro level and exchange theory becomes a framework for studying these changes. If nothing else, exchange theory redirects attention to the possible function of power resources in the shaping of retirement as an institution. It also offers an explanation of why retirement exists today and is flexible enough to account for the ever-changing aspects of retirement. At best, exchange theory underscores the interactive, or negotiable, characteristics of retirement and squarely places it within the societal context.

Walker and Price (1974) and Kimmel, Price and Walker (1978) have attempted to capture the complexity of the retirement process through the use of a systems perspective (see McPherson, 1983: 381). But it is Atchley (1982) who has proposed the most sophisticated version of a systems theory of retirement. Atchley begins with a systems theory of institutions as a foundation for his systems approach to retirement. He suggests that retirement is a "modest institution that primarily centers around the goal of providing an orderly means of shifting older workers, or allowing them to shift, out of the labour force with a minimum of financial hardship in consideration of their past contributions" (Atchley, 1982: 264). There are four interrelated elements that centre around this goal: alternatives for accomplishing retirement, a set of criteria that can be used to select from among the alternatives, constraints that tend to restrict the process of selecting among alternatives, and people and organizations who select and must bear the consequences of their choices (Atchley, 1982: 264). The alternatives for accomplishing retirement are comprised of retirement policies or the rules for retirement, such as eligibility, length of service for retirement, and the age of retirement. The set of criteria for selecting alternative policies (currently) would, for example, include the need to keep unemployment down, to provide old age pensions and to increase job opportunities for younger workers. These alternatives would be influenced by certain demographic, economic and ideological trends. The constraints (currently) would include such factors as age discrimination and the current mix of routes to retirement, such as mandatory retirement or retirement due to ill health. The actors in the process include employers, workers, retirees, unions and governments, all with different and sometimes conflicting interests in retirement.

Atchley (1982: 264) views this perspective as only a first approximation to a new theory that will guide much needed research on the societal aspects of retirement. Although no researchers have applied this perspective, it highlights the socioeconomic processes at work at the societal level and emphasizes the dynamic interplay between society, the individual, and groups. It is a long-overdue theory that warrants serious investigation.

The application of the political economy perspective to gerontology arose in direct reaction to the structural functional approach underpinning the individualistic studies of aging (see Estes, 1983; Minkler, 1984). It also opposed those theories that appeared in the 1960s to criticize the conventional perspectives of disengagement, activity, and continuity theories, such as symbolic interactionism. For example, symbolic interactionism (see McPherson, 1983: 125) focuses on how people react to aging rather than on socio-cultural factors that shape the aging experience and the management of aging in our society (Minkler, 1984: 12).

From the political economy perspective, the problem of aging is a structural one that "... begins with the proposition that the status and resources of the elderly, and even the trajectory of the aging process itself, are conditioned by one's location in the social structure and the economic and political factors that affect it" (Estes, Swan and Gerard 1984: 28). Although this is not a theory of retirement, retirement is a crucial intervening element in this paradigm. Retirement is viewed as a marginal and dependent position occupied by the aged that is a culmination of the operation of economic, political, and social structures prior to retirement. These very same structures continue to sustain the position of the aged in post-retirement through the minimization of potential conflict between generations, social classes, or interest groups. Factors assumed to influence retirement include state-fostered ideologies (Guillemard, 1977, 1980, 1983), social policies (Myles, 1984a; Wanner and McDonald, 1986), social class (Estes, Gerard and Swan 1982), the division of labour and the labour market (Walker, 1981; Dowd, 1980; Hendricks and McAllister, 1983; McDonald and Wanner, 1986), and occupational structure (Hardy, 1985; McDonald and Wanner, 1986). For example, Myles (1984b: 175) succinctly notes, "Both the right to retire - and hence to become old - and the rights of retirement are today the products of national legislation. Politics, not demography, now determines the size of the elderly population and the material conditions of its existence."

While this perspective requires further development and empirical verification, it assiduously directs attention to the structural issues of retirement and exposes some of the less apparent aspects of retirement that have been obscured by individualistic arguments (Graebner, 1980). For these reasons, the perspective is a very useful adjunct to individual explanations of retirement and holds considerable promise for expanding our understanding of retirement. If there is a problem with this perspective, it is an over-reliance on structural explanations, portraying the retired person as a mere victim of social forces.

CONCLUSIONS

This chapter underscores the often-repeated observation that retirement is a complex process. Retirement not only concerns older Canadians, it concerns all of us and is inextricably bound to the socioeconomic and political structures of Canadian society, which have been shaped by particular historical circumstances. From the review of the various definitions of *retirement* and the theories that have influenced research in the area, it is apparent that retirement researchers have not yet managed to capture this complexity in a dynamic picture of the phenomenon. That is, it is necessary to expand and develop an understanding of the societal aspects of retirement to at least a level comparable to that found in individualistic explanations, and no less so the interaction between the individual and society.

While these observations are of importance to those who produce retirement research, they are also important to the consumers of retirement research. The practitioner must be ever mindful of the underlying assumptions and implications of the research used to guide practice, in order to reduce biases, resist over-simplified and premature conclusions, and leave open the possibility of alternative solutions. In other words, the retired person need not always be "helped" by the practitioner to adjust to the system. The political, economic and social systems can also serve as the target of intervention for the practitioner, as the next chapter will illustrate.

CHAPTER 2

THE HISTORY OF RETIREMENT
IN CANADA

There is little disagreement among scholars that retirement is a social invention characteristic of modern industrial societies (Atchley, 1976a, 1982; Achenbaum, 1978; Fischer, 1978; Haber, 1978; Graebner, 1980). The emergence of retirement as a social institution has been documented for the United States (Haber, 1978; Graebner, 1980) and for many countries of Western Europe (Townsend, 1981; Walker, 1981, 1985; Parker, 1982; Phillipson, 1982; Guillemard, 1983), but has remained unexamined in Canada by social gerontologists and social historians alike (Martin Matthews and Tindale, 1987). Although it has been argued that the history of retirement has been very similar in most industrial societies (Atchley, 1982: 275), an understanding of the political, economic, and social conditions unique to the Canadian scene would make contemporary retirement patterns all the more comprehensible. This chapter makes a modest attempt to examine the evolution of retirement in Canada, using Atchley's systems perspective, outlined in Chapter 1, as a guiding framework. The basic position taken here is that the spread of the practice of retirement was driven by changes in the Canadian economy and supported by the enlightened self-interest of various political, economic and social groups.

THE PREINDUSTRIAL PERIOD

Even though retirement emerges largely as the result of industrialization, withdrawal from work among the elderly of Canada's indigenous peoples and during Canada's agrarian period is described here first to highlight the tremendous change wrought by industrialization. The term *retirement* as applied to this period has a meaning very different from its present one. Instead of an institution surrounded by a pension system, a planning industry, and a culturally conditioned lifestyle, *retirement* in this early period simply meant that a man or woman ceased engaging in the work that had occupied them for a lifetime.

The Indigenous Peoples

The idea of retirement was unknown to the indigenous peoples of Canada, though both Inuit and Indian societies were faced with the problem of what to do with older persons when their physical prowess began to fade and they could no longer contribute to the economic activity of the group. Given the extreme harshness of the Canadian environment and the major goal of group survival, there were apparently two fundamental mechanisms available to deal with the elderly: a shift in the nature of their contribution to society or the engineered demise of the older person through abandonment or killing. The solution chosen appears to be related to whether or not there was a surplus of food, whether the society was stable or nomadic, and what supporting cultural values operated at the time.

The alternatives for achieving "retirement" for the Inuit (usually meaning withdrawal from full participation in community life as a result of biological aging) were several. Men were considered old when they could no longer hunt year-round, while for women, the process was less obvious since they could withdraw into the home (Guemple, 1980). The men could forestall complete withdrawal by hunting in the spring and summer when conditions were easier than at other times of the year, or they could undergo symbolic renewal by marrying a younger woman. The women, who did not marry younger men, could carry on their primary functions by adopting children. In doing so, both men and women changed their contributory function. As another alternative, the elderly person could rely on others (children, in-laws, or influential hunters in the community) to make their contribution to the community. When elderly persons no longer commanded these resources for an extended period of time, they gradually came to be viewed as dependent and were seen as a burden on the society. It is well documented that the Inuit sometimes abandoned their old, leaving them behind on the trail or assisting them in putting an end to their lives (Freuchen, 1961; Guemple, 1980). The criterion for selecting among alternatives, then, appeared to be whether or not the older person could contribute to the overall production of the community, either directly or through others on their behalf. In the Inuit cosmology, old people did not die, but rather the name and the social identity attached to the person separated from the body, returned to the underworld and waited until it could enter the body of a newborn child (Guemple, 1980: 98-100). The Inuit cosmology supported this abandonment, making the decision on the part of the older person and his or her children straightforward.

Among Canada's numerous aboriginal Indian societies, there was great diversity in attitudes toward old age and the treatment of elderly people. However, typical of the tribes that roamed Canada's western plains were the Blackfoot. Blackfoot hunters had an old proverb for male children: "It is better to die in battle than of old age or sickness" (Ewers, 1967: 103;

Grinnell, 1921: 189-90). When the Blackfoot had only dogs for moving camp in the "dog days" and buffalo were hunted on foot, there was little comfort for the person who survived to old age. If women became too weak to perform their chores, from rearing children and feeding and clothing the family to dismantling and carrying the camp equipment, they were abandoned to face death alone (Ewers, 1967: 17). The old men, no longer possessing the agility and fleetness of foot to hunt, were also abandoned if they were too enfeebled to move from camp to camp (Ewers, 1967: 106). The deceased, it was believed, entered upon a new life similar to the one he or she had on earth. When a Blackfoot died, the spirit travelled to a hummock between the Red and South Saskatchewan Rivers, and there it ascended to a delightful, plentiful country well stocked with animals. As in the case of the Inuit, death by abandonment of older, non-productive members of society meant to the Blackfoot that they would be moving on to another life.

With the acquisition of the horse, the fortunes of the aged who could not produce changed. They were now transported by an A-shaped horse travois, and although given the worst side of the lodge and less choice pieces of meat, they were still cared for by the community (Grinnell, 1921: 189) and not left to die. With the coming of the fur trade and the establishment of forts, the "worn-out hunters" had yet another alternative. The testimony of Dr. John Rae before the Parliamentary Select Committee on the Hudson's Bay Company in 1857 suggests that there were three or four "old families" who were "unfit to hunt" who were received at the various forts and were cared for permanently. Dr. Rae stated, " we never forced them into the Fort; but if they came and asked assistance and wished to stay, they did so" (Rae, 1857 in Thomas, 1975: 27). As Dr. Rae noted, the number of older Indians "varies according to the privations which the Indians have suffered," and gratuitous medical advice was given "to every one that came, or that we heard of".

The examples of the Inuit and the Blackfoot illustrate that although retirement was non-existent as we know it today, withdrawal from productive work due to biological aging was a reality. While the Inuit had several alternatives for accomplishing "retirement," constrained by the criterion of contributing to the whole, the availability of alternative resources and the supporting Inuit cosmology, the Blackfoot initially had but one alternative. With the introduction of the horse,which increased chances for survival through better food supplies and easier travel, the alternatives were broadened for the older Blackfoot. The establishment of the fur trading posts and the desire of the Hudson's Bay Company to maintain strong positive ties with the Indians (for economic reasons) added yet another choice. In the aboriginal societies discussed here, the old were supported as long as they were productive. When their productivity was not crucial to the society because of a better food supply and stability of community, they were more likely to be maintained after they could no longer work.

Agrarian Canada

In a staples economy where farming predominated until the latter half of the nineteenth century, retirement in Canada was probably infrequent. During the frontier stage of agricultural development, wresting a livelihood from an inhospitable wilderness frequently meant subsistence living, endless rounds of tasks with too few hands to finish, hard labour and certain isolation (Cross, 1974: 9; Guest, 1985: 15). Many farmers needed to generate cash income to supplement their farming. Whether to buy seed, pay off debts or buy more land, farmers were often forced to seek employment in the fur trade, in timbering, or in fishing, on a temporary basis. Retirement under these conditions was most likely unfeasible, particularly because most farmers did not survive these rigours to live into old age. Also, there was no economic surplus, and frequently farmers could not gain clear title to their farms because of government costs charged against homesteads at start-up (Cross, 1974: 40-41). Farmers would have to keep working until they dropped.

Even when farming became established and the staples trade in wheat was one of the few sources of cash income for the farmer, there were still economic problems that militated against retirement. The French-Canadian farmer experienced an agricultural crisis in the nineteenth century resulting from the inadequacy of farming methods that made Lower Canada a major importer of wheat. With the waning of the fur trade as an extra source of money, the habitant and his sons were in "sore straits indeed" (Ouellet, 1982: 47). In New Brunswick, agricultural development lagged behind that in the other colonies because so many young men were lured away from the farm by the high pay and adventure of the timber trade (Cross, 1974: 4). Upper Canada, which later became Ontario, was the richest agricultural area in Canada. However, this area also experienced difficulties. In the 1850s, Canada West, as it was called, witnessed a severe drop in property values, agrarian indebtedness soared dramatically and sons could no longer succeed their fathers on the family homestead (Gagan, 1981: 293). Using data from Peel County, Gagan (1981) shows that through the crisis of the 1850s, the older farmer maintained ownership of the farm and delayed a takeover by his heirs. Although the information from Peel is not representative, it is quite plausible that the same processes operated in the other distressed colonies, making retirement highly unlikely.

Notwithstanding questions of longevity and the economic circumstances of the farmer, the culture of the "family farm," which placed a premium on the value of family land, family work and landed inheritance, most likely weighed against retirement. With the ownership of property, the older farmer could continue to work but could also gradually decrease his heavier farm responsibilities by delegating them to sons and sons-in-law without losing control over farm production. Large numbers of children made this possible. As one essayist wrote, children "are in Canada his [the poor man's] greatest blessing and happy is the man who has a quiver full of them" (Philpot, 1871: 119). Children provided a vital labour force on the farm (Cross and Kealey, 1982). There is also considerable literary evidence that farmers were anxious to guarantee the independence of their adult children, especially sons, by passing the farm on to them (Gagan, 1981: 100). This, of course, was the fundamental promise of the Canadian wilderness and served to attach adult children to the farm.

Even if the farmer became physically disabled, he apparently carried on (Katz, 1975: 102; Philpot, 1871). The "Armless and Legless Wonder of Moose Jaw," in an application for a patent for his homestead, wrote, "... in the winter of 1887-8 I was frozen - losing both legs and arms and did no active work personally after that, though I had a crop or two put in and some plowing done after that" (Rodwell, 1965: 38). If the farmer died, his will often contained provisions for the surviving wife (Synge, 1980). A Peel County farmer who died in 1867 left his son the farm, providing that:

> 1st he shall find and furnish all the Flour, Pork and Butter and milk, potatoes and other vegetables with plenty of good firewood ready for use and ... Keep 1 horse [and buggy] ... the above shall be found and supplied during ... the life of ... his mother. [Gagan, 1981: 107]

Some farmers did, of course, retire, but few available records document this process. If one could determine who deeded their farms over to their children and at what age, one might have some idea about who retired. Synge (1980) provides some evidence that this probably occurred when she notes in her study of Anglo-Canadians in the Ontario countryside that the younger or older couple might move to a new house built on the property or nearby. She further indicates that sons did not delay marriage until middle age when parents became too feeble to run the farm (Synge, 1980: 138); families reached a compromise that most likely involved deeding the property to the son, a practice still used today. Fischer (1978: 54) notes that in Colonial America, these deeds contained covenants that stipulated that the son provide his father with financial support for life. Gagan (1981: 106-7) provides similar evidence for Canada, at least for the County of Peel, intimating that this practice was mainly found among the wealthier farmers.

Paternalistic Labour Organization

There is little evidence to suggest that retirement was common in the workplace in nineteenth century Canada. Non-property owners who were in the employ of others appeared to work until the end of their days. A major reason for this may have been the long period of labour shortage through the 1850s that was accommodated by the development of a paternalistic and personal relationship between employer and employee, which preceded the impersonal relationships of industrial capitalism (Pentland, 1981: 26). When slavery, the indenture system and imported convict labour proved unsuitable as a source of labour for early French and British employers, they developed a well-integrated system of organizing labour to ensure their supply of workers and, hence, their profits.

In this system, best described by Pentland (1981), the employer had to first "catch" his labourer, usually by recruiting in Europe. But, more importantly, he had to adopt measures to hold the worker once he was snared. The employer had to offer continuous employment even if he did not require it, and the worker stuck with his employer because he needed continual employment to survive. The economic relationship was one of mutual dependence on both sides. The employer, afraid to use the sanction of dismissal, substituted incentives to ensure a high quality of work. As Pentland (1981) states, the employer "cultivated desired attitudes by an abundance of personal (superior-inferior) contacts, by expressing and demonstrating his paternal interest in the welfare of his charges, especially in their lifetime employment and care in old age" (Pentland, 1981: 25). In early nineteenth century Canada, there were many examples of the paternalistic labour organization, including certain fur trading organizations (the Hudson's Bay Company), timber firms (Calvin and Company), iron-making firms (the St. Maurice Forges), and water transport employers (the St. Lawrence Bateaumen). Father and son frequently worked for the same merchant, "and the merchant and his son looked after their men down the years" (Pentland, 1981: 54).

As was the case in rural Canada, some workers did retire, but, again, this appeared to be related to wealth. Thomas (1979) details the retirement of some of the fur traders. While Sir Alexander MacKenzie found the fur trade "nasty , brutish and rough," it was something that had to be endured to make enough money to retire to the life of an affluent Scottish laird (Thomas, 1979: 14). Apparently, fur traders who successfully struggled to provide for themselves often turned to retirement in the Red River (Winnipeg), one of the first retirement havens in Canada. David Thompson, another heroic fur trader, was less fortunate in setting aside monies for retirement. He ended his days in the direst of poverty, begging for a job at the Hudson's Bay Company (Thomas, 1979: 14) In the testimony of Sir George Simpson before the Parliamentary Select Committee on the Hudson's Bay Company about the company's officers and servants during 1820-70, it was evident that there was some provision made for the "servants in case of sickness or old age." The Company would allow a small pension in "any case which was deserving." The Company also had a crude annuity plan that paid four percent on any monies the worker left with the Company. As Simpson testified, "I have known labourers retire with from 200£ to 300£, Orkney labourers who are extremely economical in their habits" (Simpson, 1975: 33-34). Those labourers who did "retire" likewise headed off to Winnipeg and took up other occupations in the settlement. Katz (1975), in his study of the people of Hamilton, also notes that the entrepreneurs of the city, if they enjoyed continued financial success, retired and passed their businesses on to their sons. But for every successful businessman who retired, there were those who failed and became dependent upon the charity of friends (Katz, 1975: 195-96). Comparable to the Hudson's Bay "servants," the "retired" entrepreneurs moved back and forth between retirement and business, depending upon the economic opportunities that presented themselves.

Although this information is sketchy, it is indicative that retirement was the exception rather than the rule in preindustrial Canada. The methods for achieving retirement, when it did occur, were entrenched in the Canadian system of inheritance for both farmer and entrepreneur, in the ability to save, and in the good graces of the employer in the case of the worker. Older farmers or entrepreneurs could determine for themselves the timing and degree of withdrawal from work while still reaping the benefits of control over their enterprise. The older worker was not quite as fortunate and undoubtedly suffered certain hardship in his endeavour to save for retirement, given the miserly salaries paid at the time. Retirement, in either case, was more a privilege of the wealthy and does not appear to have been related to physical incapacitation, which was soon the situation in industrialized Canada. The constraints that impeded retirement included economic insolvency and an emphasis on the value of family work for farmers and businessmen and the paternalistic organization of labour for the worker.

The social ideology that flourished at the time also served to discourage retirement. There was a strong belief in individualism and free enterprise that was part of the colonial dream; a chance to build a new life in the New World was assumed to be open to all. Supported by certain tenets of Protestant theology that appreciated the values of thrift, hard work, self-help and self-discipline, to be poor or to avail oneself of private charity was a sign of personal failure, if not moral turpitude (Bryden, 1974; Guest, 1985). Indeed, the only old persons who were deemed a problem were those so unlucky as not to own property or not to have a job (Myles, 1984a; Guest, 1985). The major actors involved included only family and the employer and employee. As we shall see, the number of players with an interest in retirement increased dramatically with the advent of industrialization.

CANADA'S ERA OF INDUSTRIALIZATION

During the time that the British American colonies experienced their industrial revolution between 1849 and 1896 and the subsequent consolidation of industrial capitalism from 1896 to about 1930 (Cross and Kealey, 1982), the groundwork was laid for the establishment of retirement as an institution in Canada. The institution of retirement, however, was only fully realized following World War II, when retirement became a universal phenomenon characterized by the withdrawal of Canadians from economic activity in advance of biological and physiological decline (Graebner, 1980).

The Early Industrial Period

Following Confederation in 1867, Canada witnessed the completion of a transcontinental railway, large-scale immigration, the opening of the West and the rapid development of industry protected by special tariffs. Although plagued by economic depression, with only brief periods of respite, from 1873 until the end of the century, the process of urbanization and industrialization was well underway, changing the face of Canada within a few decades.

Labour force participation of older people most likely remained high during this period, as it did in other industrializing nations (Myles, 1984a: 8), because the paternalistic system outlined above carried over to the factories, and agriculture was still the principal industry (Census of Canada, 1851). Nevertheless, there were several trends that presaged the development of retirement. In the hands of politicians, charity workers and urban reformers, old age and incapacity became linked and the indigent old were singled out from the usual profligates as the "deserving poor." Industrialists at the time, confronted with the problems of controlling the labour force, began to impose mandatory retirement sporadically through the provision of pensions, and a new ideology of retirement, promulgated by a rapidly industrializing Germany with a strong national government, was also put into place (Atchley, 1982: 267-68). The worker unfit to continue in the labour force because of old age had a right to be cared for by the state.

Sir John A. Macdonald, faced with an election in 1887 and anxious to maintain his working class support, established the Royal Commission on the Relations of Labour and Capital in Canada. Besides detailing the grim exploitation of men, women, and children in urban industrial society, the Labour Commission, as it became known, recommended the creation of a government annuity system "under which working people and others might make provision for old age by periodical or occasional payments of small sums," in the hopes that this would "remove from many the fear of dependence upon relatives or charity in their declining years" (Labour

Commission, 1889: 13). It is informative that the politicians saw old age as a time of decline and dependency. Those older people who were unfortunate enough not to own property or have a job and who had no family support were faced with institutionalization in a poorhouse. The doctrine of "less eligibility," the basis of the British poor-law reforms in 1834, which was calculated to deter relief and force people to work by avoiding the misery of the poorhouse, did not apply to the elderly. They were deserving, yet the poorhouse was still the place where they eventually went. According to a statement by the Trustees and Managers of the House of Industry, Toronto in their annual report of 1886, "The inmates are chiefly old and infirm people. The retired pensioner takes kindly to our Institution, and the managers feel that they have discovered the method of taking care of those who in their time were the guardians of the Empire" (House of Industry, 1886, quoted in Cross, 1974: 204). In 1891, an Ontario Royal Commission on the Prison and Reformatory System decried the numbers of homeless old people who were lodged in local jails on charges of vagrancy because they had no place to go (Guest, 1985: 34). This was to be avoided, and it was recommended that each county in Ontario be required to operate a poorhouse for these homeless folks.

One of Canada's most famous urban reformers, Sir Herbert Brown Ames (a well-to-do manufacturer), launched a study of urban conditions in Montreal's working district in 1896. In reporting on the "poorest of the poor" (a sample of 323 families), he writes, "With 27 families, or 9 percent, old age had unfitted and with a like number sickness had prevented the workers from earning the requisite support" (Ames, 1897: 75). These "deserving poor," as he called them, should have a right to charity.

The forerunner of the modern private pension began with the railways in Canada. The Grand Trunk Railway, now a part of the Canadian National Railway, set up in 1874 what is believed to be the first industrial pension plan in Canada (Coward, 1959: 175). Although railway executives stressed their concern for the welfare of the older worker, their motives were not entirely benevolent (Haber, 1978: 81). Private pensions were developed as a means of stabilizing the workers, who were difficult to manage because they were so spread out across Canada. That this was no easy task was part of the reason why the RCMP patrolled the railway work camps (Saunders, 1897). To quote the president of Canadian Pacific Railway, the purpose of their pension was to assure an income for the aged workers who were "no longer fitted to perform their duties," but also "to build up amongst them a feeling of permanency in their employment, an enlarged interest in the company's welfare, and a desire to remain in and to devote their best efforts and attention to the company's service" (*Labour Gazette*, 1903: 553). All officers and employees were to be retired at age 65, and the benefits received were a gift that could be revoked at any time (*Labour Gazette*, 1903: 553). This was a fairly significant development, since the CPR was the largest employer in the Dominion at the time. However, the unions were fairly muted on the program and adopted a wait-and-see attitude (*Labour Gazette*, 1903: 553).

The seeds were sown for the relation between old age and incapacitation, the notion of mandatory retirement, and the idea of the "deserving" old. The role of the government in securing the welfare of wage earners in industrial society was also sketched out by Bismarck in Germany in the 1880s. As Bismarck stated:

> "The State must take the matter into its own hands, not as alms giving but as the right that men have to be taken care of when, from no fault of their own, they have become unfit for work. Why should regular soldiers and officers have old age pensions, and not the soldier of labour?" [Quoted in Donahue, Orbach and Pollack, 1960: 351]

Canadian response to social insurance "ranged form horror to an ironic appreciation of Bismarck's political astuteness" (Wallace, 1950: 390). The apprehensive Professor Mavor of the University of Toronto saw all pension schemes as a method of subsidizing low wages and objected to social insurance on the grounds that malingering would make the system unworkable (Wallace, 1950: 390). It was not until 1951 that the role for government advocated by Bismarck was fully embraced in Canada.

The Acceleration of Industrialization

With the acceleration of urbanization and industrialization, which produced massive demographic and technological changes, a number of factors converged that contributed to the growth of retirement. The economy was transformed from one of many smaller units of production to one of fewer but larger corporate enterprises. Labour became a commodity to be bought and sold in the marketplace, and productivity meant profit (Myles, 1984a: 11). Work became increasingly rationalized, demanding standardization, coordination and uniformity. All this found expression in the impersonal forms of bureaucratic organization that emphasized a specialized division of labour, a hierarchical chain of command, formal rules, and centralized authority (Atchley, 1982: 269). These structural changes in the workplace moved management out of the hands of the owner-entrepreneur and into those of a new breed of managers devoted to efficiency and effectiveness in the name of corporate profit (Myles, 1984a: 12).

"Scientific management," popularized by Frederick Taylor (1947), emphasized the division of the whole production process (by management) into small, quickly learned and routinized operations, with quantity, quality and time standards for each task. This trend initially reduced the need for skilled workers. During this transitional period, the older worker lost any prestige that might have been his due, because skills associated with his craft were no longer valuable. The principles of the approach also gave much attention to the physiological aspects of workers, namely, the speed at which they could work and muscle fatigue.

At the same time, the "wear-and-tear" theory of aging gained ascendency (Achenbaum, 1978), supporting the principles of scientific management. Although several physicians before him had noted the dissipating strength of the elderly (Haber, 1978: 86), Dr. William Osler of Tecumseh, Ontario helped to publicize this view in Canada. In 1905, in his farewell address at the anniversary exercises of Johns Hopkins University (he was on his way to the Medical School at Oxford), he stated two views. First, he stated that men above 40 years of age were comparatively useless and secondly, that men above 60 years of age were useless and there would be "incalculable benefit ... in commercial, political and professional life if, as a matter of course, men stopped work at this age" (*The Globe*, 1905a: 1). Indeed, he recommended "peaceful departure" by chloroform after one year of retirement (*The Globe*, 1905a: 1)! That an elderly man chloroformed himself in St. Louis several days later indicated that the thrust of his message was not ignored (*The Globe*, 1905b: 7).

The adoption of machine technology in the workplace and the speed at which it was operated served to underline the need for physical agility among workers (Graebner, 1980). The new machines were expensive, and employers wanted the maximum output from their investment. At the same time, some Canadian unions were agitating for the nine-hour day and higher wages (Kealey, 1980). A suitable compromise between management and the unions was to increase the work rate, which gave workers shorter work hours and assured management the profit they desired.

Alongside the growing belief that older workers were useless was the observation that their numbers had increased. This did not escape the watchful eye of economic analysts. In 1871, those aged 45 to 64 represented 11.1 percent of the total population, but by 1931, they made up 16.8 percent (Bryden, 1974: 30). An increasingly common view was that older workers and their lack of productivity could be a national menace to overall economic activity (Myles, 1984a: 9; Debates of the Senate, 1927: 148).

The convergence of these developments spelled difficult times for the older worker by the 1930s. Changes in the organization of work, the speed at which the new technology was to be operated, and the prevailing ideologies of scientific management and the "wear-and-tear" theory of aging created the conditions for retirement. The impersonal procedures of the organization provided a means to move the worker out of the labour force easily, while scientific management and the "wear-and-tear" theory of aging provided the rationale. The growing recognition of the increasing numbers of older workers lent credence to the rationale. Retirement became mandatory after a certain number of years of service (depending on the company, but usually at age 65). The purpose of mandatory retirement was to serve the needs of the industrialists and, indirectly, the unions, and its spread was influenced by the ideological climate of the time. The employee does not appear to have had much say in the matter (Myles, 1984a), but there is some indication that labour force participation rates among older men were beginning to decline. The only reliable labour force participation rates for Canada date back to 1921. Census data indicate that for men aged 65 and over, labour force participation rates dropped from 59.6 in 1921 to 56.5 in 1931, and the drop for women was from 6.6 percent to 6.2 percent for the same years (Bryden, 1974: 21).

The contribution of the Canadian government to retirement as an institution was minimal during this time and was consistent with the welfare ethos of the day. While the Canadian trade union movement had been asking for public pensions similar to plans operated in Germany beginning in 1889, Denmark (1891), New Zealand (1898), Australia (1901 and 1908) and Britain (1908), the federal government's response was to extend the hours of the post office savings departments, which served as banks on Saturday evenings. In 1905 the federal government did demonstrate some initiative, however, when it came to pensions for privy councillors, giving them $3,500 per annum if they had served five years or more as head of a department (Guest, 1985: 34). The issue of old age pensions was first raised in the House of Commons in 1906, and from then until 1914 two special committees of the House studied the issue. But the government was never in favour of pension schemes.

Amid discussions of the "deserving poor" (estimated to be about one-quarter of Canada's elderly), the needs of the "soldiers of labour," the problems of "discouraging thrift," the problem of a pension being a "work of charity" and fear of "socialist experiments," the Government Annuities Act was passed in 1908 (House of Commons Debates, 1907-08). As Laycock, in his analysis of this Act noted, "The whole Act insofar as it was intended to serve the needs of the working men was based on a misconception of their way of life" (Laycock, 1952: 31). They could barely afford the annuities plan, given their wages. Bryden (1974: 52) points out that by 1915, a random sample of annuity contracts revealed that only four percent of sales was accounted for by labourers.

The agitation for an old age pension scheme continued despite the passage of the Government Annuities Act of 1908. The Social Service Congress of 1914 passed a resolution calling for public pensions (Social Service Council, 1914). The Liberal convention of 1919 promised to take action, and the Trades and Labour Congress of Canada at their 1921 convention demanded old age pensions. A special Committee of the House of Commons was appointed in 1924, but it was not until 1927 that the Old Age Pensions Act was finally passed under MacKenzie King. The impetus for passing the Act came from two of Canada's Labour members, J.S.

Woodworth and A.A. Heaps, who were concerned about the poverty of older workers. The need for King to secure his power in the 1925 federal election also helped (Guest, 1985: 75).

The same types of argument prevailed in the House of Commons debates over the Old Age Pensions Act as surrounded the Annuities Act of 1908. In its final form, the purpose of the Old Age Pensions Act was to supplement, not replace, the income of the older worker. The Act was primarily a reflection of the then current approach to welfare of providing subsistence income to destitute older workers and their families. What was obvious from witnesses to the various parliamentary committees set up in 1911-12, 1912-13 and 1924 was the debilitating poverty faced by many older workers because of industrial conditions and the inability of poorer families to provide for their aged members (House of Commons Debates, 1921: 3860; Bryden, 1974: 42). In order to be eligible, a person had to be 70 years of age or over, a British subject, and had to have lived in Canada for 20 years and for 5 years in the province that would make the payment prior to commencement of retirement. Natives as defined under the Indian Act did not qualify. The amount of the pension was set at $240 per year and was subject to a means test. Overall, the person could earn $365 per year, including the pension amount, because a dollar per day was believed to be enough for an older person to subsist on (Bryden, 1974: 62). Due to difficulties of divided jurisdiction between the federal and provincial governments, the old age pension system took nine years to become national in character.

What is important about the Old Age Pensions Act is that it was restricted to those who were most likely to need benefits - those 70 years of age and over and the indigent (those making less than $365 per year). At the same time, personal thrift was still expected, since the benefits were fairly low (Debates of the Senate, 1927: 95-99). As was the case in the United States, this first form of social assistance was more a response to forced retirement of "wornout," and hence poor, workers than a cause of it (Graebner, 1980). It is difficult to imagine most workers having anything less than a negative view of retirement, because it implied uselessness and poverty.

From the Depression to Universal Retirement

The Great Depression of the 1930s was a time of mass unemployment and seriously depressed standards of living. At the worst point in the Depression in 1933, nearly one-quarter of the labour force was unemployed, and about 15 percent of Canadians were on social relief (Guest,. 1985: 83). While the beginnings of social security became the hallmark development in other countries (the United States Social Security Act was passed in 1935 and the New Zealand Act in 1938), attitudes redolent of the Elizabethan poor laws prevailed in Canada. A combination of declining government revenues, the inability of older workers to secure employment, and the change from a 50-50 federal/provincial sharing of the costs of the 1927 pension plan to a 75 percent federal contribution led to stricter controls to achieve economy (Bryden, 1974: 99-100). For example, in 1935, the administration of the Act was transferred from the Department of Labour to the Department of Finance; in 1938 the regulations for the 1927 pension plan were tightened to include a thorough investigation before a pension could be granted, with annual check-ups thereafter. Contributions that children could reasonably be expected to make to their parents were included as income, whether they made them or not (Bryden, 1974: 100). Several trade unions and Members of Parliament originally found the Act inadequate and, during the 1930s, lobbied for a reduction in age eligibility, mainly because there was little security for those workers being forced to retire before age 70 and also to encourage older workers to retire earlier and create jobs for the unemployed. The tightened regulations also received attention, although the older worker was not a top priority in the 1930s. At best, the social nature of human need was more clearly understood and accepted.

During World War II, the growth of private pension plans was given further impetus because of labour shortages and wage controls. As was the case in the early industrial period, pensions were used to manipulate the labour force, but this time this was achieved by offering benefits to offset wage freezes and to compete for labour in a tight market (Myles, 1984a). The result was an increase in compulsory retirement schemes, as business and industry adopted one of the group annuity policies offered by life insurance companies. Some 243 companies offered their staff these plans in 1937 in Canada. By 1942, the figure had increased by about 50 percent to 363, and by 1947 this figure had doubled to 753 (*Financial Post*, 1949: 15). Unions at the time also pressured companies to have retirement schemes included in union contracts, and there was a growth in private employer trust schemes (*Financial Post*, 1949: 15). As the *Financial Post* noted, "the order of the day in business and industry is fast becoming 100 percent compulsory retirement at age 65" (*Financial Post*, 1949: 15). Labour force participation rates based on census data do indicate a substantial drop for men 65 years of age and over from 56.5 percent in 1931 to 37.9 percent in 1951.

It was not until economic expansion following World War II, however, that universal pensions were instituted in Canada via the Old Age Security and Old Age Assistance Acts of 1951. These contributed to the already steady increase in the practice of retirement. From 1951 to 1961, the labour force participation rate for men aged 65 and over dropped from 37.9 percent to 29.3 percent (see Table 3.1). The Old Age Security Act, financed and administered by the federal government, paid a pension of $40 per month to all Canadians at the age of 70, with no means test involved. The Old Age Assistance Act, shared with the provinces, provided a pension of up to $40 per month for those 65 to 69 if need was established by a means test.

Both of these Acts represent the converging interests of a number of groups, and both were suited to the post-war ideology of Canada. On the heels of a devastating depression and the greatest war in world history, Canada, along with other Western nations, wished to avoid at all costs in its period of reconstruction the conditions of the Depression. The Keynesian revolution in economics pointed the way to avert the disasters of the thirties through emphasis on government responsibility for economic growth and social security. The broadly read Marsh Report (1943) highlighted the notions of "universal risks" (old age being one) and of a "social minimum" (Marsh, 1943: xxi, 56). In light of the flaws in the 1927 pension plan and the dominant ideology of comprehensive social security, considerable debate ensued about the means test component of the 1927 pension. The means test was viewed as "humiliating" by some groups, such as the CCF (Co-operative Commonwealth Federation) and the Canadian Congress of Labour, while others saw it as a threat to the spirit of thrift and self-reliance. There was not much point in saving, because if savings were available one would not receive the pension, so the thinking went. Whatever the motivation, most groups wished to abolish the "retirement test."

The focus of the debate was universalism, favoured by such groups as the CCF, The Canadian Congress of Labour, and the Canadian Life Insurance Officers (Bryden, 1974: 120), versus a contributory plan, favoured by the government of the day (House of Commons Journals, 1944-45), the Canadian Chamber of Commerce (Lesage, 1950), the Canadian Manufacturers Association (Bryden, 1974), the Canadian Association of Social Workers (Bryden, 1974: 120), and the Canadian public (Canadian Institute of Public Opinion, 1950). Universalism won out mainly because attaching benefits to contributions created difficult administrative problems and would, as a result, defer the elimination of the means test (Bryden, 1974: 121). In the long run, business also came to see that the more Ottawa paid, the less they had to pay (Myles, 1984a: 78). Forty dollars per month was viewed as a compromise representing the demands of the various groups. The means test at age 65 kept costs down for both federal and provincial governments and was justified by the belief that those 65 years of age could support themselves through employment.

The important implication of these developments was that the concept of universal retirement benefits was pitted against the concept of retirement as a deserved reward for long service. The universal pension was still viewed as a defence against destitution resulting from retirement. Business and industry, on the other hand, were promoting the view that retirement was a reward for service. The tension between these two views was not to be resolved until the 1960s, and then it was resolved in favour of business and industry, but implemented by the Canadian government in the form of the Canada Pension Plan.

In the public mind, retirement was well entrenched in Canada, if public opinion polls, popular media accounts and "expert" advice are any indication of the times. The popular view at the time seemed to indicate that retirement was seen as a chronological guillotine that assured a drop in income, the onset of boredom and a threat to health, if not death (*Financial Post*, 1949, 1957; *Labour Gazette*, 1957; *Macleans*, 1961). The perceived association among uselessness, poverty, and retirement appears to have lingered on from the beginnings of industrialization, as did compulsory retirement. But the idea that incapacitation occurred at age 65 or 70 was now being questioned, challenged by the growing awareness that people were living longer.

The Consolidation of Retirement

The last major step in the evolution of retirement in Canada into the social institution that we know today came with the restructuring of the Old Age Security Act (OAS) of 1951 through the 1960s into the 1970s, and the introduction of the Canada Pension Plan/Quebec Pension Plan (CPP/QPP) in 1965. The universal flat rate pension was retained. However, the qualifying age of 70 was reduced by one year every year starting in 1966, until it became 65 in 1970. The basic universal pension was to be $75 per month in 1963 and was subject to upward adjustment after 1967, in accordance with a specially constructed "pension index" based on the consumer price index. A temporary means-tested plan (which is still with us today), called the Guaranteed Income Supplement (GIS), was added in 1967 to fill the gap until the CPP/QPP was fully operative. As a compulsory and contributory earnings-related plan, the CPP/QPP was superimposed on the universal plan, OAS, which provided an additional old age pension as well as survivor, death and disability benefits.

As has been the case throughout the development of retirement as an institution, the interests of diverse groups fused to produce the current plan within a social climate that more and more subscribed to the belief of social security for all as opposed to social assistance for the needy (Guest, 1985: 150-51). It was becoming clearer and clearer in most countries subscribing to a flat rate benefit system (Britain and Sweden, for example) that retired workers were poor (Kaim-Caudle, 1973). Flat benefit rates were low, and although private pensions continued to grow in scope, they still benefited only a small percentage of the population (Brown, 1975: 85). Problems arose from inadequate coverage, vesting, portability and indexing (Bryden, 1974: 130; Brown, 1975: 109; Myles, 1984a: 46). Views began to shift in the direction of providing the retired with a reasonable standard of living, consistent with the standard of living achieved during their working years. In essence, there were those groups who wished to control the costs of pensions (the Diefenbaker government and, to a lesser extent, the Pearson government (Bryden, 1974: 138, 145) and business groups) and those groups who wanted to improve benefits (the CCF (1958), then the NDP (1961), and the unions, most notably the Canadian Congress of Labour (1953)). A contributory plan met both sets of interests. The only group consistently against a contributory plan was the Canadian Life Insurance Officers Association (1963), but their campaign against contributory pensions was contained by the counter-campaign of the Canadian Labour Congress in 1963 (Bryden, 1974: 161-62).

The effects of these pension reforms under the combined income maintenance program of CPP/QPP and the OAS pension were far-reaching. While there had been a long-term downward movement in the labour force participation rates of older men, Tracy (1982) demonstrated that the overall rate of decline accelerated during the five-year period following the introduction of the CPP/QPP. From 1968 to 1972, the rate dropped 13.1 percentage points, compared to 3.2 percentage points in the previous five years and 5.3 percentage points in the following five years, for men aged 65 to 69 (Tracy, 1982: 185). Reforms under these programs made retirement definitely more economically attractive, and the fact that Canadians were taking full advantage of these changes indicates that large numbers of them had come to want retirement. In other words, these pension changes fully normalized retirement in Canada. Of course, there have been numerous changes to the Acts over time. However, the fundamental structure has remained intact. Improvements to the "third tier" of the pension system, which has included personal savings and assets, private pensions and the more recent addition of the Registered Retirement Savings Plan (a form of deferred taxes), have not changed the basic structure of the system.

The restructuring of the public pension program in Canada in the 1960s and 1970s had a number of consequences. The government took over primary responsibility for retirement income, the concept of retirement was separated from the concept of poverty, public pension benefits became a deferred "wage" to which people were entitled because of their contri-butions, and withdrawal from economic activity took place in advance of physical decline. Under these conditions, retirement became an accepted social institution to most Canadians.

More recent evidence would lend support to these observations. In 1986, the labour force participation rate of men 65 years of age and over was 11.2 percent, compared to 47.5 percent at the end of World War II. For women of the same age, even though their labour force experience has been distinctively different, their labour force participation rate still dropped from 5 percent in 1946 to 3.6 percent in 1986 (see Table 3.1). Clearly, Canadians are retiring in large numbers, and it would seem that their preference is to retire even earlier. In a Monthly Labour Force Survey of Canadians over the age of 55 who were leaving the labour force in 1975, 40 percent of the retired men indicated a preference for retirement prior to age 65, while 46 percent of the women preferred to retire at or before age 60 (Health and Welfare Canada, 1977b: 4).

That the government is the primary source of income for the retired is also clear. The government provides 45.5 percent of the income of families and 51.3 percent of the income for individuals aged 65 and over (National Council of Welfare, 1984: 42). The poverty rate of aged Canadian families has dropped substantially, from 41.4 percent in 1969 to 11.7 percent in 1982, and is lower than the rate of 14.2 percent for non-aged families (National Council of Welfare, 1984). The poverty rate for aged individuals has also dropped from 69.1 percent in 1969 to 57.7 percent in 1982, though this is still higher than the rate of 30.9 percent for non-aged individuals, mainly reflecting the higher poverty rates still experienced by women (National Council of Welfare, 1984).

Companies and the corporate tax system treat employer contributions as labour costs, confirming the principle that a pension plan is a system of deferred wages (Pilkey, 1984: 437). Canadians' strong feelings about their right to retire and to a government pension were obvious from the public furor created when in 1985 the Conservative government proposed to do away with the universal aspect of Old Age Security and, when that met with disfavour, their attempt to do away with indexing the pension (*Globe and Mail*, June 20, 1985). That the government backed off testifies to the strength of the feelings of the Canadian public about pension matters.

Finally, that the age of 65 does not necessarily correspond to deterioration in the physical or mental capacities of individuals was a major position adopted by the Special Senate Committee on Retirement Age Policies (1979: 26) and is the basis for the more recent arguments challenging the legal status of mandatory retirement under provisions of the Canadian Charter of Rights and Freedoms and under provincial human rights legislation in a number of provinces (*Macleans*, 1980: 44-45).

Retirement in the 1980s

Today, in Canada retirement among the older population is the rule rather than the exception. The general goal of retirement policies, to remove older workers from jobs into retirement, has remained constant over time. Yet the reasons behind this overarching goal have fluctuated since the early 1900s. The alternatives for accomplishing the retirement of older workers are now found both in the retirement policies of private corporations and in our social security system for older Canadians. Retirement in Canada, then, currently involves a number of different systems and sets of alternatives. The criteria for selecting among alternative retirement policies tend to favour those policies that will produce early retirement, will ensure income security but keep costs under control, and favour the public sector over the private sector in providing pensions. These criteria have undoubtedly been influenced by the dual trend toward inflation and recession in the early 1980s, the financial plight of older women, the pressure the "baby boom" generation has exerted on entry level jobs, and the overall problem of unemployment. The recognized benefits accruing from control over very large pools of capital generated from pension plans and the escalating debate over individual rights (abolishing mandatory retirement) versus the economic productivity of corporations and social institutions have also constituted significant influences.

For example, many companies in the early 1980s began offering early retirement in an effort to trim their operations (Winnipeg *Free Press*, Feb. 14, 1983; *Financial Post*, Aug. 11, 1984; Winnipeg *Free Press*, Feb. 13, 1985; *Chronicle Herald*, March 30, 1985; Wolozin, 1985), as did the government in search of a leaner public service with the introduction of a voluntary retirement plan for executives in 1985 (Vancouver *Sun*, May 11, 1985; Winnipeg *Free Press*, May 9, 1985). The costs of financing public pensions have appeared in the media with regularity (Vancouver *Sun*, June 26, 1980; Nov. 29, 1979; *Globe and Mail*, Sept. 3, 6, 1985) and in a flood of reports from numerous and diverse groups - the Canadian Council on Social Development in 1975, the Economic Council of Canada in 1979, the federal government's Green Paper of 1982, the Canadian Labour Congress in 1982, the Business Committee on Pension Policy in 1982, the Canadian Association of Pension Supervisory Authorities in 1982, the Macdonald Royal Commission in 1985, and various discussion papers from the provinces (Quebec, 1978, Ontario, 1980, British Columbia, 1982, Manitoba, 1983). These groups have all alluded to the issue of who should control the large pool of capital generated by pension funds. However, it does not seem likely that the provincial governments would want to give up their major source of capital by allowing the private sector pension funds to take over. The exceedingly complex division of authority over pension policy between the federal and provincial governments requires a high level of consensus from the provinces, placing them in an advantageous position (Macdonald Royal Commission, 1985: 785).

There are also constraints that impact on current retirement practices. The potential routes to retirement represent one form of constraint, age discrimination another. Both of these constraints appear in the debates over mandatory retirement. As would be expected, the human rights advocates, strengthened by the Canadian Charter of Rights and Freedoms, would abolish mandatory retirement, deeming it an example of age discrimination. On the other side of the debate, private industry tends to favour mandatory retirement as a mechanism to streamline staff and remove the unproductive from the workplace. The unions see mandatory retirement as providing employment opportunities for younger workers (Economic Council of Canada, 1979). The Conference Board in Canada, in a report based on a study of 222 employers with 1.4 million employees (about 14 percent of the Canadian work force), said, in essence, that the elimination of mandatory retirement will affect a relatively small number of employees (Dunlop, 1980: xiii). The Board argues that, of the employees eligible to join a private pension plan, only 54 percent are in fact members and subject to company mandatory retirement policies. And, of all the employees now aged 55 and working for an employer with a plan, 70 percent will never work past 65. Fifteen percent will die before age 65, 6 percent will be laid off and not find another job, and 50 percent will retire early because of early retirement pension provisions or illness. Twenty-five percent will retire at age 65 and only 4 percent will work beyond their 65th birthday (Dunlop, 1980: xiii). These findings supported an earlier study by the Economic Council of Canada (1979).

In the public sector, the federal government announced in December 1985 that in 1987 persons entitled to a Canada/Quebec Pension Plan benefit would be permitted to draw benefits at any time between the ages of 60 and 70, with benefits adjusted downward if the beneficiary were under 65 (*Globe and Mail*, Dec. 14, 1985). In short, mandatory retirement has probably accounted for a small minority of retirements in Canada and, with the change in the CPP/QPP, has become more of a moral issue that will eventually be resolved in the courtroom. The moral aspect may still serve as a constraint and take the form of the older person being viewed as a "job snatcher," which Guillemard (1983) contends is the case in France.

Finally, the actors involved in defining retirement today are legion compared to the few involved at the turn of the century. Employers tend to see retirement as a way to reduce labour costs and to rid themselves of the unproductive (Wolozin, 1985). Workers have come to view retirement as an earned right that should be capitalized on as soon as possible. Unions now see retirement as a major vehicle for creating opportunities for promotion and for creating new jobs for younger workers. Government tends to see retirement as a means to providing financial security in old age (Macdonald Royal Commission, 1985: 785).

CONCLUSIONS

This limited history of retirement in Canada was intended to provide an overview of the major social, political and economic processes that shaped retirement into the institution we know today. Whereas retirement was non-existent in preindustrial Canada, today it is a legal right and a normatively governed social act. Throughout the evolution of retirement, major political, economic, and social interest groups have negotiated with each other under varying historical exigencies, social ideologies, political and economic conditions and a changing population structure to produce the conditions that have contributed to the spread of the practice of retirement. This history has underscored our observation that retirement as an institution is inextricably bound to the economy, politics, and government, and to understand the contemporary character of retirement we must understand the institutions that now shape this experience. This attempt to shed light on the Canadian retirement experience suggests that much more scholarship is required, presenting a significant challenge to Canadian social gerontology. At the same time, the message for the practitioner is clear. Historically, practitioners (social workers, health care specialists and urban and social planners) have contributed to the evolution of retirement through their advocacy and must continue their role according to the needs, desires and wants of the older people with whom they are closely linked. In the next chapter, we turn to a more detailed description of the effects of political, social and economic changes in Canada on the practice of retirement in the period after World War II.

CHAPTER 3

TRENDS IN RETIREMENT IN CANADA: THE SOCIETAL VIEW

Like the populations of most industrialized nations, Canada's population is aging (McDaniel, 1986). Since Confederation, the proportion of the population aged 65 or over has grown steadily, until by 1981 this group constituted 9.7 percent of the population. Yet at the same time, a shrinking proportion of people in this age group are remaining in the labour force. Indeed, as we shall see, Canadians have been retiring at ever younger ages, either by choice or under pressure from employers.

To understand retirement fully, it must be viewed from several levels of analysis. In this chapter, retirement will be viewed as a characteristic of Canadian society that changes over time. From this vantage point, we will attempt to understand retirement rates as responses to changes both in other institutional and structural features of society and in government pension policies. First, trends in labour force participation among Canadians are examined, paying particular attention to important differences between men and women. Next, these trends are tied into the massive changes that have taken place in Canada in the twentieth century as it has moved from an agrarian to an industrial to a postindustrial society. We then examine changes in the distribution and sources of retirement income among Canadians and conclude by comparing Canada to the other industrialized nations, placing Canadian trends in a world context. As documented in Chapter 2, retirement was not fully consolidated as an institution in Canada until after World War II. Therefore, it is from this period to the present on which this chapter is focused.

TRENDS IN THE LABOUR FORCE PARTICIPATION OF OLDER WORKERS

As pointed out in Chapter 1, the concept of "retirement" can be measured by a variety of empirical indicators. For present purposes, retirement will be equated with the withdrawal from the labour force of older workers, ignoring for the moment whether or not they define themselves as "retired" or are collecting pension benefits. This definition probably captures most of the retired, if these are defined as older workers leaving and not returning to the labour force. In its monthly Labour Force Surveys for 1978, Statistics Canada (1982a) found that fewer than 5 percent of men aged 55 to 64 not in the labour force had looked for work in the six months prior to being interviewed. Among men 65 years or over, virtually none had looked for work in the previous six months.

Much of the discussion that follows is focused on labour force participation before and after age 65. Despite the recent legal assault on mandatory retirement and the arbitrariness of age 65 as a universal retirement age, it remained the pensionable age under 88 percent of Canada's private pension plans in 1980 (Statistics Canada, 1982b), as well as the age of eligibility under the Canada and Quebec Pension Plans (CPP and QPP) and the Old Age Security program (OAS). Some programs do provide full or partial pensions at an earlier age, a circumstance to be explored more fully when the determinants of early retirement are examined, but the norm remains at age 65. Nevertheless, it must be recognized that age 65 as the "normal" retirement age is a fairly recent phenomenon. As recently as 1961, only about 12 percent of the men in the labour force retired at age 65, while only an additional 4 percent retired at age 64 and 5 percent at age 66 (Denton and Ostry, 1967). By 1975, however, fully 22 percent of men retired at age 65, with an additional 10 percent retiring at age 64 and 15 percent at age 66 (Ciffin and Martin, 1977). The total in the age range 64 to 66 had grown from just 21 percent in 1961 to 47 percent in 1975. Indeed, age 65 had emerged as the age of "normal" retirement in both principle and practice. In the discussion that follows, labour force participation will therefore be examined separately for those under 65 and those 65 and over.

After the waves of immigrants to Canada in the early part of the twentieth century had abated, Canada's labour force grew at a steady rate of between 15 and 24 percent per decade until the 1960s. Between 1960 and 1970, Canada's labour force grew by over 35 percent (Kalbach and McVey, 1979). Dwarfing even this enormous rate of growth, the decade of the 1970s saw Canada's labour force increase by nearly 40 percent. In large measure, this explosive growth was due to both an increased immigration rate and a dramatic growth in women's participation in the labour force. Yet despite this expansion, the numbers and proportion of older workers in Canada were declining. Table 3.1 shows labour force participation rates for Canadian men and women aged 55 to 64 from 1953 to 1986 and for those aged 65 and over from 1946 to 1986. Among the men, participation rates for those aged 55 to 64 years were quite stable up to 1965, ranging only between 85.4 percent in 1954 and 87.2 percent in 1957. Since 1965, the rate declined every year until 1980. It has fluctuated somewhat since then, but the secular trend remains downward so that at the present time

TABLE 3.1

LABOUR FORCE PARTICIPATION RATES FOR AGE GROUPS 55–64 AND 65 AND OVER BY SEX, 1946 TO 1986

Year	Males		Females	
	55–64	65+	55–64	65+
1946		47.5		5.0
1947		44.9		5.7
1948		44.0		5.1
1949		42.9		4.7
1950		40.4		4.2
1951		37.9		4.1
1952		36.7		3.9
1953	86.5	34.8	12.9	3.6
1954	85.4	33.2	14.0	3.7
1955	86.1	32.3	14.7	3.9
1956	86.4	34.0	15.8	4.5
1957	87.2	34.1	18.2	5.0
1958	87.0	32.1	19.2	5.2
1959	86.8	31.0	20.1	5.2
1960	86.7	30.3	21.3	5.6
1961	86.8	29.3	23.2	5.9
1962	86.1	28.5	23.8	5.6
1963	85.9	26.4	24.6	5.9
1964	86.2	26.8	25.6	6.3
1965	86.4	26.3	27.0	6.0
1966	86.0	26.2	28.4	5.8
1967	85.8	24.7	28.6	5.9
1968	85.4	25.3	29.0	6.1
1969	85.3	23.5	30.2	5.5
1970	84.2	22.6	29.8	5.0
1971	83.3	20.0	30.9	5.1
1972	82.4	18.6	29.7	4.3
1973	81.2	18.1	31.0	4.4
1974	80.3	17.7	29.6	4.3
1975	79.4	17.2	30.8	4.4
1976	76.7	16.0	32.1	4.1
1977	76.6	15.5	32.2	4.2
1978	75.6	15.0	32.6	4.0
1979	70.9	16.2	27.9	3.7
1980	76.2	14.7	33.7	4.3
1981	69.6	15.2	28.8	4.0
1982	73.7	13.8	34.0	4.2
1983	70.8	12.9	33.8	4.1
1984	67.0	13.7	28.6	3.7
1985	70.2	12.3	33.8	4.2
1986	69.2	11.2	33.5	3.6

Source   Statistics Canada (1982a), (1982c).
Note: Figures for ages 55 to 64 are not available from 1946 to 1952. The 1978 and 1986 figures are for June, since yearly averages are not available for those years.

approximately 70 percent of men in this age group remain in the labour force. Based on the trend they observed between 1961 and 1975, Ciffin and Martin (1977) concluded that there has been no substantial tendency toward early retirement among Canadian men. However, as the data in Table 3.1 show, the largest share of the shift toward early retirement among younger men has occurred *since* 1975.

The trend for men over age 65 is considerably more dramatic; nearly half of the men in this age group in 1946 were in the labour force, compared to just over 11 percent 40 years later. The average year-to-year decline among men over 65 was about nine-tenths of a percent, compared to an average decline for the younger age group of just over five-tenths of a percent.

This decline in labour force participation among older men, combined with an increase in the proportion of the population over age 55, has meant a large upsurge in the numbers of men not in the labour force. Between 1966 and 1985, the number of men aged 55 to 64 who were out of the labour force increased from 107,000 to 328,000, over a three-fold increase. During the same period, the number of men aged 65 and over soared from 492,000 to 921,000, while the Canadian population as a whole increased by just 26 percent. Clearly, the implications of these trends for Canada's future economic growth and the burden on both public and private pension plans (to be discussed in Chapter 6) are staggering.

At the same time that an enormous effort has been devoted to the study of retirement among men, women's retirement "has been widely neglected by social scientists" (Szinovacz, 1982: 13). As a result, not only is little known about the social and economic forces influencing trends and patterns of retirement among women, but little has been written on the trends themselves. The picture portrayed in Table 3.1 for Canadian women is considerably different from the pattern for men. As is the case for all Canadian women, the labour force participation rates of women aged 55 to 64 began growing steadily in the 1950s. By 1969, about 30 percent of the women in this age category were either working or unemployed, and the rate has increased only marginally since then to 33.5 percent in 1986. Since the labour force participation rate for all women continued to increase during the 1970s, from 38 percent in 1970 to over 50 percent in 1980 (Statistics Canada, 1985a), it is likely that the apparent stability for women 55 to 64 years is the result of two offsetting forces: an increasing propensity for women to engage in paid employment and an increasing tendency to retire early. The same might be said of the trend for women aged 65 and over. The percentage of women in this age category in the labour force has never exceeded 6.3 in the post-World War II period, though it did begin a downward trend in 1969, at approximately the same time that a decline in men's labour force participation was observed.

Another factor that likely influences women's retirement is the tendency for married women to follow their husbands into retirement. This, combined with the fact that women are likely to marry older men, particularly in older age cohorts (Kalbach and McVey, 1979: 327), would suggest higher rates of early retirement among women. Confirming this is a study of the retirement experiences of men and women by Martin Matthews (1987). She found that eight percent of the women in her sample, but none of the men, retired because of the retirement of their spouse. Table 3.1 indicates that 33.8 percent of women age 55 to 64 were in the labour force in 1985. Ten years earlier, 46.1 percent of these women (then aged 45 to 54) were in the labour force, suggesting that over 26 percent of them retired during this period. In the case of men, 92.2 percent aged 45 to 55 in 1975 were active in the labour force, compared to 70.2 percent of this cohort ten years later. As expected, the early retirement rate for women in Canada is somewhat higher than that for men.

We do not wish to leave the impression that "labour force participation" is synonymous with full-time employment. On the contrary, the proportion of workers employed part-time increases with age. In 1981, negligible percentages of men aged 25 to 65 were employed part time, yet 24 percent of employed men aged 65 to 69, and 32 percent of employed men aged 70 and over, were part-time workers (Health and Welfare Canada, 1983). The figures for women are even more striking. Although younger women are more likely than men to hold part-time jobs, among employed women 65 to 69 years of age, 43 percent worked part-time; for working women 70 and over the figure was 47 percent (Health and Welfare Canada, 1983). Many of these part-time employees had declared themselves "retired," so that estimates of the retired population using labour force participation figures are on the conservative side.

EXPLAINING THE TRENDS

Although the details may differ from country to country, Canada is not alone in experiencing a decline in labour force participation among its older population in the twentieth century. While a large body of research emphasizes individual preferences in this matter, individual preference is constrained by two major classes of structural determinants (Pampel and Weiss, 1983): (1) changes in the educational system, occupational structure, industry structure, and population induced by continued economic expansion; and (2) changes in government-sponsored social welfare and pension programs. These two explanations may be seen as parallelling, respectively, the structural-functional and political economy perspectives described in Chapter 1.

The former explanation points out that one of the major consequences of the development of industrialization has been a reduction in opportunities for self-employment. As real income per capita has increased, the relative demand for nonagricultural goods has far exceeded the demand for agricultural goods, resulting in a dramatic decline in the proportion of the labour force in agriculture, an industry in which most workers are self-employed. At the same time, as industrial economies mature, the typical firm becomes larger, more bureaucratized, and depends upon increasingly more complex technology. These firms then require a more rapid turnover of employees to ensure that younger workers with the latest skills and technological knowledge are available to maximize efficiency of production. As well, these workers tend to be less expensive than older, more experienced workers. According to this perspective, this places older workers, whose education and skills may be obsolete, at a competitive disadvantage in the labour market, resulting, in the long run, in a lower participation rate among this age group.

In contrast, the political economy perspective argues that the crucial factor in accounting for declining levels of labour force participation among older workers is the level of welfare and pension benefits set by governments. Because a society's level of economic development is, to a certain extent, independent of its political culture and prevailing class relations, nations at the same level of economic development may provide considerably different levels of pension support, and hence may exhibit different levels of labour force participation. Myles (1984a) traces these differences in levels of pension support to a value contradiction he perceives in capitalist societies that has its source in the "structural contradictions inherent in the conjunction of a democratic polity and a capitalist economy" (Myles, 1984a: 72). Unfortunately, Myles's analysis is restricted to the "welfare states" that have emerged in Western, private capitalist societies, ignoring the "public capitalist" states of the East bloc.

Pampel and Weiss (1983) suggest a third explanation that combines the industrialization thesis with the growth of social benefits thesis. They argue that it is only in the initial stages of industrialization that the requirements of industry for a younger labour force will be met by mandatory retirement policies. Once a relatively high level of economic development has been reached and retirement has become routinized, labour force participation will be more influenced by levels of pension and other social welfare benefits. The emphasis in this explanation is on the needs of employers being met by changes in retirement norms and inducements provided by government rather than by the mandatory retirement policies of an earlier era. Pampel and Weiss's (1983) own analysis of data from 18 nations at 6 time points shows that the largest effect on the labour force participation of elderly males is due to the percentage of the male labour force employed in agricultural occupations, which they argue is a surrogate measure for changes in the bureaucratization of industry and technological change. Nevertheless, some support for the political economy perspective is suggested by their finding that inter-nation differences in expenditures on social insurance do account for some variation in male labour force participation, if only to maintain the relative rankings in the face of increasingly similar industrial structures.

Cross-national research on the determinants of women's retirement rates suggests that they are not only influenced by level of industrial development and the availability of public pensions, as in the case of men's retirement, but also by a society's degree of sexual inequality and its fertility rate (Pampel and Park, 1986). In addition, Pampel and Park (1986) found that the effects of public pensions, sexual inequality, and fertility vary with level of economic development. This means that economic development has the strongest effect on women's retirement in countries with high levels of sexual equality, a well-developed public pension system, and low fertility levels. While women's retirement is certainly subject to the same forces influencing men's retirement, it is clear that additional forces are at work. In particular, the study of women's retirement must incorporate factors that influence the role of women in both the societal and the household division of labour. These will be explored in more detail in Chapter 6.

Before examining research estimating the relative influence of the industrialization process and public pension policy on retirement in Canada, we will review a series of changes in Canadian society that have likely had an important impact on labour force participation rates among older workers. Of course, rates are made up of a myriad of individual retirement decisions, and we will review research on both the structural and individual factors influencing individual retirement in Chapters 4 through 6.

Retirement and the Transformation of Canadian Society

The figures in Table 3.2 show a number of dramatic changes in the structure of Canadian society that have resulted from the ongoing process of industrialization in the twentieth century. These structural changes have had a profound influence on patterns of retirement. Perhaps most fundamental is the sizeable increase between 1931 and 1981 in the average life expectancy from birth, nearly 12 years for men and nearly 17 years for women. This factor, combined with Canada's declining fertility rate, has produced the dramatic increase in the aged population noted earlier. Although we would not claim that increasing life expectancy has directly influenced retirement rates, it has produced a considerably larger number of the retired over time. When Bismarck established the pensionable age at 65 in the Germany of the 1880s, few workers could anticipate an extensive period of their life to remain for retirement, if they lived long enough to collect in the first place. By 1981, the remaining life expectancy for men at age 60 in Canada was nearly 18 years and for women nearly 23 years, a considerable portion of their lives. Retirement could reasonably

TABLE 3.2
CANADA'S CHANGING DEMOGRAPHIC STRUCTURE, 1921–81

	1921	1931	1941	1951	1961	1971	1981
Life expectancy at birth (years)							
Men	—	60.1	63.0	66.3	68.4	69.3	71.9
Women	—	62.1	66.3	70.8	74.2	76.4	79.0
Industry Structure (percent)							
Agriculture	32.8	28.7	25.8	16.5	9.9	5.6	4.0
Agriculture and Other Primary	36.6	32.6	30.9	21.1	14.2	8.4	7.0
Manufacturing and Construction	26.5	17.3	28.3	32.3	28.4	26.0	25.3
Services	36.9	39.0	39.0	45.3	55.0	57.7	66.2
Professional Occupations (percent)	5.5	5.9	6.6	7.3	10.0	12.7	15.0
At Least Some Post-Secondary Education (percent)	—	—	4.2	5.4	6.1	21.9	35.6
Women in the Labour Force (percent)	15.4	17.0	19.8	22.0	27.3	34.3	40.8
GNP per capita (1971 dollars)	—	$1,361	$2,016	$2,531	$3,001	$4,379	$5,591

Sources: Life expectancy, Statistics Canada (1985a); industry structure, Statistics Canada (1982c); professional occupations, Statistics Canada (1982c); post-secondary education, Census of Canada, various years; women in the labour force, Statistics Canada (1985a); GNP per capita, Conference Board of Canada (1983).

be considered an important stage in the life cycle by a majority of Canadians.

In 1921, Canada's economy was still an agricultural, resource based economy, with over a third of the labour force working in agriculture and other extractive (primary) industries. By 1981, just four percent of the labour force remained in agriculture, with another three percent in other primary industries. Since farmers are considerably less likely to retire early than workers in other industries (McDonald and Wanner, 1984), this decline in the agricultural sector of the labour force alone may account for a considerable portion of the increase in early retirement already observed.

The results of Pampel and Weiss's (1983) cross-national, longitudinal study of the determinants of older men's labour force participation are consistent with this explanation. They found that the percentage of a nation's labour force in agricultural occupations had by far the greatest effect on the participation of older males, with a 1 percent decline in agricultural employment resulting in nearly a 0.68 percent reduction in participation. During the period of Canadian history covered in Table 3.2, the main flow of workers was not into manufacturing jobs, which peaked in the 1950s, but into the service industries, including such industries as education, banking and finance, and advertising. What service industries share in common is that they are more likely than other industries to provide white-collar jobs with distinct career lines attached to them (Spilerman, 1977), which ultimately result in expectations about the end of the career, that is, retirement.

Associated with the dramatic growth of service industries in Canada has been growth in professional employment and increasing requirements for educational credentials. Between 1921 and 1981 the proportion of professionals in the labour force nearly tripled, increasing from 5.5 percent to 15 percent. The proportion of Canada's population that attained at least some post-secondary (mainly university) education remained quite stable up to the 1950s, but virtually exploded in the 1960s, nearly quadrupling between 1961 and 1971. Although the percentage of individuals with university education was increasing dramatically during this period, a large portion of the increase was due to the availability of colleges providing both academic and vocational training. In view of consistent research findings that suggest that the better educated are both less likely to retire early and more likely to continue working after 65 (McDonald and Wanner, 1982; 1984; Statistics Canada, 1982a), this trend would suggest that early retirement rates should remain stable and then decline as the better-educated workers who entered the labour force in the 1960s reach their fifties and sixties.

Another unmistakable trend observable in Table 3.2 that will soon have a major impact on retirement patterns is the increasing presence of women in the labour force. Although most older women in Canada belong to a generation in which only a few held jobs outside the home, the trend toward increasing labour force participation on the part of women means that retirement will become as typical of women's life courses as it has been of men's over the past few decades. However, the great differences that remain in men's and women's careers will inevitably mean that the retirement experience will be different for women. Specifically, women are still far more likely to be paid less than men, more likely to interrupt their careers to raise children, more often found in part-time jobs, and less likely to belong to private pension plans (Statistics Canada, 1985b). Until these conditions change substantially, in retirement women will simply reproduce their inferior standing in the labour force.

Another important element of this transformation of the Canadian social structure is an increase in affluence, as measured by per capita gross national product. In constant 1971 dollars, the increase was over four-fold between 1931, at the outset of the Great Depression, and 1981, just before the lengthy recession of the 1980s. The main impact of this greater affluence has been to make retirement more affordable. Higher levels of individual income have been shown to be associated with both early retirement (McDonald and Wanner, 1984) and with a deceased likelihood of working after age 65 (McDonald and Wanner, 1982). However, it is unlikely that the higher levels of individual saving induced by greater affluence alone could have led to the dramatic increase in retirement over the past few decades. Instead, we must look to the growth of both government and private pension plans that replaced workers' lost earnings after retirement.

Retirement and Changing Pension Policies

Table 3.3 reports the growth since the 1950s of the three federal retirement pension programs for the elderly, Old Age Security, Guaranteed Income Supplement, the Canada Pension Plan and the Quebec Pension Plan. OAS is a flat rate, indexed benefit to all Canadians aged 65 and over. Low income senior citizens also receive GIS payments, which are also fully indexed. GIS benefits are one dollar less than the maximum for every two dollars of non-OAS income. Spouses Allowances (SPA) provide benefits on an income-tested basis to spouses aged 60 to 64 who are married to OAS pensioners. Six provincial governments, as well as the Yukon and Northwest Territories, provide additional transfer payments to the elderly, although the rates of payment vary across jurisdictions. Unlike OAS, CPP and QPP are aimed only at those Canadians who have been in the labour force and guarantee a pension income at age 65 equal to 25 percent of a contributor's average previous earnings. Benefits are financed by employers and employees, with the contribution (3.8 percent of covered earnings in 1987) divided equally between them.

TABLE 3.3

NUMBER OF RECIPIENTS AND EXPENDITURES PER RECIPIENT FOR CANADA'S FEDERAL RETIREMENT PENSION PROGRAMMES, 1953–82

	PROGRAM					
	Old Age Security		Guaranteed Income Supplement		Canada Pension Plan/Quebec Pension Plan	
Year	Number of Recipients	Expenditures Per Recipient	Number of Recipients	Expenditures Per Recipient	Number of Recipients	Expenditures Per Recipient
1953	671,240	$ 481				
1955	734,080	481				
1957	788,460	481				
1959	845,840	661				
1961	894,810	662				
1963	941,980	780				
1965	985,320	898				
1967	1,143,800	903	505,240	$ 78	4,586	$ 11
1969	1,406,800	922	743,960	334	73,367	88
1971	1,701,500	956	823,920	340	220,230	233
1973	1,791,400	995	1,015,900	731	337,659	333
1975	1,887,800	1,381	1,070,500	782	489,682	485
1977	1,988,606	1,669	1,090,534	933	703,170	863
1980	2,201,497	2,125	1,172,289	1,275	995,365	1,344
1982	2,342,480	2,621	1,234,823	1,816	1,159,178	1,786

Sources: Number of recipients for 1952–75, Statistics Canada (1982c); 1977–82, Statistics Canada (1985a) (for OAS and GIS) and Statistics Canada (1984) (for CPP/QPP). Expenditures per recipient were calculated from total expenditure figures from the same sources.

It is obvious from Table 3.3 that federal retirement pension programs were minimal up to 1967, the year both GIS and CPP/QPP became operational. Flat rate benefits to pensioners remained constant through the 1950s, only beginning to increase through the 1960s. The decline in labour force participation among men aged 55 to 64 that began around 1970-71 coincides quite nicely with the boost provided to federal pensions by GIS and CPP/QPP between 1969 and 1971, though the rather consistent decline for men 65 and over does not appear to be accelerated by the introduction of these two programs. The evidence for women is similar, though more indirect. The regular increase in participation among women 55 to 64 observed through the late 1960s is arrested, though not reversed, in the early 1970s. As noted earlier, the greater numbers of older women entering or remaining in the labour force are being offset by increasing numbers of women retiring in response to the earnings replacement offered by GIS and CPP/QPP. These observations on the impact of public pensions on labour force participation in Canada are consistent with Pampel and Weiss's (1983) finding for 18 nations that, with the exception of the percentage of the labour force in agriculture, the variable with the strongest effect on men's labour force participation is social insurance expenditures. Likewise, Pampel and Park (1986), in another cross-national study, found a strong effect of the number of years a nation has had a public pension program on the rate of women's retirement.

In a study designed to test the competing claims of political economy theory, which asserts that the trend toward lower rates of labour force participation among older persons is largely a function of government pension policies, and the industrialism theory, which suggests that it is primarily changes in the character of the labour force and the economy that have brought about lower levels of participation among the elderly, Wanner and McDonald (1987) estimated separate multivariate time-series models predicting the labour force participation rate for Canadian men and women both age 65 and over and age 55 to 64. The data for this analysis were collected for each year between 1953 and 1986. Wanner and McDonald found that rising levels of public pension benefits in Canada during this period significantly lowered the labour force participation rates of the younger men, but had only a minor effect on the rates of men age 65 or over. In fact, they found that changes in federal pension programs in the late 1960s had a measurable impact on the participation of the younger men, even when other factors known to influence labour force participation were controlled. Wanner and McDonald (1987) further found that the industrialism theory is more strongly supported for the older men. In particular, their results indicated that the declining proportion of Canada's labour force in agriculture has had a substantial effect on the labour force participation of men age 65 and over. Not unexpectedly, they found that neither theory seems to account for the patterns of labour force participation observed among older Canadian women.

Despite the persuasiveness of these findings, one should not get the impression that public pension policy implemented by governments always has predictable consequences. Assuming that the earnings test provision of the Canada Pension Plan, under which until 1967 benefits were payable only to persons over age 65 whose incomes from employment were below a certain level, acts as a disincentive to continued employment past 65, Parliament removed the test in 1975. It was anticipated that labour force participation rates for persons over age 65 would subsequently increase. Instead, the rates continued their downward trend (Tracy, 1982). In fact, Tracy (1982) found that for men aged 65 to 69 the rate of decline in 1976, the year after the earnings test was removed, was the largest observed between 1962 and 1980. Tracy argued that removal of the earnings test served to reinforce age 65 as the institutionalized age of retirement, because the only barrier to receiving CPP payments at that age had been removed. Once payments began, the men he studied tended not to continue in or re-enter the labour force.

Another feature to be noted in Table 3.3 is the dramatic increase in pension recipients over the two decades, an increase of over two and one-half times in the case of OAS recipients. This should certainly be no surprise in view of the precipitous decline in labour force participation. What is important about these figures, however, is the fact that, while federal pension recipients, as a proportion of the labour force, were just 13.7 percent in 1961, representing over 7 working Canadians for every retiree, by 1981 they were nearly 19 percent of the labour force, or about 5.3 workers for every retiree. As well, the percentage of OAS recipients receiving CPP or QPP benefits mushroomed from a minuscule 0.4 percent in 1967 to nearly 50 percent in 1982. The Government of Canada has already responded to the potential of these trends for the fiscal health of its retirement programs by gradually escalating contribution rates to the Canada Pension Plan, from 3.6 percent of earnings in 1986 to 7.6 percent by 2011 (Health and Welfare Canada, 1986). The same change in legislation will likely reinforce the trend toward early retirement observed previously by allowing those who retire between the ages of 60 and 64 to collect CPP benefits at a reduced level beginning in 1987.

Another element that has been largely ignored in the research on retirement is the growth of private pension plans. Table 3.4 shows the growth of such plans and their membership from 1960 to 1980. While the spurt of growth in the number of plans in the 1960s levelled off with the consolidation of many smaller plans, membership steadily grew both in numbers and as a percentage of the labour force. Membership in 1960 represented just 27.8 percent of the total labour force; by 1980 this had grown to nearly 37 percent. Also important is the growth of non-contributory plans, since members of plans in which the employer picks up the entire tab will have a larger disposable income, part of which may be

TABLE 3.4

**PRIVATE PENSION PLANS IN CANADA AND THEIR MEMBERSHIP,
1960-80**

Year	Number of Plans	Number of Members	Percent of Members in Non-contributory Plans
1960	8,920	1,815,000	20.5
1965	13,660	2,345,648	22.3
1970	16,137	2,822,336	22.0
1974	15,853	3,424,245	24.9
1978	15,095	4,193,244	28.3
1980	14,586	4,475,429	30.1

Source: Statistics Canada (1982b): 13, 18.

saved in vehicles such as RRSPs, further increasing potential retirement income. Indeed, current federal taxation policy discriminates against those employees whose pensions are contributory by allowing them to take as a tax deduction only the maximum allowable RRSP contribution minus any contribution they have made to their pension plan.

These figures conceal an important discrepancy in coverage – that between men and women. In 1980, 45.1 percent of the total male labour force belonged to plans, but just 31.2 percent of the total female labour force were members (Statistics Canada, 1982b: 15). Incredibly, the gap in coverage between men and women increased substantially after 1970, when 37.7 percent of the male labour force was covered by pension plans versus 26.9 percent of the female labour force. Although this difference can be explained by the cumulative result of labour force and earnings discrimination practised against women generally, a large proportion of the male advantage is attributable to just two factors: the concentration of employed women in industries in which few firms offer pension benefits, and the greater prevalence of part-time work among women. Women in the labour force are disproportionately concentrated in the retail trade, business service, and personal service industries, in which pension coverage is significantly lower than in the manufacturing, mining, and construction industries in which men are over-represented (Statistics Canada, 1982b). As for the influence of part-time employment, calculating the proportion of women covered by pension plans as a percentage of full-time paid workers reveals that fully 47.8 percent are members of plans, as are 57.3 percent of full-time males (Statistics Canada, 1982b). As can be seen, the gender gap narrows from 13.9 percent to 9.5 percent, compared to coverage rates calculated against the total labour force. However, pension *coverage* is not the whole story. Even if they are covered by private pension plans, the benefits offered workers are normally in proportion to their earnings while in the plan, and women's earnings remain, on average, considerably lower than those of men. In 1982 the earnings of women employed full-time were just 64 percent of the earnings of men employed full-time (Statistics Canada, 1985b). Nevertheless, as with public pension coverage, the continued growth of private pensions and enlargement of their benefits will make it easier for Canadians to retire at ever earlier ages, although the disadvantages of women in accumulating pension benefits will likely persist.

Sources of Government Pensions Policy

Although we have sketched out two main explanations of declining labour force participation, one attributing it to the growth of industrialization, and a second explaining it largely in terms of the growth of government pension programs, and indicated how developments in Canada lend support to both of them, we have not looked at the question of why governments have provided these programs. The industrialism thesis attributes the rise of the welfare state generally, and the implementation of pension programs specifically, to the dynamics of economic growth (Kerr et al., 1960; Wilensky, 1975). In this explanation, the state is seen as providing financial support for groups adversely affected by the dislocations created by industrial advancement. The mechanism that is frequently mentioned as stimulating this state intervention is the demographic aging of society that accompanies industrialization. While policies of mandatory retirement and the demand for younger workers in industry produce increasing numbers of jobless elderly, these persons themselves (Wilensky, 1975) or their children (Entwisle and Winegarden, 1984) successfully pressure government for old age pensions.

In contrast, the political economy perspective emphasizes the role of the working class, in the form of union organizations and support for social democratic political parties, in establishing welfare state programs in general and public pension programs in particular. In this view, social programs are not the direct result of the industrialization process, but emerge only when the working class achieves sufficient power to force governments to introduce such programs (Korpi, 1983). Indeed, Myles (1984a) argues that the expansion of public pension systems in the industrial nations was the result of much broader attempts on the part of the working class to improve their wages. He goes so far as to term public pensions a "retirement wage" - deferred wages to be paid to workers only after they retire. Although sharing some assumptions with other theorists in the political economy of aging, neo-Marxists go even further: they claim that the introduction of pensions was a calculated government attempt to bolster a failing capitalist system (Olsen, 1982), preserving its class structure and deflecting demands for radical change. It is probably far more reasonable to assume that, while public pensions were in most cases introduced as social policy measures to reduce poverty among older persons, they have evolved into measures to remove older workers from the labour force, solving simultaneously the "efficiency" problem faced by employers and the unemployment problem faced by governments (Graebner, 1980).

Although most of the research testing the claims of the industrialism and political economy explanations have been rather one-sided, including only variables called for by the investigator's favoured explanation, Pampel and Williamson (1985) attempted to test these competing explanations, using a sample of 48 nations at all levels of economic development over the period 1960-75. In their models predicting pension expenditures, the dominant variables were percentage of the population age 65 and over and several variables measuring level of industrialization. As well, the age structure variable had an even stronger effect on pension expenditures in nations with democratic governments, suggesting that age politics plays a more important role in those nations. In contrast, Pampel and Williamson (1985) found that their measures of class structure, political control by leftist parties, union membership, union centralization in bargaining, electoral competition, and corporatism, had little or no influence on pension expenditures.

Up to this point, we have reviewed retirement trends and their explanations for Canada. How does the situation in Canada compare to that of the other industrialized nations? Is the movement toward even earlier retirement unique to Canada, or is it occurring in other nations as well? Has the labour force participation of older workers in other nations responded to the same social forces and government policies as has that of Canadian workers? The next section attempts to answer these questions.

RETIREMENT IN OTHER INDUSTRIAL NATIONS

As the title of a recent article (Nusberg, 1986) claims, early retirement has become "ubiquitous" in the Western industrialized nations. Table 3.5 shows that for four Western European countries and the United States, there has been a strong trend toward earlier retirement among men during the 1970s. The most dramatic decline in labour force participation among men younger than age 65 occurred in France. There, over 65 percent of men age 60 to 64 were in the labour force at the beginning of the decade, while just 38 percent were by 1979. Declines in the other four nations were considerably less but still substantial, ranging between 10 and 15 percent over the decade. The decline in Canada was also within this range. The declines for men 65 and over were also sizeable during the 1970s in most of the nations represented in Table 3.5. In France and the Netherlands, only about 5 percent of these men remained in the labour force. Among these five nations, the United States has the highest participation rate in 1979, with over 20 percent of men over 65 still in the labour force. Except in the case of France, where rates declined, participation rates for women aged 60 to 64 remained relatively constant in these countries, even increasing marginally in Great Britain and Sweden. As in Canada, the trend for women in these countries is likely obscured by a countervailing trend toward increased labour force activity among women in the industrialized countries during this period.

As is the case for Canada, declining labour force participation rates in the other industrialized countries are linked to government policies permitting the awarding of pensions at ever earlier ages (Tracy, 1979). Tracy suggests that the major approach to awarding earlier pensions has been not so much to lower the normal retirement age but to introduce provisions that give workers greater opportunities to retire before that age. Nevertheless, consistent with our observation that government policies do

Retirement in Canada

TABLE 3.5

LABOUR FORCE PARTICIPATION RATES FOR THE UNITED STATES AND FIVE EUROPEAN NATIONS, 1970 AND 1979

Country	Men, 60–64		Men 65+		Women, 60–64	
	1970	1979	1970	1979	1970	1979
France	65.2	38.2	15.4	5.8	33.7	22.4
Great Britain	86.6	75.8	19.4	10.2	51.1	54.9
Netherlands	73.9	59.9	11.4	4.4	11.9	10.5
Sweden	79.5	69.0	28.9	14.0	35.8	39.4
United States	75.0	61.8	26.8	20.0	36.1	33.9

Source: Casey and Bruche (1983 : 112).
Note: All figures in the 1970 column for Great Britain and the Netherlands are for 1971.

not always elicit their intended consequences, Tracy (1979) found that workers have been retiring at earlier ages even in countries that offer few or no options for early pensions to be awarded.

Why have so many industrialized countries offered inducements to workers to retire early? During the 1960s, a period during which unemployment rates were unusually low, the principal issue surrounding older workers was how to maintain their productivity and keep them in the labour force past the conventional retirement age. In fact, the Organization for Economic Cooperation and Development (OECD) issued a series of studies addressing the issues of how older workers might be retained in the labour force and how the unemployed or retired might be returned to active employment (Casey, 1984). By the 1970s, the large birth cohorts of the 1950s were entering the labour market, as were increasing numbers of women, thereby creating a surplus labour pool. High unemployment rates in the advanced industrial nations were further exacerbated by the exporting of manufacturing jobs by multinational corporations to developing nations with lower wage and benefit scales. In the face of these high unemployment rates, governments began to introduce new provisions into their public pension Acts that, in effect, paved the way for the exclusion of older workers, ostensibly to create openings for the unemployed young.

Of the countries represented in Table 3.5, the Netherlands and France have by far the lowest rates of labour force participation for both older men and older women, and both countries have pension policies explicitly designed to ease workers out of the labour force at a relatively early age. In both countries, this policy takes the form not of early pensions, but of "bridge payments" carrying workers leaving the labour force by age 60 to the normal pensionable age of 65. In the case of France, the early retirement scheme operates through the unemployment insurance fund. Since 1977, a higher benefit level has been made available to all workers over the age of 60 who are voluntarily or involuntarily without a job. Persons as young as 56 who have lost their jobs become eligible immediately for regular unemployment benefits and, at age 60, for increased benefits. This provision has effectively lowered the early retirement age still further (Casey and Bruche, 1983). The Netherlands offers its workers a flat rate pension at age 65, with some 70 to 80 percent of the labour force covered by company-sponsored pensions, which also normally begin at age 65. However, since the late 1970s collective agreements at the company level have introduced early retirement schemes that now cover some 80 percent of employed workers (Casey and Bruche, 1983). While these plans vary from company to company, they typically grant a bridge payment from the time of retirement up to the normal age of pension eligibility that equals approximately 80 percent of final earnings. Most of these plans allow early retirement at ages 60 or 61, and in all but one plan participation is voluntary. More recently, persons becoming unemployed as early as age 57 become eligible for unemployment benefits equal to 70 percent of their final earnings until reaching the pensionable age of 65 (Nusberg, 1986).

The situation in the United States is considerably different from that in the European countries, or in Canada for that matter. As Table 3.5 indicates, the pattern in the United States of increasing early retirement seems typical of industrial countries, but there men over age 65 are considerably more likely to be in the labour force. As Casey (1984) points out, the United States has not followed the European lead in using early retirement as a means of solving its unemployment problem. In fact, in 1986 the United States abolished entirely the mandatory retirement age of 70 that had been in place since 1978 and put in place the legal machinery to increase the age at which a full public pension might be drawn in the future. Despite the fact that U.S. Social Security pensions available at age 62 are considerably less generous than their European counterparts, by 1981, 38 percent of eligible males aged 62 to 64 were receiving one (Casey, 1984).

CONCLUSIONS

In this chapter we have examined trends in Canadian retirement patterns and attempted to understand them both in the context of the dominant theories of retirement and in comparison to patterns in other industrial nations. We can conclude only that, while it differs in certain respects, the overall Canadian pattern is typical of that found in advanced industrial societies. The dramatic decline in age at retirement that has taken place over the past 30 years is the result of two major forces, one operating on persons over the "normal" retirement age of 65, the other operating primarily on those under 65. The enormous decline in participation among men aged 65 and older from nearly 50 percent to little more than 10 percent of men in that age group has been largely a consequence of the shifts in Canadian society from an agrarian period, in which most workers were either farmers or self-employed in a small business, to a "post-industrial" (Bell, 1973) period, in which a majority of workers are employees of large, bureaucratic firms or government agencies. Accompanying this shift has been the spread of mandatory retirement policies and declining earnings possibilities outside of working for others. The relatively more recent spread of early retirement, although related to these broad social forces, is likely the result of changes in government pension policies.

However useful the perspective taken in this chapter is for understanding processes in Canadian society as a whole, it does little to further an understanding of the meaning of retirement to individual Canadians. The next two chapters attempt to complement this macrosocietal view by examining retirement as an individual decision and an individual experience within the context of the retirement institution. They look more closely at the myriad individual situations that are aggregated into the social trends described in this chapter.

CHAPTER 4

ANTECEDENTS OF THE INDIVIDUAL RETIREMENT EXPERIENCE

Why people retire, how they go about retiring, and what happens to them after they retire have been a source of continuing fascination for social gerontologists since the end of the 1940s. This unabated interest in the individual retirement experience reflects the individualist theoretical tradition in social gerontology described in Chapter 1 and has generated a vast amount of research. Making sense of this ever-burgeoning literature can be confusing because of the diversity of studies, frustrating because of the gaps in knowledge, and puzzling because of often-contradictory findings.

To simplify matters, this chapter will highlight those issues that appear as common threads running through research studies undertaken in several countries, but with an eye to their relevance to the Canadian situation. In attempting to uncover why people retire, researchers have focused primarily on such factors as perceived health status, amount of unearned income, characteristics of work and occupation, and family attributes. How people go about retiring has been considered from the perspective of pre-retirement planning, making the retirement decision, and the nature of the transition from work to retirement. In determining the consequences of retirement, researchers have investigated the mental and physical health of retired people, their level of happiness, and general life satisfaction among them. Because there is a wealth of research about the consequences of retirement, that discussion is reserved for Chapter 5. This chapter will concentrate on why people retire and how they go about it. Before turning to these issues, a few precautionary notes about the existing retirement research are required to facilitate our understanding of both the individual retirement experience, noted in this chapter and Chapter 5, and the social structures that influence that experience described in Chapter 6.

THE RETIREMENT RESEARCH: SOME CAVEATS

Several general observations can be made about the retirement research in Canada. There has been no national, representative, longitudinal study of retirement in Canada, while, for example, in the United States there have been at least seven such studies (see Palmore et al., 1985). Most available Canadian evidence is drawn from surveys using smaller samples, which are not always representative of the general population and which are usually cross-sectional in nature. Studies that are cross-sectional give a "snap-shot" of a process on one occasion and therefore do not address changes in the retirement experience over time, except by using either prospective or retrospective questions. What working people say they intend to do and what they actually do can be inconsistent, because of the many factors that might intervene before actual retirement. After-the-fact explanations of retirement may also be deceptive. For example, health as a reason for retirement is more socially acceptable than dislike of work, in the face of a strong North American work ethic. Finally, Canadian researchers have sometimes relied on secondary data sources not originally designed to study retirement, such as census materials, in their quest to understand retirement on a national basis. Secondary data analysis has not always been satisfactory, because many key variables, such as health status or attitudes to work, are not often available for analysis.

To underscore these observations it is worth noting that, to date, the only national study devoted to an investigation of the retirement experiences of Canadians is a cross-sectional study done by Health and Welfare Canada in conjunction with the Monthly Labour Force Survey in February of 1975. The only Canadian longitudinal study that explores directly the transition from work to retirement and life after retirement is the Ontario Longitudinal Study of Aging (LSA), which was carried out from 1959 to 1978. This study was not based on a random sample, dealt only with retirement among males, and is only now becoming available for general use.

Gender differences in retirement behaviour is a relatively new area of research in Canada, so there is little accumulated evidence about this phenomenon. As is the case in any new area of investigation, what is known is somewhat contradictory and fragmented, partially because of the problems of small, nonrepresentative samples common in this research (Martin Matthews and Brown, 1987). In addition, male-oriented conceptions of work and retirement have often been applied inappropriately to the female experience (Connidis, 1982). There has also been the related problem of choosing the appropriate comparison group for understanding women's retirement (Connidis, 1982; Palmore et al., 1985). Using men for comparison can highlight gender differences, using non-working women as a comparison group emphasizes the effects of labour force participation among women, and using non-retired women as a comparison group for retired women emphasizes the effects of retirement. These types of studies are not comparable, but they are necessary to understand the entire range of retirement experiences of women.

Making sense of the retirement research, then, poses a number of problems for the wary reader. As outlined in Chapter 1, it is important to ascertain the theoretical framework informing the study, as well as how *retirement* is defined. At the same time, it is crucial to attend to the research methods used, the nature of the sample, and the comparison groups used for interpretation.

FACTORS LEADING TO RETIREMENT

With the rapid increase in retirement among men following World War II, researchers began asking why people retire. Riley and Foner (1968) summarized the small number of American studies at the time, stating that those who retired were older, sicker and less educated people who had held lower paying jobs. It was also more likely to be women than men who retired. As the trend toward early retirement became more evident, researchers modified the question from Why do people retire? to Why do people retire early? Early retirement was perceived to occur at any time prior to the "normal" retirement age of 65. When the options for the age of retirement were broadened in the United States with the adoption of the amendments to the Age Discrimination in Employment Act in 1979 and in Canada with the adoption of provincial human rights legislation and, later, the Canadian Charter of Rights and Freedoms in 1985, the question became Why do people retire when they do, if they retire at all? Retirement at age 65 was considered by scholars to be on-time retirement, and retirement any time after age 65 was labelled late retirement (Palmore et al., 1985).

Who retires when and why, is not an idle question. The answer has serious ramifications for the social, psychological, and economic welfare of the individuals and families involved and, at the societal level, for determining the requirements of pension funds and for the size and composition of the future labour force. Furthermore, there is growing evidence that the determinants of early, on-time, and late retirement are very different (Morgan, 1980; O'Rand and Henretta, 1982a; Palmore et al., 1985; Wanner and McDonald, 1987), as are the issues surrounding them. For example, in what ways will the early retirement of women, who increasingly have longer and more remunerative work histories, have an impact on the Canadian social security system and the size of the future work force? Similarly, knowing why people retire at the "normal" age of 65 will provide some insight about labour force changes as mandatory retirement continues to be constitutionally challenged in Canadian courts. Finally, an understanding of the determinants of late retirement can shed some light on the links among work, financial status, and retirement and assist in predicting future labour supply. The sections that follow treat separately the research and issues surrounding each of the age plateaus in the retirement experience.

Early Retirement

Canadian workers want to retire, and they want to retire early. Of the men aged 54 in the Ontario Longitudinal Study of Aging, 67 percent reported that they wished to retire before age 65 (Crawford and Matlow, 1972). The Retirement Survey of 1975 indicated that 40 percent of the retired men would have preferred to retire before or at age 60. Seventy percent of those men still in the labour force preferred to retire before age 65, and 77 percent of the working women wanted to retire before or at age 60 (Health and Welfare Canada, 1977b). In a large, random sample of Albertans, one-half of the respondents retired early or planned to retire early (Third Career Research Society, 1976). In 1984, a Gallup survey in Canada showed that 47 percent of the workers aged 18 and over intended to leave the labour force before age 65 (Canadian Institute of Public Opinion, 1984).

In an attempt to explain the desire for, as well as actual, early retirement, most researchers have identified health, unearned income, attachment to work and attributes of the marital unit as key individual explanatory factors.

Health and Unearned Income

Perceived health status and retirement income have frequently been seen as competing explanations of early retirement. On the one hand, early retirement has been viewed as an involuntary response to declining health (Parnes and Nestel, 1971; Reno, 1971; MacBride, 1976; Schwab, 1976; Statistics Canada, 1980; Baillargeon, 1982; Palmore, George and Fillenbaum, 1982; Palmore et al., 1985), and on the other, unearned income – that is income from sources other than wages, salary and self-employment, such as monies from assets and social security – is presumed to entice workers into early retirement (Barfield and Morgan, 1969; Bowen and Finegan, 1969; Cohen, Rea and Lerman, 1970; Parnes and Nestel, 1971; Boskin, 1977; Quinn, 1977; Kapsalis, 1979; Statistics Canada, 1980; Schmitt and McCune, 1981; Shaw, 1984). Several researchers have found support for both hypotheses simultaneously (Quinn, 1977; Baillargeon, 1982; Monahan and Greene, 1987). In a recent study, Palmore et al. (1985) used several longitudinal, nationally representative data sets for the United States and concluded that, for men, early retirement was a function of both self-rated health and attitudes to retirement. Both Quinn (1977) and O'Rand and Henretta (1982a), using the U.S. Retirement History Study, found that health and unearned income were the two most important predictors of early retirement for unmarried women.

Canadian studies of early retirement indicate some support for both hypotheses. The Statistics Canada Retirement Survey of 1975 indicated that poor health was the only reason men retired before age 57 and was the single most important reason for having retired at each age up to age 64 (Ciffin and Martin, 1977). In the small subsample of women who retired, no reason for retirement was associated with specific ages, with the exception of compulsory retirement, usually at age 65 (Ciffin and Martin, 1977). A Statistics Canada research report (1980), using Monthly Labour Force Survey data for men aged 55 to 64, discovered that the major reason cited for labour force withdrawal was health problems. The relation between early labour force withdrawal and income was ambiguous. In a Quebec study of 220 men and women in the public and private sectors, the reasons for retirement varied by sector (Baillargeon, 1982). Early retirement was related to poor health for men in the private sector and was associated with work-related stress and financial adequacy among men in the public sector. Only women in the public sector were studied, and their early retirement was associated with both poor health and being married.

With regard to unearned income, respondents to the 1975 Retirement Survey were asked if they would have retired five years earlier than they did if it would have made no difference in the amount of their pension. Of the retired men, 31 percent indicated that they would have retired earlier, while 22 percent of the retired women would have done so. Of those Canadians responding to this survey who were still working, 55 percent of the men and 57 percent of the women would have retired earlier than their scheduled retirement age (Health and Welfare, Canada 1977b). In a more direct test of the hypothesis and using the same data, Kapsalis (1979) found that, for men 55 to 64 years of age, a higher retirement income was associated with an earlier retirement age. McDonald and Wanner (1982), using a cross-sectional subsample from the Canadian National Mobility Study of 6,127 men and women aged 55 to 64, reported that Canadians who retired early had higher levels of unearned income than did those who continued working. The influence of unearned income was more pronounced for the men than for the women.

Although the Canadian evidence is far from conclusive, health and potential retirement income do figure in the early retirement decision. Which factor is more important for whom and in what context is not entirely clear. The indications are that health and unearned income are more salient factors for men than for women, and that the specific work context determines which variable will emerge as more important.

The implications for the individual are significant. A large proportion of men and, to a lesser extent, women may be pushed out of the labour force early, and perhaps involuntarily, because of poor health, which in turn can lead to a lower income (Health and Welfare Canada, 1977b: 7-8). These people constitute a vulnerable group that should be flagged for special attention by practitioners. At the policy level, the power of an adequate pension cannot be overlooked. If the Canadian goal is early retirement as championed by many individual Canadians, business people, and organized labour leaders, then pension benefits must continue to be attractive to lure people out of the labour force. Conversely, if reducing early retirement is the goal, to offset the purported drain on public pensions, then pension benefits should be made less attractive or delayed. The push (health) and pull (finances) toward early retirement, however, would have to be balanced so that those with precarious health are financially protected. The recent change to the Canada Pension Plan making pensions available as early as age 60 suggests that the federal government is attempting to further accelerate the trend toward early retirement.

Work and Early Retirement

A long series of studies, beginning in the early 1950s, but pursued to a lesser extent in more recent investigations of retirement, emphasize the link between people and their work and its repercussions for retirement. The assumption underlying these studies is that those people who are not firmly attached to their work will retire early, while those people who have a strong attachment to their work will retire later. If the occupational research is any indication (see Morse and Weiss, 1955; Tausky, 1960; Kaplan and Tausky, 1974; Manheim and Cohen, 1978; Vecchio, 1980; Harpaz, 1983; 1985) most people would appear to be very attached to their work. A national survey in Canada found that Canadians are committed to work. They would chose work over most leisure activities and prefer working to being on unemployment insurance (Burstein et al., 1975, in Chen and Regan, 1985: 3). It is important to remember that work is just as salient for women as it is for men (Connidis, 1982; Newman, Sherman and Higgins, 1982; Martin Matthews and Brown, 1987). The oft-repeated observation by pioneer retirement researchers that women lacked commitment to work because their primary work was in the home no longer stands up to empirical scrutiny (Miller, 1965; Irelan, 1972; Blau, 1973; Price-Bonham and Johnson, 1982).

Researchers attempted to explore the relation between work and retirement in a number of ways. One of the first lines of investigation was to examine the inverse relation between attitudes to work and attitudes to retirement (Friedmann and Havighurst, 1954; Johnson and Strother, 1962; Saleck and Otis, 1963; Palmore, 1965; Simpson, Back and McKinney, 1966; Fillenbaum, 1971; Streib and Schneider, 1971; Parnes and Nestel, 1971; Goudy, Powers and Keith, 1975; Skoglund, 1980). The results were not entirely convincing. First, there is a substantial number of studies that found only a tenuous relation between job attitudes and retirement attitudes (Simpson et al., 1966; Barfield and Morgan, 1969; Fillenbaum, 1971; Goudy et al., 1975; Sheppard, 1976). Secondly, there are some studies that reported that those people with high job commitment also have strong positive attitudes toward retirement (Seltzer and Atchley, 1971; Atchley, 1972; Morrow, 1982). Finally, there are those studies that substantiated the expected inverse relation between attitudes to work and attitudes toward retirement (Tuckman and Lorge, 1953; Freidmann and Havighurst, 1954; Saleck and Otis, 1963; Simpson et al., 1966; Parnes et al., 1970; Glamser, 1981; Price-Bonham and Johnson, 1982; Dobson and Morrow, 1984). Possible explanations for these discrepant findings are the use of diverse concepts of attachment to work (e.g., job satisfaction, job involvement, desire to work, missing work, etc.) and inconsistency in the time at which the attitudes were measured, usually before retirement or after retirement.

Studies that specifically uncovered a relation between negative attitudes to work and planned early retirement or actual early retirement are more definitive (Parnes and Nestel, 1971; Bixby, 1976; Skoglund, 1980; Schmitt and McCune, 1981; Palmore et al., 1985; Monahan and Greene, 1987). Those people who retired early were less attached to their work than those who did not retire early. However, these work attitudes were uniformly secondary in importance to financial reasons and health in predicting early retirement (Schmitt and McCune, 1981; Palmore et al., 1985; Monahan and Greene, 1987).

Another line of investigation looked at the effects of occupational status or prestige. McKinney and his colleagues were one of the first groups of researchers to discover that, for respondents in higher and middle status occupations, the more positive the commitment to their jobs, the less likely they were to look forward to retirement (Simpson et al., 1966). Higher status jobs are usually associated with higher incomes, more interest and more autonomy, making it less attractive to their incumbents to retire especially early. Low occupational status has since been consistently linked to early retirement for men, and in some studies, for women (Epstein, 1966; Epstein and Murray, 1967; Bixby and Rings, 1969; Parnes and Nestel, 1975; Powers, Keith and Goudy, 1980; Price-Bonham and Johnson, 1982; Dobson and Morrow, 1984; Kilty and Behling, 1985).

Using Canadian data, McDonald and Wanner (1984: 112) showed that it is not occupational status *per se* that leads men and women to retire early, but rather the lower educational background that they brought to their jobs. The differences in findings could be attributed to the use of different measures of occupational status, such as level of income, education, and the blue collar-white collar distinction. For example, if income is used as a measure of status, it is not surprising that it does not predict early retirement for women, since Canadian women are less likely to be rewarded financially in proportion to their occupational standing (McDonald and Wanner, 1984).

There are other work-related factors that researchers have found to be associated with early retirement, but these studies are fewer in number. For example, the desire for leisure (Palmore, 1964; Messer, 1969; Pollman, 1971; McPherson and Guppy, 1979), the need for personal growth, the length of time in job (Schmitt et al., 1979), perceived pressure to retire (Wood, 1980), and number of job changes (Pollman and Johnson, 1974) have all been found to have some effect on early retirement.

In summary, people who are not attached to their work tend to retire earlier once state of health and income level are taken into account. Low occupational status has also been linked to early retirement, particularly for men, but it is evident that more research is required to unravel the link between women, their work, and retirement. As will be seen in Chapter 6, the trend is to look more at the effects of other features of occupations on early retirement. The next step for researchers would be to consider the structural aspects of occupation together with individual attitudes and characteristics. Connidis (1982) has argued that research on female work and retirement should take into account the interaction of multiple careers (work and family) and the meanings attached to these careers in order to understand women's retirement. Keating and Doherty (1986) took an initial step in this direction by linking individual retirement plans and the organization of work and family in their studies of Canadian farmers. They reported that the individual retirement plans of farmers were vague as a result of complex family and financial issues that were consistent with the problems of a family business.

The Marital Unit

Recently, researchers have found that marital status does affect the timing of retirement. Single men and married women are more likely to retire before age 65 (Baillargeon, 1982; O'Rand and Henretta, 1982a; Atchley and Miller, 1983; McDonald and Wanner, 1984). Single men probably have fewer family responsibilities than married men and can afford to retire earlier. In the case of women, marriage may provide opportunities for women to stop working because of the increased economic resources that result from the marital union. In fact, O'Rand and Henretta (1982a) indicated that the most important late-life status in predicting early versus late retirement for working unmarried women was a change in marital status. If a woman changed from being unmarried to married or from being separated or divorced to widowed she was more likely to retire early (O'Rand and Henretta, 1982a: 372).

Several recent labour force studies have indicated that decisions about retirement should be viewed as joint decisions between husband and wife (Clark, Johnson and McDermed 1980; Clark and Johnson, 1981; Gratton and Haug, 1983; Shaw, 1984; Campione, 1987). Henretta and O'Rand (1983) found what they call "symmetry" in the retirement decision in dual worker families. Their research suggested that there is a certain amount of equality in decisions to retire, since the pattern chosen depends upon the characteristics of both spouses, not just the characteristics of the husband. For example, the older one of the spouses was, the more likely it was that the couple would follow a joint pattern of retirement. The financial situation of either spouse also mattered but did not lead to joint retirement. The spouse without pension coverage was more likely to work longer than the spouse with coverage, although the effect of the husband's pension was stronger (Henretta and O'Rand, 1983: 513-15). An example of an asymmetric effect, an effect not equal for both spouses, was the presence of dependants in the home. The presence of dependants tended to increase the labour force participation of husbands, while it decreased participation among wives (Anderson, Clark and Johnson, 1980; Clark et al., 1980).

While Shaw (1984) and Campione (1987) considered only one side of the symmetry hypotheses, they both discovered that the retirement of the husband did increase the likelihood of the wife's retirement. Shaw (1984) indicated that working women did not necessarily plan to retire at the same time as their husbands, but having a husband who was already retired did influence women to plan for earlier retirement. Women's chances for retiring were increased at the point of early pension eligibility as well (Shaw, 1984: 158). Campione found that the married woman's decision to retire was influenced by her own wage level, social security entitlement, pension benefits, and age, but also by her spouse's wage level and his retirement status (Campione, 1987: 385).

It might, therefore, be expected that, as women have more continuous employment histories, and are thus more likely to qualify for early pension benefits, they will retire even earlier than they do at present. And, if men continue to retire earlier, this would reinforce the trend for women who are influenced by their husband's retirement status, a feedback loop that would predict an accelerating increase in early retirement in the future.

To summarize, early retirement appears to be primarily a function of the person's perceived health status and his or her expected retirement income. People not attached to their work tend to retire earlier, as do men who have a lower occupational status. Single men and married women are also more likely to retire early. The marital unit also influences early retirement, such that the characteristics of both spouses affect the timing of retirement.

On-Time Retirement

Understanding why people retire at age 65 has become significant only in light of the successful challenges to mandatory retirement under provincial human rights legislation in Manitoba, Quebec, New Brunswick, Prince Edward Island, Alberta and British Columbia, as well as under the Canadian Charter of Rights and Freedoms of 1982.

The fundamental issue for governments, business, and organized labour is the effect the elimination of mandatory retirement will have on the labour force participation rate of older Canadians. The primary concern of the proponents of mandatory retirement is that older workers will not retire at age 65 once mandatory retirement is completely abandoned. They argue that the increased participation of older workers will enlarge the tax burden on future generations of workers, prevent the career advancement of middle-aged workers, result in harsher monitoring of the work performance of older workers, and add to the unemployment problem (see Gunderson and Pesando, 1980; McPherson, 1983). What is assumed in these arguments is that mandatory retirement *forces* workers to withdraw from the labour force independent of their own choice and perceptions of their health and financial circumstances.

The actual effect of mandatory retirement on the decision to retire is not so straightforward. To begin with, there is a definite trend toward early retirement, as was noted in Chapter 3. Secondly, only about 48.1 percent of Canadians are in jobs subject to mandatory retirement regulations (Economic Council of Canada, 1979: 68-69). More important, the extent of *involuntary* mandatory retirement is small (Ciffin and Martin, 1977; Economic Council of Canada, 1979; Gunderson and Pesando, 1980). Gunderson and Pesando (1980) reported that in the Retirement Survey of Health and Welfare Canada, mandatory retirement was given as a reason for retirement by less than 1 percent of those under age 65, 17 percent of those aged 65, and about 27 percent of those over age 65 (1980: 354). For all age groups, 29 percent of the male retirees and 11 percent of the female retirees had left their jobs because of compulsory retirement (Ciffin and Martin, 1977: 9). Of all the men and women in this Canadian study, over 60 percent of those who retired because of compulsory retirement and other reasons, retired at the ages they preferred, whereas only about 30 percent of the men and 45 percent of the women who retired because of poor health or being laid-off did so (Ciffin and Martin, 1977: 22). In other words, a small proportion of Canadians retire specifically because of mandatory retirement, and well over half of them prefer to do so. They are not coerced by mandatory retirement rules in the sense that they are dissatisfied with the timing of their retirement.

While more empirical evidence is required on the extent to which workers are actually constrained by a mandatory retirement age, these national results conform with more limited Canadian studies (see Martin Matthews and Brown, 1981) and similar work in the United States (Parnes and Nestel, 1981; Palmore et al., 1985). In particular, Parnes and Nestel (1981: 189) reported that only 5 percent of retirees in the National Longitudinal Surveys were forced to retire at age 65 because of mandatory retirement policies in the workplace. They suggested that a large majority of workers covered by mandatory retirement policies retired at age 65 because they simply had no desire to remain in their jobs (Parnes and Nestel, 1981: 189). This may also apply in Canada, because very few older workers state that they are available for work. In March 1986, less than 1 percent of those 65 and over who were not in the labour force reported being available for work, compared to 6 percent of those 45 to 64 years of age (Méthot, 1987: 9).

If compulsory retirement is not the only reason for "on-time retirement," what then are the other reasons? The answer, unfortunately, is mainly a matter of speculation. Mandatory retirement is more often than not linked to membership in a pension plan, so retirement at age 65 could reflect financial considerations. For example, in the Retirement Survey, a larger proportion of the men and women who retired for compulsory reasons were receiving a job-related pension than those who retired because of poor health, being laid-off, or other reasons (Ciffin and Martin, 1977: 52). Another reason may be that the socially constructed association between reaching age 65 and retirement will continue to operate for many workers. A Gallup Report in December 1985 showed that one-half of Canadians approved of forced retirement at age 65, up from a low of 34 percent in 1981 (Canadian Institute of Public Opinion, 1986). Hence, at the same time that a flexible retirement age is becoming a reality, the idea of retiring at age 65 continues to have a firm hold on the Canadian public.

Again, there is a gap in our knowledge. Long-term changes in the work environment, the capacity of older workers, the cultural value placed on work and leisure, and the adequacy of pension plans may alter these trends and will have to be monitored (Méthot, 1987: 11).

To summarize, most Canadians who retire at age 65 do not appear to be forced out of the labour force by compulsory retirement policies. They may be retiring at age 65 because this age coincides with the commencement of full pensions and/or because they believe age 65 is a good time to retire.

Late Retirement

It is important to know who will work past the normal retirement age of 65 and why they continue to work, in the absence of mandatory retirement. In 1986, only 175,000 Canadians aged 65 and over were employed, which represents approximately 1.5 percent of all employed Canadians. For men in this age group, the levels of employment have dropped sharply from 17 percent in 1975 to 11 percent in 1986, but they have remained constant for women. In 1986, less than 4 percent of women aged 65 and over had jobs outside their homes, which is only slightly less than the figure recorded in the the 1950s (Méthot, 1987: 7-8). Although the number of workers is small, workers over 65 still represent a force that will have to be recognized by governments, unions, and employing organizations. Issues that will have to be confronted include the provision of work opportunities for older workers, the feasibility of new employment arrangements (job redesign, reduced hours of work, job sharing, and graduated retirement schemes), development of performance appraisal systems, modification of benefit packages and retraining obsolete workers (McDonald and Wanner, 1982).

Who are these older Canadian workers? In 1986, employment levels were higher for those people in the 65 to 69 age range than for those 70 years of age and over (Méthot, 1987: 7-9). A large proportion of the female workers (45 percent) and, to a lesser extent, male workers (30 percent), worked part-time. This represents a substantial increase from 1975, when 20 percent of employed men and 34 percent of working women aged 65 and over were part-time workers. Interestingly enough, the majority of these workers worked part-time by choice. In 1986, 85 percent of the men and 79 percent of the women did not want full-time work. About 27 percent of the men and 12 percent of the women were employed in agriculture, and of all the employed older persons in 1986, 21 percent of the men and 18 percent of the women were self-employed. Not surprisingly, the highest levels of employment occurred in the Prairie Provinces, primarily because of the large agricultural industry in this region (Méthot, 1987: 7-9).

The evidence explaining late retirement and work after retirement is meagre relative to explanations of early retirement. However, unlike the research on early retirement, the findings are very consistent. Most studies confirm that there is little difference between the working retired and those who simply continue to work past age 65 (Palmore et al., 1985). Both groups tend to be well-educated with upper occupational status, married men and single women who enjoy reasonably good health (Fillenbaum, 1971; Streib and Schneider, 1971; Census Canada, 1976; Health and Welfare Canada, 1977b; Canada, 1982). Despite the apparent contradiction with the finding that it is upper occupational status individuals who work, a number of recent studies have indicated that financial reasons often motivate the working retired and those who retire late (Palmore et al., 1985; Boaz, 1987a). In an attempt to ascertain exactly why people work after retirement, Boaz (1987a) showed that work during retirement by both men and women was a response to low or moderate levels of unearned income at the beginning of retirement and, for men, was also a response to a decrease in the real value of income during retirement (1987a: 437). As would be expected, several studies have underscored the relation between attachment to work and retirement reluctance (Fillenbaum, 1971; Streib and Schneider, 1971; Atchley, 1976b; Jaslow, 1976; Skoglund, 1979; Powers et al., 1980; Palmore et al., 1985).

One study in the United States clarifies the inconsistency between high occupational prestige and the need to work for financial reasons. Palmore et al. (1985) found that the working retired, as compared to the retired, had the same level of health, a strong attachment to work and an increased probability of continued employment through self-employment but were less likely to have received substantial financial rewards from working (1985: 102-3). A comparable Canadian study supports these results. Canadian men and women who worked past age 65 did so out of financial need, but the financial need was greater among the women than among the men (McDonald and Wanner, 1982: 176-77). These late retirees were better educated and were more likely to be self-employed than were those retired early or on time. Self-employment is a key variable, because the self-employed are not constrained by mandatory retirement policies. Nevertheless, some part of the involvement of the self-employed in the labour force was related to financial need, because the majority were in small businesses and farming (McDonald and Wanner, 1982).

What the available evidence suggests, then, is that the reasons for late retirement are almost the exact opposite of those for early retirement. Individuals who are healthy and attached to their work but need money continue to work. Part-time work and self-employment would appear to be the major mechanisms used to meet these needs. While no Canadian researchers have studied the effect of attachment to work on late retirement, the available evidence does suggest the importance of economic need. A number of Canadians, most notably women, are being pressured into working into old age by financial hardship. Many of these women are not "on-time" in their career-retirement sequence because of broken career lines and delayed career entry due to family responsibilities (O'Rand and Henretta, 1982a). Their concentration in lower paying jobs with poor pension coverage simply compounds the problem (McDonald and Wanner, 1982). Again, this disadvantaged group should receive the special attention of policy makers and retirement practitioners.

The implications for employing organizations are that job sharing, reduced hours of work, and graduated retirement schemes will be required to help older Canadians meet their needs, especially if public pension policy is not about to be changed. The problem of the obsolete worker and retraining may not be as serious as was originally thought, since most late retirees are well educated (Rosen and Jerdee, 1985). The self-employed present a different problem. The situation of the self-employed may necessitate a change in public pension policy that results in more adequate financial protection in retirement for this group.

To summarize, Canadians who retire later than age 65 would appear to have acceptable health, are attached to their work, need additional income and have the opportunity for continued employment, through self-employment or on a part-time basis. Women, more so than men, experience a more pressing financial need to work past age 65.

THE TRANSITION FROM WORK TO RETIREMENT

The process of retiring has been considerably less studied than have the antecedents and consequences of retirement. One of the major reasons social gerontologists have been remiss in examining the work-retirement transition is that the majority of early gerontologists assumed that retirement was a crisis for people and moved on to explore other related phenomena, such as pre-retirement planning. If retirement is a crisis, then pre-retirement planning should help to ease the transition (Atchley, 1980). As a consequence, researchers have given considerable attention to demonstrating that pre-retirement planning "works" in changing peoples' attitudes to retirement and in helping them to "adjust." And, to assist the pre-retirement planners in their mission, researchers have used complex decision-making models to dissect how the retirement decision is made. This section looks first at retirement as a crisis and then at pre-retirement planning and decision making, since the latter two processes are related to how the retirement process has been conceptualized.

Retirement as a Crisis

In early studies of retirement, many gerontologists argued that because of the significance of work for people, retirement posed a major adaptive challenge for older persons (Cavan et al., 1949; Baron, Strieb and Suchman, 1952; Friedmann and Havighurst, 1954). The thinking at the time was that work is a source of income, structures time, provides status and identity, offers meaningful social interaction and is a source of accomplishment (Friedmann and Havighurst, 1954; Beck, 1982). Without work people will experience a sense of loss to the degree that these elements are no longer available after retirement. Withdrawal from the paid labour force represented a form of personal crisis and could lead to poor adjustment and/or decreased life satisfaction. This notion lingered in the gerontological literature and in practice for some time.

Today, a number of researchers point to 40 years of inconsistent research results regarding the relation between the loss of work and the psychological adjustment of older persons as solid evidence that retirement does not necessarily bring on a crisis (MacBride, 1976; Beck, 1982). For example, on the basis of a thorough review of the literature, MacBride (1976: 554) concludes that "people do quite well physically, mentally and socially after retirement and that the negative stereotype [crisis] is a myth." Many researchers tend to ignore a major tenet of crisis theory that people can experience a crisis and be well adjusted after the event if the crisis is handled appropriately (see Golan, 1978). In other words, some researchers conclude that because people appear to be fairly satisfied with retirement, they did not undergo a crisis when making the transition from work to retirement. This type of *ex post facto* explanation lends credence to the positive stereotype of aging noted by Connidis (1987) that can obscure the true nature of the aging process and, in this case, retirement.

Fortunately, a few researchers have investigated the issue directly. Bell (1975), using a non-random, all-male sample, found that retirement was not a major disruption for people in the areas of family, voluntary associations and community. Based on a random sample of 300 recently retired men and women in southern Ontario, Martin Matthews et al. (1982) reported that retirement was not a particularly critical life event when compared with other critical life events, such as death of a spouse, birth of children, and getting married. In fact, retirement ranked 28th of 34 life events in descending order of importance (Martin Matthews et al., 1982: 32). Looked at another way, 82 percent of the events were rated by the respondents as having more of an effect on their lives than retirement did. As well, retirement appeared to have slightly more impact on men than on women. While retirement was not perceived as a crisis, it is very important to note that there was substantial variation in the extent to which retirement affected peoples' lives, since there was almost a fifty-fifty split between those affected very little and those affected a lot (Martin Matthews et al., 1982: 35).

In a second study using the same data, Martin Matthews and Brown (1987) showed that the key variable having an effect on retirement as a critical life event for both men and women was attitude to retirement. The less likely the respondents were to retire when they preferred, the more critical retirement was perceived to be in terms of its negative impact. The effect was more pronounced for women and may reflect what the authors hypothesized to be the unscheduled nature of women's reasons for retirement; that is, women were more likely to retire for reasons that have to do with the circumstances of others, particularly the health of a spouse, or a spouse's retirement (Martin Matthews and Brown, 1987: 564). The authors also found that the cumulative effect of life events was more devastating for men than for women. "As the number of experienced life events increases, the *more likely* are men and the *less likely* are women to report a profoundly negative effect of retirement from work" (Martin Matthews and Brown, 1987: 565).

What little research there is suggests that retirement is not a crisis for everyone, but it does affect some people negatively. To be able to distinguish between those who will have problems in making the transition from those who will not, as well as under what circumstances, is an important item for the research agenda. There are indications that attitudes and income influence whether or not retirement is perceived as a crisis, and it is quite likely that health status plays a part as well. The importance of the timing of the event, the amount of control the individual has over the event, and the nature of the socioeconomic environment at the time of the event would be logical factors to consider. To be forced to retire during a recession or depression could conceivably lead to a crisis definition of the event (Minkler, 1981).

Atchley (1976a) is one of the few authors who has offered a model of the retirement process based on continuity theory, which deviates considerably from the crisis perspective. He describes two phases that precede the event of retirement (the remote and near phase) and five phases that follow (honeymoon, disenchantment, reorientation, stability, and termination phases). But, as Atchley himself stated, not everyone experiences every phase, the order of the phases varies among individuals and the phases are not necessarily tied to chronological age. As a result, the model is impossible to support or refute and is therefore questionable in its application (George, 1980). However, Atchley's model does sensitize us to the possibility that there are alternative explanations of the retirement process to that offered by crisis theory.

Pre-retirement Planning and Preparation

Retirement preparation programs have essentially two goals, namely, education and counselling (Doering et al., 1983; Giordano and Giordano, 1983; Peterson, 1984). Retirement education involves the dissemination of objective facts about retirement, such as financial planning, the workings of private and public pensions, health promotion, housing, social services, use of leisure time, and new employment. Pre-retirement counselling deals with the attitudes and emotional responses people may have to retirement (Kasschau, 1974; Peterson, 1984); that is, the retirement counsellor will focus on people's social psychological needs to facilitate adjustment after retirement.

In 1975, the Canada Survey of Retirement found that 8.6 percent of those men still working and 8.9 percent of the active women had taken part in some sort of retirement preparation program, compared to 8.1 percent of the retired men and 3.1 percent of the retired women (Ciffin and Martin, 1977: 88). The primary factor that influenced participation was whether or not the person was in a job-related pension plan. Three-quarters of the men and about one-half of the women who had been in retirement preparation programs received or expected to receive a job-related pension. Because of the relation between program participation and a job-related pension, it is no surprise that these people were more likely to be in the public sector than in the private sector; they were not likely to be self-employed; they were in higher status jobs; and they were likely to be part of a bargaining unit. They were also more likely to be men than women (Ciffin and Martin, 1977: 89). Of those individuals who had not participated in a preparation program, 34.7 percent of the men and 32.8 percent of the women wished to do so (Ciffin and Martin 1977: 88). While these figures require up-dating, they are similar to those reported in the United States that indicate that only 5 to 10 percent of the population approaching retirement participates in retirement preparation programs, and this proportion has not increased substantially over the past 20 years (Atchley, 1981: 80). In both Canada and the United States, it would appear that retirement preparation is probably not systematically available to most persons contemplating retirement.

Since the inception of some of the first pre-retirement preparation programs in the American steel industry in the early 1950s, there has been considerable debate in the literature about the analytical framework for pre-retirement preparation programs (information dissemination or counselling or both), the optimal age for participation, the mix of participants (inclusion of spouses), the length of programs, and the different methodologies for delivering programs (Kasschau, 1974; Reich, 1977; Lynch et al., 1979; McMahon, 1981). As a result, in Canada there appears to be a wide variety of programs according to goals, format and learning/counselling methods (McMahon, 1981).

At the same time, findings based on retirement preparation studies have been described by Kasschau (1974) and Morrow (1980) as inconclusive and/or contradictory. Kasschau has argued that the confusion is a result of offering retirement adjustment programs but using planning content as the curriculum. In other words, the goals being evaluated are not consistent with the program being delivered. As Kasschau (1974) has implied, there are a number of methodological flaws in the studies of retirement preparation programs. Almost all of the evaluative research suffers from inadequate control in the research design, use of non-representative samples, low response rates, limited use of pre- and post-tests, and underuse of longitudinal designs (Doering et al., 1983).

As a result, there are a number of studies that suggest that information dissemination and counselling goals are accomplished through retirement preparation programs and a number that suggest they are not. Participants' knowledge of retirement issues has been shown to improve after program involvement (Hunter, 1968; Fillenbaum, 1971; Glamser and Dejong, 1975; Kenny and Portis, 1982; Poser and Engels, 1983), and attitudes toward retirement have been observed to become more positive after counselling (Barfield and Morgan, 1969; Charles, 1971; Smyth and Holder, 1981; Bond and Bond, 1980; Shouksmith, 1983). The University of Oregon compared three distinct teaching/learning models for retirement preparation programs and found that all of the program methods listed produced statistically significant treatment effects (Lynch et al., 1979). These researchers also found that the multi-group workshop was more effective as a method for influencing behaviour, knowledge, and attitudes than were unstructured/information methods and facilitated interaction methods for small groups (Lynch et al., 1979).

In contrast, a study by O'Rourke and Friedman (1972) found no attitude change among labour union members after an eight-month preparation course. Morrow (1980) has claimed that a positive attitude change was observed in her study of university employees, but there was no pre-test of attitudes to determine whether there was in fact a program effect. The respondents to the Canada Retirement Survey indicated that the knowledge provided in retirement preparation programs was minimal (Ciffin, Martin and Talbot, 1977). Glamser (1981), using a rigorous experimental design with a follow-up six years later, found no significant differences between those who took a program and those who did not in terms of life satisfaction, retirement attitude, and felt job deprivation.

Some researchers have reported that there are no gender differences when it comes to retirement preparation (Newman et al., 1982), while others have found differences along several dimensions. Behling et al. (1983) noted that professional women were disadvantaged in terms of financial planning and expected retirement income, implying that the planning needs of women were different from those of men. Kroeger (1982) and Block (1984) found that men had more access than women to formal retirement preparation programs, mainly because more women were employed in service industries and small businesses, where retirement preparation programs were not likely to be available. However, if formal programs were available, women tended to use them at a higher rate than did men (Kroeger, 1982; Kaye and Monk, 1984). And, if no formal programs existed, men were more likely to avail themselves of informal sources of information than were women (Kroeger, 1982: 104). Part of the reason for this finding was that the women in this study lacked advanced education, were in low status jobs, and had friends who expressed unfavourable opinions about retirement.

To summarize, it would appear that retirement preparation programs are not readily available, people are not taking advantage of them to the extent that they might, it is not clear that they benefit participants, and there are differences in the needs of women and men. Atchley goes so far as to state, "Most retirement programs, even the comprehensive ones, are in a rut" (1981: 82). Fortunately, there are changes on the horizon.

In the 1980s, there has been a growing awareness that retirement preparation is really part of long-range career planning and that the whole issue would be best presented in these terms throughout the individual's working life (Atchley, 1981; Kaminski-daRossa, 1984; Rosen and Jerdee, 1985). Long-range career planning benefits both the organization and the individual. The organization can continually assess present and future staffing requirements and establish the kind of corporate culture that respects and supports the contributions of individual employees in every age category. Engaging the employee in career planning can lead to early identification of needs for training, transfer, job redesign, retirement and work after retirement. For example, a two-day workshop immediately prior to retirement is too little, too late to be of much value if major changes are required. Making retirement part of career planning would leave the door open to the options of continued work, new work, and part-time work. In fact, Kremer and Harpaz (1982a) reported that the intention to continue work after retirement was the single most important factor predisposing workers to have a negative attitude toward pre-retirement counselling.

Many retirement counsellors have also hypothesized that the reluctance to attend retirement preparation programs is a reflection of a fear of aging, futility in planning for the unknown, or being pressured into retiring (Raffel, 1980). The use of career planning could help alleviate these fears, because retirement would be seen as only one option, carefully chosen from among many by the individual. The high drop-out rate from retirement preparation training among blue-collar workers could be avoided if the workers were included in career planning early on in their work life (Harpaz and Kremer, 1981). Finally, career planning for everyone would at least draw attention to the unique needs of women (Rosen and Jerdee, 1985). While the arguments for long-range career planning are persuasive, it would be necessary to empirically assess the results of such programs to avoid slipping into yet another "rut."

The Retirement Decision

An examination of how the retirement decision is actually made is a relatively new area of study that attempts to gauge the influence of social psychological factors on the decision. The rationale for dissecting the retirement decision is to assist retirement practitioners in offering information and counselling that meet the specific needs of widely different groups. The few researchers who have studied the decision-making process have used one form or another of expectancy theory (Fishbein, 1963; Vroom, 1964; Triandis, 1971), in which behaviour (retirement) is viewed as the end point of a chain of psychological events that begins with a subjective evaluation of the possible outcomes of courses of action (to retire or not to retire). After an evaluation is made, a course of action is decided upon and the behavioural intention is believed to be a close predictor of actual behaviour.

The research indicates that the expectation-intention-action chain is operative in retirement decision making (Eran and Jacobson, 1976; Parker and Dyer, 1976; Jacobson and Eran, 1980; Hwalek, Firestone and Hoffman, 1982; Prothero and Beach, 1984). Prothero and Beach (1984) found that 78 percent of the time, expectations about retirement predicted intentions, and intentions predicted retirement actions 76 percent of the time. As was the case with studies predicting the timing of retirement, positive expectations about retirement were related to intentions to retire, and negative expectations were related to intentions to continue working. Participants who acted as was predicted on the basis of their expectations tended to have a much stronger positive or negative attraction to retirement

(Prothero and Beach, 1984: 169-73). Jacobson and Eran (1980) in a study of predictors of physicians' preferences for retirement, reported that attributes of work affect the decision chain. Predictions of intentions were most accurate for those physicians who were dissatisfied with their jobs, had a low evaluation of their professional competence, and experienced high levels of work-related stress (Jacobson and Eran, 1980: 19-20). Hwalek et al., (1982) showed that social pressures were more important in predicting early retirement intentions than either health or expected retirement income. It is important to note that none of these studies used random samples, so it is not clear whether the findings apply to all workers.

The few studies cited indicate that attitudes toward work and retirement have an effect on the retirement decision. The new information to be gleaned from studying the decision to retire is that the expectancy model is *not* useful for the prediction of choices in ambiguous situations (Jacobson and Eran, 1980; Prothero and Beach, 1984); that is, it is difficult to predict what course of action people will take if they do not feel strongly either way about retirement. Translated into practice, this would suggest that those without firm attitudes about retirement would probably benefit from more information about the alternative choices of working or retiring, so that they could formulate an opinion and go on to plan accordingly. Those persons who intend to retire are already committed and would need a slightly different retirement planning package than those who intend to continue working.

The fundamental message found in the research on the process of retirement is that retirement is not a crisis for everyone, but some people are, in fact, affected substantially and need to be singled out for further study and practical help. Indeed, the entire retirement process requires a conceptual overhaul that could begin with phenomenological studies of people in the process of retiring. One American researcher is currently involved in the study of the actual experiences of people who are in the process of retiring, and more studies of this type would enhance our knowledge (Richardson, 1988).

The glaring deficits in basic information about retirement preparation in Canada demand immediate attention as retirement practitioners begin to shift their focus to long-range career planning. Studies of the retirement decision-making process reinforce the research on why people retire and are suggestive of how people might be treated differentially in practice. Overall, it would be very useful for researchers to return to this area of study and to be guided by the needs of practitioners, because the results have immediate application for retirement consultants and their clients.

CONCLUSIONS

This chapter has reviewed the individual retirement experience, addressing the questions of why people retire and how they go about retiring. From the studies reviewed here, it is evident that health and potential retirement income are the primary factors leading to early retirement. People who are not attached to their work retire earlier than do those attached to their work, when health status and income level are taken into account. Married women and single men are also more likely than others to retire early. There have been no empirically supported reasons concerning why people retire at age 65, but it is clear that the majority of Canadians are not being forced out of the labour force on the basis of age status alone. Choosing to retire late appears to be a function of good health, attachment to work, and the need for additional income.

Investigations of the retirement process have challenged the notion that retirement is a crisis for all people, although it does appear to affect a significant number of people adversely. If the retirement process does not necessarily represent a crisis, and if Atchley's retirement phases (although widely accepted) continue to elude substantiation, it would seem that the time has come to move forward and develop new conceptual models of the retirement process that are based upon the actual experiences of those in the midst of retiring.

The available studies on pre-retirement preparation are less than definitive, which is not to suggest that these programs are inadequate. Part of the problem of conflicting findings can be attributed to the application of less than rigorous program evaluation techniques and to the fact that the whole field has taken a new direction in the last decade, which has made it difficult for researchers to keep pace with these developments.

Research on retirement decision making is fairly recent and in some ways complements the work on why people retire, by emphasizing the social psychological factors that influence the decision. This avenue of research has particular value for the practitioner in terms of client assessment and individualized intervention and for these reasons needs to be continued. Overall, the existing studies suggest strongly that the actual process of retirement is one of the least understood aspects of retirement, in contrast to the consequences of retirement, which are considered in the next chapter.

CHAPTER 5

THE CONSEQUENCES OF THE INDIVIDUAL RETIREMENT EXPERIENCE

When it comes to studying life after retirement, researchers have left few stones unturned. The enormous effort devoted to examining the consequences of retirement began with attempts to test the micro theories of aging mentioned in Chapter 1, because retirement provided the "natural exit" that lead to decreased, increased, or similar levels of activity and, depending upon the theory, different levels of happiness or morale in retirement. To test disengagement theory, the researcher would attempt to show that retirement is a form of letting go of society and that the reduced activity is functional for the individual. The activity theorist would attempt to show that after retirement, people are happily engaged in other forms of social activity. The continuity theorist would attempt to demonstrate that the individual is content to spend more time in roles developed prior to retirement. As a result, there is a huge body of literature that addresses the relation between levels of activity and happiness, morale, or general life satisfaction in retirement. And, when the notion of retirement as a crisis is made explicit, it comes as no surprise that adjustment to retirement becomes a heavily researched issue. For example, does retirement precipitate a breakdown in physical or mental health or perhaps a financial crisis? As the "sociology of happiness" (Marshall and Tindale, 1978-79; Marshall, 1981) and the notion that retirement is a crisis for all have fallen by the wayside, researchers have become more attuned to what contributes to a satisfying retirement. That is, other independent variables affecting well-being have been considered that may or may not be a direct result of retirement. In this chapter, life after retirement is considered in the areas of health, financial adequacy, and well-being, along with those issues that must still be resolved by social gerontologists.

HEALTH

The research conclusions about the impact of retirement on physical health are fairly straightforward. With only a few exceptions, most studies from the 1950s onward have found that retirement does not lead to significant deterioration in physical health or increases in the risk of death (Emerson, 1959; Martin and Doran, 1966; Ryser and Sheldon, 1969; Streib and Schneider, 1971; Hayes, McMichael and Tyroler, 1977; Portnoi, 1981; Shapiro and Roos, 1982; Ekerdt and Bosse, 1982; Ekerdt, Bosse and Goldie, 1983; Ekerdt, Bosse and LoCastro, 1983; Palmore et al., 1985).

It would appear, however, that not all gerontologists are prepared to accept these results. For example, Minkler (1981) has warned that the studies are suspect because of methodological problems. Her list of concerns is lengthy. There is a fundamental problem differentiating analytically between disease processes, the processes of normal aging, and the disease outcomes that can be specifically related to retiring. There is a problem in isolating the effects of retirement *per se* from the effects of such factors as changes in income or number of social contacts that might occur in conjunction with retirement. That the unhealthy tend to select themselves out for early retirement contributes to what Minkler has called the "well worker" bias. When the retired are compared to those who continue to work on the health variable, it is not unexpected that the retired would report poorer health, since that is why many retired in the first place. Finally she also cites the widely discussed problem of the validity and reliability of self-reports of health (Minkler, 1981: 122-23).

Ekerdt (1987), in an attempt to explain why the "retirement harms health" myth persists, stated that Minkler is an example of those who choose to underplay "the consistency of these findings in favour of reciting their methodological flaws" (Ekerdt, 1987: 456). He went on to say that the myth prevails because of the availability of vivid anecdotes, the tendency to interpret big events (like retirement) as major causes of illness, the cultural celebration of work, theoretical perspectives in gerontology that portray retirement as disruptive, and the misinterpretation of research results (Ekerdt, 1987: 454). The views of both researchers are probably correct, as the few Canadian studies of the retirement/health relation indicate.

A Statistics Canada study on retirement and mortality found that mortality for men was higher during the second year of retirement than was that of the general male population (Adams and Lefebre, 1980: 19). However, the study only considered those receiving CPP benefits, and males were over-represented in the sample. Health prior to retirement was not controlled, so the well-worker bias may have been in effect. Yet, according to the authors, stress from retirement was the enemy, a conclusion that is weakly supported at best. Shapiro and Roos (1982), using the Manitoba Study on Aging, reported that, in their representative sample of 2,211 working and retired persons, the retired reported poorer health statuses and more health problems, but when serious illnesses were controlled, retired persons made no more visits to physicians than did the employed. They also found that the retired had a higher admission rate to hospital than did the employed, but this higher rate was not related to their employment-retirement status. They simply had more serious medical conditions (Shapiro and Roos, 1982: 191). These authors controlled for the well-worker bias to show that retirement did not affect health. These findings are similar to the major studies in the United States by Ekerdt and his associates (Ekerdt and Bosse, 1982; Ekerdt, Bosse and Goldie, 1983; Ekerdt, Baden, Bosse and Dibbs, 1983). These authors, using the Normative Aging Study, compared pre- to post-retirement changes in physical health. They found that once age was controlled and men who retired due to illness were excluded from the sample, there were no significant differences between retirees and those who continued to work. What is more, they reported that the pre- to post-retirement health change for retirees was not significantly associated with mandatory retirement or a reduced standard of living (Ekerdt, Bosse and Goldie, 1983).

There are, indeed, some methodological problems with the research on retirement and health, but most of these problems can be managed in carefully crafted studies, such as that of Shapiro and Roos (1982). And, while the view that retirement negatively affects health should be abandoned, there are still issues that remain to be investigated. For example, there has been very little research conducted on the effects of retirement on mental health, and those few studies that do exist have not produced conclusive findings (Hinds, 1963; Spence, 1966; Lowenthal and Berkman, 1967; Gurland, 1975; Lipton, 1976; Miller, 1979; Seidon, 1980). A recent Health and Welfare report identified the retired as a high risk group for suicide, suggesting that the loss of status, mandatory retirement, and the stress and feelings of uselessness attached to retirement could be factors contributing to suicide (Health and Welfare Canada, 1982b: 11). The high rate of suicide for those 65 years of age and over in Canada when compared to the total population - 16.2 per 100,000 senior citizens compared to 14.3 for the total population – is indicative of the need for research into changes in mental health around the time of retirement (Health and Welfare Canada, 1982b: 18).

The fact remains, however, that there are no available Canadian studies that assess the effect retirement has on mental health. Predictive and prospective studies of the physical and mental health of female retirees are also required because larger cohorts of career women are approaching retirement age and because most of the previously mentioned studies have been conducted on men. Another avenue of research includes the experiences of different occupational groups and the link between work, retirement, and health (Hardy and Pavalko, 1986). And, finally, a major shift in mental gears will have to be made to assess the possibility that retirement may actually improve physical and mental health for some people (Thompson and Streib, 1958; Tyhurst, Salk and Kennedy, 1966; Ryser and Sheldon, 1969; Ekerdt, Bosse, and LoCastro, 1983).

INCOME ADEQUACY

Retirees generally have to make do with lower incomes than they had when they were working. A National Council of Welfare report has clearly shown that there is a substantial reduction in cash income for many Canadians after they retire. The median income of families with heads 65 to 69 years old in 1981 was only 61 percent of the median income of families led by persons 55 to 64 years old, while the median income of unattached persons aged 65 to 69 was 75 percent of the median income for those 55 to 64 years old (National Council of Welfare, 1984: 47). If private income is not included, public programs (OAS, GIS, CPP/QPP) in 1983 replaced little more than half of a single person's pre-retirement income, 56 percent of a two-earner couple's income, and 77 percent of the pre-retirement income of a one-earner couple (National Council of Welfare, 1984: 50). That 45.5 percent of the income of older couples and 51.3 percent of the income of single older individuals came from public sources is indicative of the importance of the public pension system. Single women were the hardest hit, since they received 53.3 percent of their income from government income security programs, compared to 46.6 percent of the income for men (National Council of Welfare, 1984: 43). About 29 percent of older peoples' income was based on private investments, and 11 percent came from private pensions.

Low-income aged Canadians also feel the pinch, because public programs account for almost all the money they receive. In 1981, elderly couples living below the poverty line received 93.2 percent of their income primarily from Old Age Security and the Guaranteed Income Supplement. The situation was not quite as severe for the unattached older person, who received 86.8 percent of his or her income from the same sources (National Council of Welfare, 1984: 43).

It is particularly important to note that many middle-income Canadians may join the ranks of the poor and near-poor at the time of retirement. The evidence comes from the number of Canadians receiving Old Age Security benefits who also receive the Guaranteed Income Supplement. Remembering that the GIS is directed to low-income pensioners, one-half of the 2.4 million older persons receiving OAS also received the GIS, and one-quarter of these individuals received the full amount because they had no other source of income (National Council of Welfare, 1984: 51). Because there are not enough low-income people of working age to account for the numbers receiving GIS, many of these people must have been middle-income earners prior to retirement. The National Welfare report concluded: "As many as two-thirds of middle-income Canadians must contend with a drop of 25 percent or more in their standard of living when they retire" (National Council of Welfare, 1984: 51).

Given that income drops with retirement, one might assume that retirement is the sole culprit causing this drop. As was the case with health status, once pre-retirement characteristics are accounted for, the actual effect of retirement on income level is not as large as would be expected. Palmore and his associates found that pre-retirement characteristics (age, race, education, etc.) accounted for one-fourth to one-half of the income differences between working and retired men in the United States (Palmore et al., 1985: 47). In other words, actual retirement accounted for only part of the income drop. These findings pertain to the American scene and need to be tested in the Canadian context.

Cash income, of course, does not represent all the economic resources of the retired. Over three-quarters of families with heads 65 years of age and older own their own accommodation, as do 40 percent of single individuals in the same age group, and most have paid off their mortgages (National Council of Welfare, 1984: 75). Older Canadians also benefit from a number of subsidies that allow them to consume more goods and services than their incomes would warrant. Retired persons do not have to pay CPP/QPP, unemployment insurance premiums, or union dues, and all older Canadians receive special federal and provincial tax concessions, are covered by national health insurance, and are eligible for subsidized social services (homemakers, meals-on-wheels, home repair services, etc.) in their communities. Two Canadian researchers have estimated that if the value of non-money sources of income and unreported cash gifts were taken into account, the total income of older Canadians would be some 30 percent greater (Stone and MacLean, 1979: 24).

Setting aside the objective economic picture of the retired for the moment, what appear to be most relevant are the subjective meanings retired persons attach to their income (Peterson, 1972; Liang and Fairchild, 1979; Liang, Kahana and Doherty, 1980; Brown and Martin Matthews, 1981; McPherson, 1983; Snell and Brown, 1986). As McPherson (1983: 394) has noted, the definition of an adequate retirement income is based upon how people feel about their financial situation in comparison to their income before retirement and in comparison to the income of other retired persons. At the same time, education, social status, ethnicity, and a number of other specific conditions of retirement influence feelings of satisfaction (McPherson, 1983; Brown and Martin Matthews, 1981). Snell and Brown (1986), using a random sample of 450 men and women, demonstrated how peoples' perceptions of their financial status predicted the types of strategies they used in handling their income in retirement. These researchers considered four strategies that the retired utilize in managing their retirement income - reducing expenditures, home production, changes in assets, and post-retirement employment. They found that expenditure reduction was the most frequently used strategy, and that actual income, morale, and savings practices were not related to any of the four strategies. Peoples' subjective assessment of the adequacy of their income in relation to others and to previous times was the most important factor in determining economic management strategies. "Those who felt most economically deprived, regardless of income level, restrained their spending, while those who felt least deprived were the ones who made changes in their asset portfolios" (Snell and Brown, 1986: 17).

The limited evidence reviewed here supports the view that retirement is a less than affluent time of life for most Canadians. Canada's retirement income system is barely adequate in serving poor older persons, particularly single or widowed women. Middle-income earners will also experience some drop in income upon retirement, although this issue must be investigated further. That private pensions account for only 11 percent of older persons' incomes points to problems with private pension plans. Do subsidized services and other benefits bestowed by governments and the private sector actually allow the retired to compensate for income drops? Are retired Canadians "house rich and cash poor," given the high costs of maintaining a residence? What effect do economic conditions such as inflation have on retirement income? These questions and observations can be related to the nature of the socioeconomic structures of Canadian society, as discussed in the next chapter, but the retirees' views of these matters must be considered seriously in future research if pension policy is to be relevant and if pre-retirement planning and counselling are to be useful.

WELL-BEING IN RETIREMENT

Recent longitudinal research has shown no systematic effects of the retirement event on measures of well-being (George and Maddox, 1977; Mutran and Reitzes, 1981; Beck, 1982; George et al., 1984; Palmore et al., 1985). If people are unhappy, dissatisfied or have low morale in retirement, it is because of other factors, many of which operated prior to retirement. Most people fare quite well in retirement, depending upon the personal resources they bring to retirement and upon certain socioeconomic characteristics they possessed prior to retirement.

Personal resources refer to such factors as a person's health, income, personality, and coping skills, their social networks, and the nature of their leisure activities. Socioeconomic characteristics can include peoples' previous occupation, gender, and marital status. Defining well-being is not quite as simple and, in fact, presents a number of tricky measurement problems for social scientists.

The constructs and scales used for happiness, life satisfaction, and morale have gained widespread popularity among researchers as indicators of adjustment to, and subjective well-being in, retirement. The constructs have been used inconsistently and interchangeably, with little attention being paid to conceptual clarity (Campbell, 1976; George, 1981; Sauer and Warland, 1982; Horley, 1984; Roadburg, 1985). Life satisfaction, happiness, and morale are probably indicators of well-being and are probably related to each other, but they are not identical constructs (Stones and Kozma, 1980; Horley, 1984). For example, satisfaction has been viewed as the result of a comparison of aspirations with achievements and hence requires some passage of time before an assessment can be made; in contrast, happiness represents an evaluation of a current situation (Smith, 1979; Stull, 1988). Or, one can adjust to retirement in the sense of accepting it, but that does not necessarily mean one is happy or has high morale in retirement (MacLean, 1983: 4; Roadburg, 1985: 142).

Indicators of subjective well-being can also be used at a number of levels of specificity. The global level is aimed at evaluations of well-being in general, while the domain level refers to evaluations of well-being in specific areas, such as health, retirement, family, and marriage. One Canadian researcher has maintained that even the domain levels can be broken down further into the day-to-day elements of life, such as baby-sitting grandchildren and caring for a chronically-ill spouse (Horley, 1984).

The effect of these measurement problems can be seen in the outcomes of the research on well-being in retirement. For example, what predicts adjustment to retirement does not necessarily predict enjoyment of retirement (MacLean, 1983). Similarly, an assessment of gender differences in retirement adjustment is influenced by whether a domain-specific or global measure is utilized (Martin Matthews and Brown, 1987: 567).

Personal Resources

Health and Wealth

The old proverb that health and wealth are the ingredients for a happy old age (Larson, 1978) and a successful retirement (Roadburg, 1985) has been partially validated by the empirical evidence. Perceived health has been found to be related to virtually every measure of well-being for retired men and women (Barfield and Morgan, 1970; Streib and Schneider, 1971; Jaslow, 1976; Fox, 1977; Kimmel et al., 1978; Snider, 1980; Atchley, 1982; Beck, 1982; Riddick, 1985; Roadburg, 1985; Palmore et al., 1985; Seccombe and Lee, 1986; Martin Matthews and Brown, 1987). When comparisons are made between workers and retirees, the lower levels of satisfaction reported among the retirees have usually been a result of poorer health (George, 1980; Foner and Schwab, 1981; Beck, 1982; Shapiro and Roos, 1982). Several gerontologists have gone so far as to suggest that health is the single most important factor in evaluating life satisfaction in retirement (Snider, 1980; Beck, 1982; Riddick, 1985; Seccombe and Lee, 1986).

These conclusions augur well for Canadian retirement. Despite the pervasiveness of chronic conditions in the older population (Chappell, Strain and Blandford, 1986), most older people perceive their health to be good or excellent. In the United States, 41.1 percent of older, non-institutionalized persons report good health and 28.3 percent report excellent health (Wolinsky, 1983). There are no comparable national data for Canada. However, regional studies have produced similar results (Chappell, 1983). Presumably most older Canadians have the potential to experience satisfaction in retirement, given their perceptions of good health.

It was noted earlier that health is one of the main factors leading to early retirement, and, as would be expected, those who are forced to retire early because of poor health have lower levels of life satisfaction in retirement than do others (Palmore et al., 1985). Palmore and his colleagues found that those retiring because of poor health suffered the most negative consequences in retirement, followed by those retiring for other compulsory reasons. Voluntary retirees enjoyed the most positive effects of retirement (Palmore et al., 1985). How to assist those persons with poor health in making a better adjustment to retirement is an important question for practice that is only now being investigated. For example, Beck and Page (1986) reported that the number of leisure activities had a greater positive impact on psychological well-being for retired men in poor health than for those in good health.

Like health, wealth is a key resource contributing to well-being in retirement (Chatfield, 1977; Fox, 1977; George and Maddox, 1977, Foner and Schwab, 1981; Beck, 1982; Block, 1982; MacLean, 1983; Dorfman, Kohout and Heckert, 1985; Riddick, 1985; Seccombe and Lee, 1986). Higher incomes reduce financial worries, allow people to retain their standard of living, and permit them to engage in meaningful and pleasurable activities.

Although the weight of the evidence from the United States is substantial, Canadian studies of the importance of income to well-being in retirement are uncertain. A national cross-sectional retirement survey (Ciffin, Martin and Talbot, 1977) confirmed this relation. However, Snider (1980) and Martin Matthews and Brown (1987), using random samples, found no such relation. The contradictory results underscore earlier comments about problems with measurement of well-being, since a number of different indicators were used and at different levels of specificity. There is, of course, the possibility of cultural differences in how Canadians evaluate their income. However, it is hard to imagine that income does not contribute to well-being, especially when it is an important predictor of early and late retirement and the subjective assessment of income has been demonstrated to affect financial management strategies. Future research programs must consider the influence of income on well-being, if for no other reason than to assist Canadians who plan for a satisfactory retirement and for those who provide professional help through pre-retirement planning.

Personality and Coping Skills

A small group of social scientists has considered retirement adjustment or well-being from the perspective of personality predisposition. Basically, people with different personalities exhibit different "retirement styles," presumably some being more conducive to adjustment in retirement than others. Four personality typologies have been generated that are fairly similar. Only one typology includes women.

In one of the first studies of personality and retirement adjustment, Reichard, Livson and Peterson (1962) described five types of personalities, which they contended were the most reliable predictors of retirement adjustment. "Mature men" were characterized by a healthy realism, the "armoured men" had sophisticated defence mechanisms that precluded the perception of stress, and the "rocking chair men" were passive-dependent in nature and willingly accepted what life presented. These three personality types adjusted successfully to retirement. The "angry men," who were typically rigid, aggressive and bitter, and the "self-haters," who channelled their anger against themselves, did not exhibit very positive adjustment to retirement.

Ten years later, Gutmann (1972) proposed an untested personality typology that included two active mastery types, two passive mastery types and one magical mastery type. He speculated that the active mastery types would experience the most stress in retirement, because they valued work and achievement, but that they would have more personal resources at their command for a better retirement adjustment.

Walker, Kimmel and Price (1980-81) suggested yet another set of retirement styles, which they inferred from the work-related retirement activities of men: the reorganizer, holding on, rocking chair, and dissatisfied styles. The reorganizers and rocking chair group were more satisfied with retirement than the holding on group or dissatisfied group. The reorganizers were actively involved in a newly formulated life pattern, and the rocking chair group intentionally opted for reduced life activity. The holding on group did not accept aging or the need for retirement, while the dissatisfied group had low levels of activity and found it difficult to keep busy.

More recently, Hornstein and Wapner (1985) outlined four adjustment styles derived from the retirement experiences of a small, non-random sample of men and women. The styles were distinctive in how the retirement experience was viewed. Some viewed retirement as a transition to old age, others as a beginning of a new phase in life. Others saw retirement as of no particular significance other than the opportunity to continue pre-retirement activities in a more self-directed way. Finally, for some, retirement was viewed as an imposed disruption and was a time of frustration and lack of focus. The authors implied that all four types adjust to retirement, but they presented no evidence to substantiate their conclusions.

A somewhat related avenue of research has examined a person's locus of control. People who are internally controlled believe that their desired goals are largely determined by their own effort, skill and motivation. Externally controlled persons place a greater emphasis on chance and environmental factors as determinants of their goal achievement (Reid, Haas and Hawkings, 1977). An Australian study has shown that Rotter's locus of control scale was a significant predictor of most aspects of retirement satisfaction (activities, relationships, finances, and health) for men but not for women (O'Brien, 1981b). The interpretation of these findings was that those in retirement have more free time available than the employed, and the structuring of this free time may be related to personal initiative, a characteristic the internally controlled are more likely to exhibit. Why locus of control does not matter for women remains unclear.

One Canadian study has investigated the dimensions of happiness contributing to happiness in retirement and has found that affective environmental encounters (ratio of positive to negative encounters) contribute more to happiness than do personality dispositions (Stones and Kozma, 1980). The results suggest that counselling for retirement adjustment should focus more on lifestyle alterations than on changing personalities.

The area of personality and adjustment to retirement is somewhat underdeveloped. Whether retirement style is actually related to personality characteristics or social constraints or a combination of both is a question for further research. For example, in the dissatisfied group of the study by Walker et al. (1980-81), the majority of men were forced to retire, had poor health and had the lowest income. At best, this research provides some information about the retirement experience and emphasizes that there are many ways to adjust to retirement.

Social Relationships

Common sense would suggest that involvement in a social network can contribute to any person's sense of security, personal worth, and competence, as well as to life satisfaction. Roadburg found that 51 percent of the respondents in his study of retirees stated that friends became more important with age (1985: 119). The social relationships of older persons, including informal networks (family, friends and neighbours) and formal networks (civic and religious organizations), have been linked to retirement with varying degrees of success.

The effect of the actual retirement event on participation in social relationships would appear to be minimal at best. Levels of social participation prior to retirement have been found to be the best predictor of post-retirement participation in informal relationships for men (Wan and Odell, 1983; Palmore et al., 1985). There is limited evidence that retirement induces a decline in participation in formal organizations for men (Rosencranz, Pihland and McNevin, 1968; Wan and Odell, 1983), and an increase for retired women (Depner and Ingersoll, 1982). In the case of men, the decrease seems to be associated with those organizations related to occupation (Rosencranz et al., 1968), and for women the increase has been attributed to more involvement in church organizations (Keith, 1982). Overall, retired women reportedly have larger social networks than do men (Depner and Ingersoll, 1982), which is consistent with the general findings on the older population (See Strain and Chappell, 1982).

Do these relationships contribute to satisfaction in retirement? The answer is a qualified yes. A long string of studies has shown that informal contacts do contribute to retirement satisfaction (Livson, 1962; Lowenthal and Haven, 1968; Rosenberg, 1970; Lemon, Bengston and Peterson, 1972; Blau, 1973; Bell, 1976; Mutran and Reitzes, 1981; Keith, 1982). However, more recent studies have not supported this relation (Gigy, 1985-86; Martin Matthews and Brown, 1987; Stull, 1988). Part of the problem can be attributed to the use of domain-specific and global measures of satisfaction, and also to whether quality as opposed to quantity of relationships was measured. The quality of the relationship is emerging as the crucial factor. In a study of rural retirement satisfaction, Dorfman et al. (1985) showed that contacts with confidants, namely intimate and special friends, was consistently related to satisfaction in retirement, more so than contacts with relatives, friends and neighbours. And, while some earlier studies found that family interaction was negatively associated with retirement satisfaction (Kerckoff, 1966; Bell, 1976), this rural study has shown that if the relationship with relatives is characterized by affectionate closeness, it does contribute to retirement satisfaction, particularly for men (Dorfman et al., 1985).

Involvement in formal organizations has been consistently related to satisfaction in retirement (Keith, 1982; Dorfman et al., 1985; Palmore et al., 1985). Organizational involvement may constitute an accommodation to withdrawal from work for both men and women in the sense that social contact is increased or maintained and the skills required at work can be used in other organizations. In sum, close and intimate relationships cultivated earlier in life would appear to be important to retirement satisfaction.

Leisure Activities

Once people have retired, they are confronted with a large block of unstructured time. Two Canadian researchers estimated that those over age 65 have the most time for leisure activities relative to younger persons - over seven hours per day (Kinsley and Graves, 1983: 17). The decision concerning how this time is allocated, and to what pursuits, is a function of a variety of factors, such as age, gender, marital status, level of education and income, the presence of children in the home, and pre-retirement leisure patterns, especially those established during middle age (Curtis and White, 1984; Roadburg, 1985; McPherson and Kozlik, 1987). There can also be barriers to leisure participation, such as poor health, absence of companions and lack of transportation (Ciffin et al., 1977; Hoffman, 1985).

Social scientists have specifically investigated the numbers and frequency of leisure activities and the quality of the activities and have tested complex models in an attempt to explain the relation between leisure participation and well-being in retirement. The current evidence suggests that relatively few people develop new leisure patterns after retirement and few people increase the number and frequency of their activities (Ciffin et al., 1977; McPherson and Kozlik, 1980, 1987; Bosse and Ekerdt, 1981; Roadburg, 1985). In particular, Roadburg (1985) found that the older persons in his convenience sample increased or maintained those activities that did not require physical exertion and were inexpensive. Those activities that fell by the wayside tended to require physical involvement and the participation of other people.

Whereas the number and frequency of leisure activities do not appear to change much with retirement, there is evidence to suggest that the sheer numbers of activities are related to an increase in life satisfaction (Peppers, 1976; Markides and Martin, 1979; O'Brien, 1981a; Fly, Reinhart and Hornby, 1981; Hooker and Ventis, 1984; Palmore et al., 1985; Riddick, 1985; Rosma, Bandy and Bleham, 1985). There is a growing awareness that solitary activities provide just as much satisfaction as social activities (Peppers, 1976; Kremer and Harpaz, 1982b) and that the usefulness or meaningfulness of the activities is conducive to subjective well-being (Beveridge, 1980; Bond, 1982; Hooker and Ventis, 1984; Beck and Page, 1986).

A test of one of the more complex models of retirement satisfaction indicated that, for women, income had a sizeable effect on well-being via its influence on leisure activity. The more disposable income women had, the more they could participate in leisure activities and the more satisfied they were in retirement (Riddick and Daniel, 1984). In another report, Riddick (1985) showed that employed women exhibited more life satisfaction than did retired women or homemakers, and that leisure activity was the strongest predictor of life satisfaction among the retirees and homemakers. For men, involvement in community activities may be an intervening variable between retirement and well-being (Mutran and Reitzes, 1981). In contrast, Kremer's (1985) model of retirement satisfaction showed that male retirees' evaluation of free time or shared leisure activities played a minimal role in overall retirement satisfaction.

If leisure patterns are fairly stable from pre-retirement to post-retirement (Bosse and Ekerdt, 1981), and if leisure activity does contribute to retirement satisfaction, then the cultivation of an interest in leisure activities earlier in life becomes very important to a satisfactory retirement.

Sociodemographic Characteristics

Certain social structural characteristics can place people in advantageous circumstances when it comes to adjusting to retirement. Those characteristics that have received the most attention from researchers include occupational status and occupational attachment, marital status, and gender.

Occupation

Several studies have indicated that adjustment to retirement is a function of the person's occupational status prior to retirement (Loether, 1964; Simpson et al., 1966; Chatfield, 1977; George and Maddox, 1977; Larson, 1978; O'Brien, 1981a). The argument underlying the link is that higher status occupations equip people with the skills (initiative, self-discipline, broader interests, etc.) that facilitate adjustment to retirement. More recent studies, however, have indicated that income covaries with occupation and is the factor that accounts for the effects of occupation (Beck, 1982; Seccombe and Lee, 1986). Whether or not the skills attached to work actually enhance retirement adjustment has never been studied. An Australian study categorized leisure activities according to work characteristics that had been found to contribute to job satisfaction - skill utilization, influence, variety, pressure and interaction (O'Brien, 1981a). The researcher then related these leisure traits to retirement satisfaction but found no relation between them.

Another line of research assumed that people forged their identity through work and that the loss of the work role would therefore make retirement adjustment problematic. A long string of studies has produced mixed results (Atchley, 1972; George and Maddox, 1977; Skoglund, 1979; Goudy et al., 1980; Martin Matthews and Brown, 1987). In the one available Canadian investigation, the male retirees with high work saliency reported low morale, but no such relation existed for the women (Martin Matthews and Brown, 1987). The confusing results undoubtedly reflect wide variation in the measures of work attachment and retirement satisfaction used in this research.

Marital Status

The presence of a wife or husband can be a social resource for retired persons, and several studies have confirmed that marital status does add to well being in retirement (George and Maddox, 1977; Keating and Cole, 1980; Synder, 1980; Mutran and Reitzes, 1981; Beck 1982; Palmore et al.,

1985; Seccombe and Lee, 1986). A recent analysis of the marital dyad indicated that the husband's happiness in retirement was a predictor of the wife's happiness in retirement, and vice versa (Stull, 1988). The importance of having a companion to share experiences with in retirement is underscored in a study of multiple changes that can occur at retirement. Stull and Hatch (1984) found that social interaction became an important predictor of happiness in retirement for those men who lost a wife at or near the time of retirement, whereas it was not a significant predictor for those men whose marriages remained intact.

Keating and Cole (1980) have offered a description of how marriage might contribute to retirement satisfaction. In their sample of retired male teachers and their wives, both the husband and wife placed a high value on their marriage. For the male retiree, the marital relationship became a primary source of social reinforcement in the absence of work. The women expressed a need to be supportive of their retired husbands and did so by making qualitative changes in the housewife role. The husbands responded positively to the changes, which, in turn, had a positive effect on the women's self-esteem (1980: 87). The process occurring when both husbands and wives retire has yet to be explored.

Gender

A handful of studies has indicated that retirement may be more difficult for women than for men (Atchley, 1976b; Jaslow, 1976; Fox, 1977; Levy, 1980-81), but more recent studies have shown that there are few, if any, sex differences in retirement well-being (Atchley, 1982; Collette, 1984; George et al., 1984; Palmore et al., 1985; Seccombe and Lee, 1986). Having made this observation, we must agree with Connidis (1982: 19), who has cautioned that it is not productive to try to determine which gender is better at adjusting to retirement. Time would be better spent examining the male-female differences in the process of adjustment to retirement (1982: 19). From the review of the literature, it is readily apparent that women, as compared to men, arrive at the threshold of retirement with fewer financial resources, less preparation for retirement, a different work and family history, and a dissimilar social network. New theoretical models oriented to women's retirement that take account of these factors, as suggested by Connidis (1982), need to be formulated and tested.

CONCLUSIONS

Life after retirement may not be smooth sailing for everyone, but few people suffer adverse consequences as a result of the act of retiring. If people's perceived health status was good prior to retirement, it will likely continue to be good after retirement and will contribute to a satisfactory life style. The effect of retirement on income is a little more complicated and warrants more complex methods of investigation, which should include the influence of perceived financial adequacy on retirement satisfaction.

It is quite likely that personality and/or coping skills do influence retirement satisfaction, but the dearth of research in this area makes any conclusion premature. Investigations of social relationships point to the salience of close relationships with friends and family developed earlier in the life cycle. Research into the relation between leisure and retirement satisfaction is suggestive of the same principle - the cultivation of an interest in leisure activities earlier in life will be carried over to retirement and will likely enhance satisfaction.

The link between prior occupational status and adjustment to retirement is not clear cut, specifically in regard to the skill carry-over effect and the influence of the degree of attachment of people to their occupations. One of the most advantageous sociodemographic characteristics for a satisfactory retirement would appear to be the presence of a spouse. That the resources people bring to retirement vary as a result of gender differences strongly indicates the need for different adjustment models for men and women. Although the factors examined in this chapter are not exhaustive and represent only the major research interests, the message of this research is fairly consistent: retirement satisfaction is a function of the personal resources that have taken a lifetime to accumulate.

The view, taken in this and the previous chapter, of retirement as an individual-level process that is linked to other social structural and institutional changes obscures important differences in retirement processes, experiences and outcomes across groups in Canada. Although a number of differences between men and women have been highlighted, a large body of research indicates that retirement is by no means a uniform phenomenon across ethnic groups, occupations, industries or income groups in Canada. In the next chapter, we will explore the influence of an individual's structural location in society on his or her retirement experiences, as well as the impact of retirement as both a demographic phenomenon and an institution on the economy, the political process, and other institutional sectors of society.

CHAPTER 6

THE STRUCTURAL VIEW OF RETIREMENT

The previous two chapters reviewed the individualist perspective on retirement, which views retirement behaviour as the result of a voluntaristic decision, with the only external constraint represented by the presence of a mandatory retirement policy in the workplace. This chapter describes a newer, very different perspective on retirement, the structuralist perspective. This approach to understanding retirement assumes that social, economic, and political forces external to the individual shape and constrain both the retirement decision and circumstances after retirement. As Myles puts it, "To understand old age as it is lived today, we must transcend the ethnographic description of the many individual expressions of this experience (even those descriptions based on national surveys) and link it to the institutional structures that provide its content" (1984a: 2). The key institutional structure referred to by Myles is the welfare state, which has been largely responsible for the establishment of the modern institution of retirement in industrial societies. However, other social and economic formations also condition the individual experience of retirement, often mediated by governmental policies. These include the structure of the labour market, particularly industry structure, occupational structure and the distribution of unemployment, and status positions ascribed to individuals, particularly ethnicity and gender.

This chapter also examines several structural consequences of retirement, that is, consequences of aggregate changes in retirement patterns for Canada's system of inequality, labour force, and public policy. Specifically, we will review the impact of increasing numbers of retirees on income and poverty levels, the supply and demand for labour, and federal and provincial pension programs.

STRUCTURAL EXPLANATIONS OF RETIREMENT: AN OVERVIEW

It should be apparent by now that most explanations of retirement have been informed by individualized conceptions of aging. The review of the research on retirement presented in previous chapters indicates that the influence of individual factors, such as attitudes toward work, job satisfaction, personal health, and the ability to save, have gained the attention of a majority of researchers. Peter Townsend (1981: 6) succinctly captures the essence of this approach when he refers to this individualistic bias "as acquiescent functionalism or the kind of theory of aging which attributes the causation of problems to the difficulties of individual adjustment to aging, retirement, or physical decresence, while acquiescing in the development of the state, the economy, and inequality"

More recently, a number of gerontologists have been challenging this bias. The elderly are not necessarily responsible for the inflation that has eroded their retirement savings (Estes, 1979); they are not responsible for retirement policies that were formulated to facilitate economic development in industrial nations (Estes, 1979; Graebner, 1980); they are not responsible for inequalities prior to labour force withdrawal that are reproduced in retirement (Walker, 1981). The elderly may indeed be poorly adjusted in retirement, dissatisfied with life, or poor, but part of their condition may also be explained by supraindividual factors. This alternative perspective, sometimes called the political economy of aging, looks to the structural features of society to explain the condition of elderly persons. Although the perspective exhibits considerable diversity, there is an apparent common denominator: retirement is viewed as a socially constructed dependent position in society that is as influenced by the operation of forces such as government policies, social class dynamics, and the labour market, as are other status positions in society.

RETIREMENT AND STATUS MAINTENANCE

One form this approach takes is to establish the position of the elderly in a society's overall system of stratification, particularly inequality in income. Sociologists studying "status attainment" find that persons who come from families in which the parents have more education and occupy higher ranking occupations, who themselves obtain more education and enter professional or managerial occupations generally earn higher incomes than those who do not. Do the effects of these factors on income inequality persist after retirement? Henretta and Campbell (1976), using data from the United States, showed that they do. Terming this phenomenon *status maintenance*, they found that the effects on income of parental status, and particularly of education and previous occupation, persist into retirement for the cohort of men they studied. What this implies is that the existence of a government pension system does not result in a levelling of income inequality in retirement: the same forces that produce income inequality before retirement maintain it into the retirement years.

Myles (1981) found similar status maintenance into retirement in Canada, though he more carefully distinguishes the forms it may take. The form studied by Henretta and Campbell (1976), in which a person maintains his or her position relative to others in the same age cohort, Myles terms *intragenerational* or *intracohort status maintenance*. A second form, *intercohort status maintenance*, refers to the degree to which a retired person is able to preserve his or her status position, compared to others in the same occupational group still in the labour force. Myles showed that, for Canada in 1973, while retired professionals and managers preserved their income advantage over those who worked in other occupations, the incomes of all groups fell dramatically after retirement. Nevertheless, there was some tendency for the incomes of white-collar workers to fall less than those of blue-collar workers. The third form of status maintenance discussed by Myles compares an individual's pre- and post-retirement status. This form emphasizes the degree of continuity in a person's life style as he or she ages, rather than intracohort or intercohort comparisons.

What the status maintenance concept suggests is that research on retirement cannot be carried out by studying only the retired. Retirement is best viewed as an important stage in the life cycle that can be understood only in comparison with other stages. The emphasis on inequality in this research, particularly income inequality, is a natural outgrowth of its roots in status attainment research, but also reflects the emphasis in the political economy of aging perspective on the material conditions of the elderly and how they are affected by social forces often beyond the ability of the individual to control. We next examine the effects of the structure of the labour market itself on retirement patterns.

RETIREMENT AND THE LABOUR MARKET

An individual's location in the labour market, particularly the firm, industry, and occupation within which he or she works, establishes the most direct context within which retirement takes place. While individuals in industrial societies do have some choice in the nature of the jobs they pursue (although even these choices are circumscribed by parents' status and educational attainment), once entered, those jobs set limits on further career opportunities and, ultimately, opportunities for and conditions of retirement. This section focuses on the impact on retirement of work in a segmented economy in which jobs may be clean or dirty, simple or complex, skilled or unskilled and situated in firms that are large or small, unionized or non-unionized, in competitive industries or oligopolistic industries.

Economic Sector

Beginning with Averitt (1968), advocates of the dual economy perspective have argued that the trend toward concentration and centralization of wealth and resources has caused the development of advanced capitalism increasingly to polarize the economy into two main sectors, each characterized by different forms of social and economic production organization. It is the organization of production that more immediately influences the careers and, ultimately, retirement patterns of individuals employed within each sector. The core industrial sector is dominated by large corporate enterprises, as represented in durable manufacturing, the construction trades, and extractive industries. Firms in the core economy are noted for high productivity, high profits, intensive utilization of capital, a high incidence of monopoly elements, and a tendency to have a high degree of unionization. The general result is high wages and better working conditions and fringe benefits. The state sector (government employment) is assumed to be very similar to the core sector in terms of conditions of employment (Averitt, 1968).

In contrast, at the periphery of the economy are smaller firms concentrated in agricultural production and in portions of nondurable manufacturing, retail trade and subprofessional services. Firms in this sector are noted for labour intensity, low productivity and profits, intensive product market competition, and lack of unionization. These factors are translated into lower wages and fringe benefits. Since firms in this sector generally aim to maximize short-term profits, most jobs are not likely to develop a worker's skills, are characterized by high worker turnover, and are not often organized into labour markets internal to the firm.

One of the most important features distinguishing core firms from periphery firms is the way in which jobs within them are organized into career paths (Tolbert, 1982; Wanner and Lewis, 1983). Spilerman (1977) has distinguished between *orderly* and *chaotic* career lines. Among the characteristics of orderly career tracks are requirements that earnings and occupational prestige increase steadily over time. In contrast, chaotic career lines are posited to exhibit no such regularity in earnings or prestige increments. It is likely that such career lines extend as well to the end of the career, that is, to retirement. It might be expected, therefore, that employees in core industries will be more likely to exhibit an orderly career exit; that is, they should be more likely to work up to a conventional retirement age, usually 65, more likely to remain out of the labour force after retirement, and more likely to collect private pensions from the firms for which they worked.

Most research testing these ideas has been carried out using the longitudinal data bases collected in the United States over the past two decades. Palmore et al. (1982), using the U.S. National Longitudinal Studies data, found that workers who spent their careers in core firms were less likely to work beyond age 65. McDonald (1983), using the same data, found that sectoral placement made a crucial difference in retirement across the retirement age spectrum, above and beyond individual differences. She found that workers in the periphery sector were considerably less likely to retire early, probably because their generally lower paying jobs and fewer benefits make this financially difficult.

Table 6.1 presents some data suggesting the impact of sector of employment on retirement for Canadian men and women who withdrew from the labour force just prior to the 1981 Census of Canada. As expected, those who left core sector firms were better educated, were in occupations with higher average status, and earned higher wages prior to leaving the labour force. Also consistent with the expectations of dual economy theory, a much larger proportion of both men and women in periphery industries were working part time before retirement. For men, the timing of retirement clearly differs in core and periphery. A larger percentage of men who worked in core industries retired between ages 60 and 64 (27.6 compared to 22.3 percent) and at age 65 (17.7 compared to 12.7 percent), often considered "on time" retirement in an orderly career. A far greater percentage of men in periphery industries were age 66 or over before leaving the labour force. These patterns are muted for women, though the fact that women have far different career lines than men should not make this unexpected (Connidis, 1982).

Financial conditions after retirement differ considerably between core and periphery workers. A larger percentage of both men and women who worked in core industries received pensions beyond the basic OAS benefits, while fewer men who worked in the core received other government transfer payments. McDonald and Wanner (1987) found further that the way in which factors such as education, income prior to retirement, and self-employed status influence retirement differs across sectors of the economy. All this suggests that retirement in Canada is certainly not a uniform phenomenon, operating in the same way across the economy. Persons who work in core firms can anticipate retiring earlier with a greater certainty of receiving a private pension than can those who work in periphery firms.

The emphasis in dual economy theory is on the workplace, the firm or industry within which work takes place. But what of the occupational structure surrounding work? We have seen that dual economy theory implies that core and periphery sectors are characterized by distinct labour markets, but is there something about the nature of occupations themselves that influences the timing of retirement from them? This issue is considered next.

Retirement in Canada

Table 6.1

Means and Percentages for Men and Women Who Withdrew From the Labour Force, 1980–81, by Economic Sector, Canada, 1981

Socioeconomic Characteristics	Men Core	Men Periphery	Women Core	Women Periphery
Age				
55 to 59	19.0%*	19.3%*	31.5%	37.4%
60 to 64	27.6%*	22.3%*	30.4%	29.5%
65	17.7%*	12.7%*	10.9%	7.2%
66 or over	35.7%*	45.7%*	27.2%	25.9%
Level of Education	9.4	9.2	10.4*	9.6*
Occupational Status [a]	44.3	43.3	52.4*	44.8*
Class of Worker				
Self-Employed	7.5%*	27.6%*	2.8%*	12.1%*
Paid Worker	92.5%*	72.4%*	97.2%*	87.9%*
Amount of Work				
Part Time	21.2%*	34.4%*	45.7%*	60.8%*
Full Time	78.8%*	65.6%*	54.3%*	39.2%*
Weeks Not Worked	24.4	26.0	30.1	29.2
Wages	9806.*	6003.*	4452.*	2982.*
Total Income [b]	16806.*	14841.*	9453.*	7161.*
Received OAS	45.8%*	52.0%*	61.0%*	61.7%*
Received Other Pension [c]	35.2%*	28.9%*	26.5%*	15.0%*
Received Other Transfer Payments [d]	16.8%*	21.6%*	13.3%*	10.7%*
Number of Cases	871	606	533	580

Source: Tabulations by the authors from the 1981 Census of Canada Public Use Sample Tape.

Note: Separate F or χ^2 tests for differences in means or percentages across economic sectors were performed. Significant differences at $\alpha < .05$ are indicated by asterisks.

[a]   Blishen-McRoberts (1976) scale of occupational status.
[b]   Total income from all sources.
[c]   All regular income received as a result of previous employment of the respondent or a deceased relative.
[d]   All other government transfer payments from federal, provincial, or municipal governments.

Occupational Structure

As pointed out in Chapter 4, when the question of the effect of occupation on retirement patterns has been addressed, almost uniformly the focus has been on the status or prestige of occupations (Palmore, 1964; Palmore et al., 1982) rather than on other occupational characteristics that might reasonably be assumed to predispose workers either to leave the labour force or to remain in it, such as their substantive complexity, physical and environmental demands, and the degree of social and manipulative skill they involve. As shown in Chapter 3, Canada's occupational structure has been undergoing a rapid transformation over the past several decades. If the implications of this change for retirement trends are to be understood, the relative effects of the various characteristics of occupations, not just their prestige, on the timing of labour force withdrawal must be known.

Walker (1981) is the only proponent of the political economy perspective who refers directly to the role of occupational structures in retirement. He argues that labour market experiences are socially divided with two distinct extremes. On the one hand, "jobs are boring, arduous, or alienating, offering little or no prospects for promotion, few fringe benefits and relatively little security; while on the other hand, there are relatively high paid jobs offering a wide range of fringe benefits, a great deal of autonomy and security of tenure" (Walker, 1981: 77-78). He goes on to state that these job-related characteristics ultimately translate into inequalities in retirement experiences, most notably in terms of economic advantage or disadvantage. While he attempts to demonstrate that job tenure and occupational pensions make a difference in retirement, he never pursues how such job characteristics as level of interest, arduousness or autonomy influence the retirement experience.

Walker's (1981) simplistic, attenuated treatment of job structure is typical of the research on retirement and occupations in general. To our knowledge, there are but a handful of studies that investigate the association between retirement and occupational structures, none of them using Canadian data. Jacobson (1972), a British industrial psychologist, studied the effect of job strain on retirement intentions. With a small sample of semi-skilled British operatives, he found that men with jobs involving high levels of strain were more likely than others to retire willingly before the pensionable age. Quinn (1977), using data from the U.S. Retirement History Study, examined the effects of job autonomy, working conditions and strain on actual retirement decisions by using a cross-classification matrix created for the U.S. Department of Labor that gives for each census occupation the probability of holding each of the approximately 14,000 jobs listed in the *U.S. Dictionary of Occupational Titles*. This matrix allows for the derivation of expected job characteristics for each U.S. census code - the probability that the occupation has each of the specified attributes. Quinn (1977) found the effect of strain on the early retirement decision to be the largest, followed by the effects of low autonomy and bad working conditions, although none is statistically significant by conventional standards.

Hayward (1986) and Hayward and Hardy (1985) have examined the effects of occupational characteristics on early retirement, which they operationally define as complete withdrawal from the labour force. Hayward looked at the effects of substantive complexity, physical and environmental demands, social skill and manipulative skill on the probability of being out of the labour force and found that, in the United States, for men retiring before age 62, only social and manipulative skill levels of their occupations have small effects; for men ages 62 to 64, none of the occupational characteristics has a significant effect on the probability of retiring, net of the effects of the other socioeconomic variables in his model. In contrast, Hayward and Hardy (1985) looked at how the early retirement process in the United States varies across the work context. They found that the effects of a number of important predictors of retirement are quite different in jobs with higher versus lower substantive complexity, social skill requirements, or physical or environmental demands. For example, they found that health limitations are more likely to increase the odds of retirement for workers in jobs with higher substantive complexity, requiring more social skill and presenting fewer physical demands.

Also, using data from the U.S. National Longitudinal Studies, McDonald and Wanner (1986) examined the effects of the substantive complexity, motor skills, physical demands, and desirability of working conditions associated with occupations on early, on-time (age 65), and late retirement. They found that substantive complexity, as an indicator of high levels of training, intellectual demands, and diversity, sustains labour force participation across the entire retirement age spectrum, and that it is a more important explanatory factor than financial resources. They also found that workers experiencing unpleasant or hazardous working conditions tend to remain employed through the early retirement period, but are most likely to retire at age 65 when government, and possibly private, pensions become fully available.

Unfortunately, the research does not exist currently to determine the degree to which these findings for other countries apply to Canada, although the worker trait data used in compiling the *Canadian Classification and Dictionary of Occupations* might be used to examine the extent to which non-status characteristics of occupations affect retirement patterns (see Hunter and Manley, 1986). What is clear, however, is that, controlling for a number of other socioeconomic characteristics, occupational status does not significantly affect the likelihood of either early or late retirement in Canada (McDonald and Wanner, 1982; 1984).

Despite the absence of occupational status effects on retirement, the data in Table 6.2 indicate that there are gross differences in retirement patterns across occupations in Canada, which suggest the operation of other

TABLE 6.2

OCCUPATIONAL DISTRIBUTIONS OF OLDER CANADIAN MEN NOT IN THE LABOUR FORCE AND OLDER EMPLOYED MEN, 1978

Occupational Category	Employed Men		Men Not in the Labour Force	
	55–64	65+	55–64	65+
White Collar	50.0 %	54.8 %	43.2 %	46.1 %
Managerial and Professional	19.7	16.5	16.1	13.7
Clerical	7.4	6.3	6.8	7.7
Sales	10.1	15.7	8.0	8.8
Service	12.8	16.4	12.3	15.9
Blue Collar	50.0	45.2	56.8	53.9
Primary Occupations	11.0	25.7	12.8	14.4
Processing, etc.	18.7	9.6	18.0	17.9
Construction Trades	10.2	4.9	14.0	11.8
Transportation	5.9	2.5	7.2	4.9
Materials Handling, etc.	4.2	2.5	4.8	4.8
Total	100.0	100.0	100.0	100.0
Estimated Population N (000's)	691	131	125	243

Source: Statistics Canada (1982a), Table 16.

Note: "Men not in the labour force" includes only those who have worked sometime in the past five years. Excluded are men who are permanently unable to work, have never worked, or have worked more than five years prior to the date of the survey.

occupation-based factors. Among men 55 to 64 years, half of the employed labour force is in white-collar occupations, but 43.2 percent of those not in the labour force had prior jobs that were white-collar. The largest differences are to be found among those in managerial and professional occupations, for white-collar workers, and among those in construction trades for blue-collar workers. That blue-collar workers are retiring earlier in Canada is consistent with the finding for the United States that the physically demanding nature of much blue-collar work is responsible for this pattern.

The crude contrast between white-collar and blue-collar workers for men 65 years and over is misleading. It is for the most part the result of there being such a large proportion of men in primary occupations, mostly self-employed farmers, remaining in the labour force past age 65. This is consistent with other research showing that self-employment has an extremely large effect on labour force participation after age 65 in Canada (McDonald and Wanner, 1982). Men in all other blue-collar occupations are more likely to have withdrawn from the labour force than men in white-collar occupations, with the sole exception of clerical workers. Again, it is likely the physically demanding nature of the blue-collar occupations and the extent to which workers in them experience occupationally related health problems that impel workers to withdraw from the labour force, although the specific nature of this relation remains to be explored in Canada.

The link between type of occupation and reason for retirement has been documented by Ciffen and Martin (1977). While just over 11 percent of Canadian men in managerial, professional, or technical occupations reported poor health as a reason for retirement, 42.4 percent of those in primary blue-collar occupations and 37.6 percent of those in other blue-collar occupations did so.

In contrast, the major reason for retirement among managerial, professional and technical workers was a compulsory retirement policy, with nearly 49 percent reporting it as a reason for retirement. Just 5.1 percent of those in primary occupations cited compulsory retirement as a reason for their retirement. As in the case of reason for retirement, it is likely that the effects of other variables influencing retirement behaviour differ across occupations in Canada, as Hayward and Hardy (1985) found for the United States.

Thus far, we have seen how the locus of employment, the sector or occupation within which a person works, can constrain individual retirement behaviour. It also seems likely that the stability of the occupational career, number of job entries and exits or spells of unemployment will influence the timing of retirement. This question is examined in the next section.

Unemployment and the Unemployment Rate

The effect of unemployment on retirement patterns may take the form of either a high local unemployment rate making it difficult for an older worker to find a job or a long spell of personal unemployment discouraging the worker from continuing the job search so that he or she withdraws from the labour force by retiring. It has been argued (Bould, 1980) that retirement can sometimes be viewed as a mechanism for dealing with long-term, chronic unemployment among older workers in that it provides a "respectable" route out of the labour force, eliminating the stigma attached to unemployment. In this view, the availability of public pensions would make it easier for older workers facing a long spell of unemployment simply to declare themselves retired and begin collecting benefits. A part of the effect of public pension benefits so frequently found in research on early retirement is seen as mediating the effect of unemployment, though this would likely be true only of workers in lower status jobs in periphery firms.

For the United States, Bould (1980) found that, controlling for a variety of factors known to be related to early retirement, previous unemployment has a significant effect on retirement among both white and black men ages 52 to 64. Its importance is underscored by Bould's observation that the effect of each additional week of previous unemployment on the probability of retiring is approximately equal to the effect of each additional one thousand dollars of assets. Although unemployment itself may influence retirement, Parnes, Gagen and King (1981) found that being a "displaced worker," that is, one who has been employed for several years by the same employer before being permanently laid off, does not necessarily increase the probability of retiring. In their study in the United States of men aged 45 to 54 in 1966 who were displaced by their employers in that year, they found that by 1976 these men were no more likely to withdraw from the labour force than a control group of men who had not been displaced. However, the displaced workers were much more likely to end up in lower status occupations paying considerably less than their former jobs. In contrast, a study using the U.S. Retirement History Survey by Boaz (1987b) found that the major factors influencing withdrawal from the labour force among men between ages 58 and 61 were early separation from a long-term job and the subsequent lack of steady full-time work. She argues that the "push" out of the labour market created by job loss and the inability to find suitable employment is a major source of early retirement, and policy measures designed to delay retirement must respond to this by expanding employment opportunities for older workers.

Proneness to unemployment generally, and not just loss of a long-term job, may influence early retirement. McDonald and Wanner (1984) found that the number of periods of employment of three months or more experienced by workers significantly affects the likelihood of early retirement for Canadian men and women, although the effect disappears for women in the presence of controls for other socioeconomic variables. That workers who had a larger number of spells of unemployment were considerably more likely to retire early suggests that they were "discouraged out" of the labour force at the earliest possible date by the uncertainty of employment they experienced.

It seems reasonable to expect that personal experience with unemployment will influence the retirement decision, but what about the state of the local labour market? Would a higher local unemployment rate further discourage older workers into early retirement? Again for the United States, Quinn (1977) found that married white males were more likely to retire early when the local unemployment rate had been increasing, while McDonald (1983) found that the absolute level of the local unemployment rate produces a significantly higher level of early retirement. That is, men who lived in places with high unemployment rates were more likely to retire before age 62, although McDonald's research does not get at the mechanism linking local unemployment rate to the retirement decision. It is likely that higher rates simply translate into longer, more discouraging job searches that eventually result in labour force withdrawal.

The data available for Canada suggest that unemployment may have similar effects in this country. On a national level, it is clearly not a difference in the unemployment rate between older and younger workers that impels early retirement among the former. In 1986 the unemployment rate for workers aged 55 to 64 years was in fact slightly lower than the unemployment rate for 25 to 54 year olds - 7.3 percent compared to 8.2 percent - although since the beginning of the current economic recovery in 1982, the unemployment rate for the younger workers fell from 8.8 percent to 8.2 percent, while the rate for the 55 to 64 year olds actually increased from its level of 6.9 percent in 1982 (Akyeampong, 1987). What is probably crucial in this regard is the large difference in the duration of unemployment between older and younger workers. Again in 1986, 25 to 55-year-old workers averaged 22.5 weeks of unemployment before finding another job, while workers aged 55 to 64 years averaged 31.3 weeks. At the extreme end of the distribution, 18.6 percent of the older workers were unemployed for 53 weeks or more, compared to just 10.6 percent of the younger workers (Akyeampong, 1987).

In view of this discrepancy, are older workers more likely to become discouraged and leave the labour force for retirement? To answer this question, we must examine the behaviour of both older and younger workers after a job loss. Table 6.3 reports data gathered in a special Labour Force Survey in January of 1986 on the labour market adjustment experiences of workers laid off from their jobs between 1981 and 1984 for such reasons as plant closure or workload reduction (Picot and Wannell,

TABLE 6.3

**LABOUR MARKET OUTCOMES FOR WORKERS LOSING FULL-TIME JOBS, 1981-84,
AS OF JANUARY 1986 BY AGE, CANADA, 1981-85**

	Age of Workers	
	25-54	55-64
Percent employed	65.2	39.1
Percent unemployed	21.0	19.5
Percent not in the labour force	13.8	41.4
Unemployment rate	24.3	33.3
Average weeks spent in successful job search	27.0	36.8
Average percent change in weekly earnings	-1.9	-12.3

Source: Statistics Canada (1987), p. 108.

1987). These workers, had no job to which they could return and were forced either to seek other employment or to leave the labour force. It is apparent from Table 6.3 that there are marked differences in the labour force experiences of the 55 to 64-year-old workers and those aged 25 to 54. While over 65 percent of the younger workers had found another job by January of 1986, just 39.1 percent of the older workers had succeeded in doing so. Only a small proportion, 13.8 percent, of the younger workers had withdrawn from the labour force (i.e., were not employed or still seeking work), whereas a sizeable 41.4 percent of the 55 to 64 year olds were no longer in the labour force. Since January 1, 1987, workers can begin receiving Canada Pension benefits on an adjusted basis any time between ages 60 and 70, a provision likely to boost the already large proportion of older displaced workers who opt to retire.

It is likely that many of these older workers were "discouraged" into retirement by the labour market conditions they faced. As Table 6.3 indicates, the older laid-off workers who did find another job averaged 9.8 weeks longer to find one than the younger workers. When they did find one, the remuneration they received was over 12 percent less than their earnings from their previous job. In contrast, the younger workers were able to find jobs at approximately the same level of compensation, losing only about 1.9 percent of earnings on the average. In fact, the pay reductions experienced by the older job changers is obscured by the overall average; the one-half of workers age 55 or over who actually took pay cuts lost, on average, one-third of their wages in the job change (Picot and Wannell, 1987)! While such earnings discrimination against older workers is by no means limited to those seeking employment, it is more pronounced among those changing jobs late in life (Wanner and McDonald, 1983) and likely a factor in the early retirement decision.

While in Canada the proportion of those retiring early as a consequence of being "discouraged out" of the labour force is probably small, the actual numbers involved is sizeable. An estimated 82,000 persons aged 55 or over experienced permanent lay-offs in the last major economic recession (Akyeampong, 1987). Approximately 33,948 of these workers (41.4 percent) withdrew from the labour force, often because they were unable to find another job or the jobs available to them paid less than their accrued pension benefits. Of course, some of these workers stopped looking for work for other reasons, such as health problems, but these figures still describe a problem of major proportions for Canadian society.

RETIREMENT AND ASCRIBED STATUSES

That an individual's location in the paid labour force, whether in a specific firm, industry, sector of the economy, or occupation, has a direct impact on the timing and conditions of his or he retirement may be obvious. But we have argued more broadly that occupying any position in society that has status implications will influence the manner in which the individual encounters the institution of retirement. Two such positional systems are ethnicity and gender. In a sense, traits of this kind are characteristics of individuals. However, to the extent that ethnic and gender groups have differential access to social and economic resources, membership in such groups influences both treatment under government programs and labour market location and outcomes. It is in this sense that ethnicity and gender will be treated as structural features of Canadian society that affect both the timing of retirement and life circumstances after retirement.

Ethnicity and Immigrant Status

It is well known that Canada's aged population is not an ethnically or culturally homogeneous one. Unlike the United States, where a "melting pot" image of the cultural assimilation of ethnic groups prevails, Canada has consistently encouraged multiculturalism and ethnic diversity as official government policy. Indeed, in 1981, 11 percent of the Canadian population over age 65 spoke a language other than English or French at home (Health and Welfare Canada, 1983). It is not surprising that there is little disagreement among Canadian social gerontologists that the impact of ethnic variation on aging is significant (Gerber, 1983; Marshall, 1987; Driedger and Chappell, 1987). While there is a growing body of research on ethnic variations in the aging experience, represented particularly by a 1983 special issue of *Canadian Ethnic Studies* devoted to ethnicity and aging, studies of ethnicity and retirement are rare. The most recent, comprehensive treatment of aging and ethnicity in Canada has but a single index entry devoted to retirement, a simple statement that retirement age has been institutionalized in modern societies (Driedger and Chappell, 1987). Researchers have offered evidence that the aged members of certain ethnic groups are disadvantaged on a number of characteristics, ranging from education, occupation, and income to health, nutrition and housing (see, for example, Jackson, 1980; Quinn, 1977; Watson, 1982). More specifically, the multiple-jeopardy perspective, which argues that being simultaneously elderly, female, and a member of a minority ethnic group combine to reduce considerably an individual's access to social and economic resources, has found some empirical support (Dowd and Bengston, 1978; Havens and Chappell, 1983; Penning, 1983). However, none of this research addresses directly the effect of ethnic group membership on retirement in Canada. Though it has few implications for the Canadian situation, research in the United States does suggest that race influences the timing of retirement; blacks tend to withdraw from the labour force earlier and more completely than do whites, reflecting their generally poorer health, lower incomes, and location at the periphery of the American economy (Parnes and Nestel, 1971).

TABLE 6.4
LABOUR FORCE ACTIVITY OF CANADIAN MEN AND WOMEN AGE 55 AND OVER BY PLACE OF BIRTH, 1981

Labour Force Activity	PLACE OF BIRTH									
	Canada	United States	Western Europe	Ireland or United Kingdom	Eastern Europe	Southern Europe	Other Europe	Asia	Africa	South or Central America
Men Aged 55 to 65										
Working full-time	61.7%	69.5%	75.1%	74.0%	74.8%	76.4%	68.9%	60.3%	69.2%	72.1%
Working part-time	6.0	8.6	5.5	4.6	4.2	1.7	4.4	4.0	0.0	1.9
Unemployed	4.4	2.0	2.4	2.8	4.9	5.6	3.7	8.1	11.5	6.0
Not in labour force	27.9	19.9	17.0	18.6	16.1	16.3	23.0	27.6	19.2	20.0
Not in labour force and receiving OAS/CPP/QPP	7.1	5.3	4.2	3.7	4.3	5.1	4.4	3.2	0.0	0.0
Men Aged 66 and over										
Working full-time	9.8%	10.6%	6.3%	6.3%	9.4%	6.8%	8.2%	15.8%	12.0%	27.9%
Working part-time	5.8	6.3	5.0	6.3	5.7	1.2	4.7	6.2	8.0	3.1
Unemployed	0.4	0.4	0.4	0.2	0.3	0.0	0.5	5.0	0.0	0.0
Not in labour force	84.0	82.7	88.3	87.2	84.6	92.0	86.6	73.0	80.0	69.0
Not in labour force and receiving OAS/CPP/QPP	83.7	81.1	86.2	85.9	83.9	84.7	86.1	43.3	45.0	31.0
Women Aged 55 to 65										
Working full-time	20.3%	21.3%	27.0%	24.9%	29.3%	25.1%	19.1%	20.2%	26.5%	33.7%
Working part-time	10.6	10.3	13.0	14.5	13.0	4.7	12.7	8.7	11.7	12.0
Unemployed	2.0	1.3	1.8	1.6	2.5	3.8	1.8	3.4	0.0	3.7
Not in labour force	67.1	67.1	58.2	59.0	55.2	66.4	66.4	67.7	61.8	50.6
Not in labour force and receiving OAS/CPP/QPP	17.0	13.2	9.4	11.1	10.3	15.4	11.5	3.4	8.8	6.2
Women Aged 66 and over										
Working full-time	2.5%	2.0%	1.9%	1.3%	2.6%	1.4%	4.3%	5.3%	0.0%	5.1%
Working part-time	3.2	2.6	3.0	1.8	3.5	1.2	3.4	1.8	3.6	2.6
Unemployed	0.2	0.0	0.0	0.2	0.1	0.0	0.5	0.9	0.0	1.5
Not in labour force	94.1	95.4	95.1	96.7	93.8	97.4	91.8	92.0	96.4	90.8
Not in labour force and receiving OAS/CPP/QPP	93.9	91.4	88.7	93.7	91.5	87.1	89.6	55.2	64.3	43.1

Source: Tabulations by the authors from the 1981 Census of Canada Public Use Sample Tape.

To assess ethnic differences in retirement patterns, Table 6.4 reports the labour force activity of Canadian men and women age 55 to 65 years and over age 65 who were born both in Canada and in other regions of the world. The data reported in the table come from a sample of respondents to the 1981 Census of Canada.

Here, ethnicity is defined in terms of country of birth rather than on the basis of ethnic self-identification, because that definition unambiguously assigns respondents to a single ethnic group. As well, any effect of ethnicity on retirement is likely to be more pronounced for first-generation immigrant members of an ethnic group. From Table 6.4 few differences are observable in patterns of labour force activity among men age 55 to 65, although unemployment rates are noticeably higher among Asian- and African-born men. While the labour force withdrawal rates of the younger Asians, Africans, and Latin Americans are not unusual, these groups are less likely than others to be out of the labour force and collecting Old Age Security, Canada Pension, or Quebec Pension benefits. Indeed, none of the African-born or Latin American-born in the sample were collecting public pensions before age 66.

The second panel of Table 6.4 indicates that the differences between the labour force experiences of the Canadian and European-born men, on the one hand, and that of the "visible minorities," on the other, become striking in the older age cohort. The proportions of Asian-, African-, and Latin American-born men continuing to work full time are considerably higher than proportions for the other groups. For Asians, this value may even be underestimated, since 5 percent of the respondents were unemployed and looking for work. The other major contrast in this panel is for the proportions of the various ethnic groups not in the labour force and receiving some form of public pension. Among the Canadian- and European-born men, it is a consistent 83 to 86 percent, while among Asians, Africans and Latin Americans it is about half that. Indeed, only about 30 percent of the Latin American men not working receive OAS, CPP, or QPP. Although these social insurance programs are intended to be universal, these new Canadians are not benefiting from them. This is likely the result of their failure to meet the statutory requirements for receiving benefits, since the vast majority of members of this group immigrated to Canada after the 1967 alteration of immigration policy.

The labour force participation patterns for women shown in the third and fourth panels of Table 6.4 are, as expected, quite different from those of men, but the patterns of differences across ethnic groups are quite similar to those observed for the men. A considerably smaller proportion of the women age 55 to 65 are in the labour force than is true of men, but in the older cohort the difference narrows, at least in absolute terms. In addition, the rates of part-time employment for women under 66 are typically two to three times those of men, suggesting that, while unemployment does not appear to be a major problem among older women, underemployment may well be. For women over age 65, labour force participation rates are generally low, but for most ethnic groups the proportion of part-time workers exceeds the proportion of full-time workers. As in the case of the men, there is a distinct dichotomy between the Canadian and European born and those born in Third World regions, in terms of receipt of social insurance benefits among those no longer in the labour force. The rates at which these women receive OAS, CPP or QPP are typically a half to a third less than the rates for Canadian or European-born women.

The greater propensity of more recent immigrants from Third World countries to remain in the labour force after age 65 observed in Table 6.4 is likely the result of their failure to qualify for full pension benefits under current Canadian policy. Indeed, Wanner and McDonald (1986) found that, although ethnicity itself has only a minor effect on the incomes of older Canadians, the variable with the single largest effect on income among older men was the period of immigration; those arriving after the 1967 policy change had substantially lower incomes. Although changes in Canadian immigration policy in 1967 did away with "preferred nation-alities" and purportedly the last vestiges of ethnic and racial discrimination among immigrants, these changes were not linked to policy for the retirement income system (Canada, 1983).

Three major problems exist for those who immigrate to Canada during their working career. Those who immigrated after 1977 and who have accumulated no retirement benefits from their country of origin, the majority of such immigrants, will not receive full OAS benefits unless they live in Canada for at least 40 years. This is true even if they become Canadian citizens during this period. Instead, they will receive partial OAS benefits of 1/40 of the full benefits for each year of residence, providing they have lived in Canada for 10 years continuously prior to retirement. Unlike native-born Canadians, for whom GIS benefits are not reduced by the receipt of OAS, if immigrants are eligible for GIS benefits, they will be reduced by the amount of any foreign pension received, even if that pension provides benefits smaller than those of OAS. Immigrants to Canada after 1966 who receive no retirement benefits from their country of origin may not receive a full pension from the Canada or Quebec Pension Plans if they arrived after age 18, because they will not have worked the full contributory period in Canada. Wanner and McDonald (1986) found that these policies impact most heavily on immigrants from developing nations, particularly those of Asia and Africa, which provide no public pensions or with which Canada has no reciprocal agreement on social security.

Gender in the Social Structure

Chapters 3 and 4 have already alluded to the substantial difference in retirement patterns and their determinants between men and women. Much of the difference is likely a result of a majority of the present generation of older women in Canada never having held jobs outside the home. With the rising level of labour force participation among younger women, increasing numbers of women experiencing the transition to retirement can be anticipated. Nevertheless, it is not reasonable to expect a convergence of retirement patterns and experiences between men and women as long as gender exerts such a powerful influence on opportunity in the labour force.

Conceptualizing gender as representing a set of structural positions in society rests to a large extent on the nature of the sexual division of labour, both in the labour force and in the household (Stone and Minkler, 1984). Specifically, the delays and interruptions that characterize married women's careers are to a considerable extent the result of their culturally defined responsibility for the rearing of children, despite falling fertility rates in all industrial societies. Indeed, a national study carried out in 1982 found that the most important reason for leaving the labour force among Canadian women under age 40 was child-rearing responsibilities (Boyd, 1985). As well, the division of labour within the household sees the great majority of childcare and housework tasks still being carried out by women (Meissner et al., 1975), even when both husband and wife are retired (Brubaker and Hennon, 1982). Thus, women's traditional role as caregivers is not substantially altered by changes in their labour force participation. In fact, women who have retired from the labour force often enter a "career" of caring for husbands or, in some cases, elderly parents, whose health is deteriorating (Simon, 1987).

As in all industrial societies, women in Canada are likely to have very different life chances than are men. Although the labour force participation rate among women has been growing, women are less likely to have a job on a full-time basis; if she has a full-time job, a woman is far more likely to be working in a "woman's" job, in which the majority of other workers are also women and the likelihood of promotion is relatively low; her job is more likely to be in the periphery sector of the economy; she is probably paid less than a man in a comparable job; and her job is less likely to have a private pension entitlement attached to it. Being a woman thus represents a distinct status position in Canadian society, a status position that restricts access to scarce resources as well as to other desirable positions. Gender is more than an attribute of individuals for purposes of understanding labour force behaviour generally or retirement behaviour specifically. It represents a set of distinct structural positions in society, both in the division of labour and in the stratification hierarchy, that has important consequences throughout the life cycle.

In view of all this, it makes sense that the study of patterns of retirement among women must consider their very different labour force experiences. Few studies have done so. Typically, models containing the same predictor variables are estimated for both men and women. Utilizing this approach to predict "objective retirement" (simultaneous withdrawal from the labour force and receipt of a pension) using data drawn from the U.S. Retirement History Study and the Duke Second Longitudinal Study, George et al. (1984) rather surprisingly found that nothing but age significantly affected women's retirement in either sample. None of the other variables in their model, education, occupational status, health limitations, pension coverage, years in longest job, or years worked since age 21, had any substantial effect on the probability of women retiring, though all these factors had significant effects in the case of the men in their samples. While these results may be partially a function of the extremely small sample sizes for women, they may also be related to the absence of retirement predictors in the women's models that measure contingencies unique to women's careers.

In contrast to these results, Campione's (1987) study of married women's retirement decisions using data from the University of Michigan's Panel Study of Income Dynamics found that not only age but also indicators of potential Social Security wealth, wage wealth, and pension wealth significantly predicted retirement. In addition, she found that the retirement of a married woman's husband increased the probability of her own retirement, independent of the financial factors. Although their retirement models for men and women were the same, McDonald and Wanner's (1984) Canadian results substantiate Campione's findings; women who were married, self-employed, better educated and had prospects for a higher unearned income were more likely to retire early. In fact, after controlling for a large number of socioeconomic characteristics, McDonald and Wanner found that age had no significant effect on early retirement in their sample of women. Consistent with all other research on women's retirement, though, McDonald and Wanner observed that a much smaller proportion of the variance in early retirement was explained by their model for women than by their model for men, suggesting either that, as with their careers generally, women retire in a more "disorderly" fashion than do men or that a number of variables salient to women's retirement were not included in the model.

The concentration of women in a limited range of jobs offering little economic security and few opportunities for advancement has serious consequences for the financial side of retirement. As in the case of men, women's retirement incomes are influenced by their occupational status, earnings, and industrial context of employment. But unlike men, women's retirement incomes are affected directly and indirectly by their family role and early family events. O'Rand and Landerman (1984), for example, found in the United States that the birth of each child and each year of delay in entering the full-time labour force influenced negatively women's occupational status and, ultimately, their retirement incomes. They further found that being self-employed or a worker in a family business enhances men's but not women's assets, which are a source of retirement income. The effects of discontinuity in the career and beginning first job at a late age appear to be similar for women who are married and unmarried at the time of retirement in the United States (O'Rand and Henretta, 1982a).

Although the Canadian research on women's retirement income does not include any studies of the effects of early career contingencies, it is likely that the lower earnings, less stable careers, and lower probability of receiving a private pension among Canadian women all produce lower retirement incomes. While Statistics Canada always reports its income data by age rather than by labour force status, the figures comparing unattached men and women age 65 and over are revealing. Unattached persons are those who were either never married or widowed or divorced and live in a single-person household. In 1982, the $9,965 median income of unattached elderly women was 72 percent of the $13,759 average for unattached elderly men, underscoring the maintenance of the gender gap into retirement (Statistics Canada, 1985b: 75). Even considering Canada or Quebec Pension Plan benefits, unattached women received approximately 63 percent of unattached men's benefits, almost perfectly reflecting women's earnings as a percentage of men's in Canada (Statistics Canada, 1985b: 76). The only source of income for which unattached elderly women's incomes exceeded that of their male counterparts was income from the Old Age Security and Guaranteed Income Supplement programs, the latter expressly designed for low income persons. Indeed, in 1986 the poverty rate for unattached elderly women was over 46 percent, compared to 32 percent for men (National Council of Welfare, 1988: 67).

This section has documented the influence of some features of the labour market and the social structure on patterns of retirement. While "individualist" research informed by functionalist theories has emphasized the voluntary nature of the retirement decision and the influence of personal preferences on it, the structuralist view attempts to underscore the limits placed on the retirement decision by a person's location in the labour market, as well as the possession of certain ascribed statuses that influence employment opportunities. Just as social structures can alter the probability of retirement at any given age, they are themselves influenced by the growth of retirement as an institution. These consequences are considered next.

THE SOCIETAL CONSEQUENCES OF RETIREMENT

The rise of the institution of retirement in industrial societies, particularly the dramatic increase in early retirement that has taken place over the past two decades, has had consequences not only for the individuals undergoing the process, as documented in previous chapters, but also for society as a whole. Arguments favouring the liberalization of opportunities for early retirement have often been couched in terms of the social good it can provide: greater employment opportunities for younger persons; permitting firms to replace workers whose skills are outmoded with those whose training is more recent; the reduction of unemployment rates among the young; facilitating promotions for younger workers who are in fixed career tracks, thereby motivating them in their work. Yet we know relatively little about the extent to which these objectives have been achieved, not to speak of the potentially negative consequences of increasing levels of early retirement.

The focus of most research at the societal level has been on the consequences of an aging population, and the research has not recognized that the number of aged persons and the number of retired person are not necessarily congruent. As well, a great deal of research attention has been drawn to the issue of the rising cost of public pension programs, almost to the exclusion of other equally compelling consequences of an expanding retired population. In addition to the effects of increasing levels of retirement on public pension programs and government expenditures, this section considers the impact of retirement on poverty and the income distribution and on employment opportunities and the labour force. As these issues are discussed, it will become apparent that they are in reality tightly interrelated. Certainly, other features of the social structure, such as migration and family structure, may be heavily influenced by changes in retirement patterns, but little research is available linking them to retirement. Such issues as housing and health care for the elderly are not considered here, because they really constitute societal consequences of population aging rather than of retirement *per se*, particularly in Canada with its universal health insurance program (see McDaniel, 1986).

Retirement and the Distribution of Income

It is perhaps too obvious to observe that, except in the case of a few individuals with sizeable amounts of nonsalary income, wages and salaries must be replaced as employment ceases. Therefore, the consequences of retirement for the incomes of Canadians are mediated almost entirely by the public and private pension systems, as well as by the savings rates of individuals. Government policy wholly determines the structure and benefit levels of public pensions and has enormous influence on both private pensions and savings, mainly via tax legislation. As a result, it is impossible to assess the effect of rising levels of retirement on the Canadian income distribution independently of the effect of pension policy. This is not to say that government policy is the only factor involved in individual retirement incomes. As the concept of status maintenance would suggest, for individuals pre-retirement income is likely the best predictor of post-retirement income.

In research using longitudinal data from the U.S. Retirement History Study, Burkhauser, Holden and Feaster (1988) found that married couples, both of whom survived for at least 10 years after retirement and who had private pension income, rarely fell into poverty. Even those intact couples in the study without private pension income seldom experienced incomes below the poverty level. However, the death of the husband greatly increases the likelihood of the surviving wife facing poverty. What all this suggests is that the relation between retirement and income is not as simple and straightforward as would first appear.

The introduction of a comprehensive public pension system in Canada has had salutary consequences for the incomes of retired Canadians, who have experienced substantial gains in their average incomes since the 1960s. Between 1969, shortly after the introduction of the Canada Pension Plan, and 1986, families headed by Canadians aged 65 or over saw their real incomes rise by 57 percent (National Council of Welfare, 1988). Elderly unattached individuals also experienced similar income gains over the period. In contrast, the incomes of families headed by persons under age 25 remained virtually constant between 1969 and 1986, when average 1969 income is expressed in 1986 dollars.

An equally optimistic picture of the improving financial circumstances of the retired is portrayed by improvement in poverty rates among the elderly since the 1960s. Table 6.5 shows trends in the poverty rate for both families and unattached individuals for various years since 1969. While these figures should be treated with caution because of the assumptions required in defining the low-income cut-off points in various years, the trends for elderly persons and families are so striking that methodological refinements are unlikely to change them. The poverty rate for elderly families dropped precipitously from 41.4 percent in 1969 to just 9.5 percent in 1986, lower than the rate for any age group except those 45 to 54. The largest part of this decline took place during the 1970s as Canada and Quebec Pension benefits were being phased in.

The picture is not quite so bright for elderly unattached persons, nearly 43 percent of whom had incomes below the low-income cut off in 1986. Yet while the poverty rate among unattached persons under age 65 remained fairly stable from late 1960s to 1986, the rate among those age 65 and over dropped over 26 percentage points. Figures on a yearly basis for the 1980s reveal that a sizeable decline in the poverty rate took place among the unattached in 1984 after improvements in GIS benefits were introduced (National Council of Welfare, 1988), again underscoring the immediate impact of changes in government programs on retirement income levels.

TABLE 6.5

TRENDS IN POVERTY RATES AMONG ELDERLY AND NON-ELDERLY CANADIAN FAMILIES AND UNATTACHED INDIVIDUALS, 1969 TO 1986

Year	Families		Unattached Individuals	
	Under Age 65	Age 65 and Over	Under Age 65	Age 65 and Over
1969	17.7%	41.4%	31.6%	69.1%
1979	11.8	21.9	30.3	66.3
1983	16.4	11.1	37.6	57.5
1986	14.6	9.5	34.8	42.7

Sources: National Council of Welfare (1984), p. 34, and National Council of Welfare (1988), pp. 37–38. The poverty rates for persons and families under age 65 in 1983 and 1986 were calculated from the latter source as weighted averages for the age groups presented there.

Although these improvements in the financial circumstances of retired persons suggest a redistribution of income from persons in the labour force with higher incomes to those out of the labour force with lower incomes, no such trend is detectable in Canada's overall income distribution. In fact, the National Council of Welfare observes that "income [in Canada] is distributed in a highly unequal and regressive manner, and there has been little progress in redistributing income over the last thirty-five years" (1988: 105). This lack of change is consistent with Myles's (1984a) interpretation of old age pensions as representing a form of "citizen's wage" that must be offset by lower employment earnings. In this view, the growth of public pension plans represents a shift of the wage setting process from the marketplace alone into a combination of the market and the political arena. "Public pension benefits - a deferred wage - become part of a broader wage-setting process mediated by the state" (Myles, 1984a: 78). As Myles hypothesizes and demonstrates empirically, the quality of public pension plans in the Western capitalist democracies is strongly related to both the degree of electoral competition and the political power of the working class. That is, in countries where elections have been closely contested and labour has both successfully organized and influenced the political process, public pension benefits have been of a higher quality. Nevertheless, as the data for Canada show, this has not resulted in a more equitable distribution of income as public pensions are phased in.

Retirement and the Pension System

An issue that has sustained an often-heated debate in public policy circles in Canada, as in most other industrial countries, is the implications of an aging population for government expenditures, particularly on health care and pensions. We do not propose to embroil ourselves in this debate, since it is well covered elsewhere (see Economic Council of Canada, 1979; Herzog, 1982; McDaniel, 1986; Myles, 1984b). However, the implications of an increasing rate of early retirement for Canada's pension system are certainly of interest here. Simply put, the fear expressed by many is that the aging of the post-war baby boom generation, combined with Canada's low fertility rate since the late 1960s and increasing longevity, will produce an ever-expanding dependent elderly population requiring increasing proportions of the country's gross domestic product to underwrite their needs.

That the percentage of Canada's population 65 years and over will grow in the future is not in dispute. By 2021, roughly 20 percent of the population will be in this age group, depending upon future trends in fertility, mortality and migration rates (McDaniel, 1986). There is also general agreement that this growth in the numbers of the retired will entail a greater financial burden on those in the labour force. Department of

Insurance projections of CPP contributions required to maintain 1982 benefit levels show them growing from 3.6 percent of earnings to nearly 10 percent by the year 2020, given several assumptions about the economy and demographic structure of the population (Hamilton and Whalley, 1984). Perhaps even more serious will be the impact of increasing numbers of retired persons on the OAS and GIS programs. These are directly financed out of general government revenues and contain no contributory plan. Therefore, the sizeable increase in the benefits paid under these programs will affect directly federal tax rates or the size of the federal deficit (Hamilton and Whalley, 1984). How large this impact is likely to be is difficult to assess, since no research on the question currently exists for Canada (Foot, 1987a). But in an admittedly rough approximation, Hamilton and Whalley (1984) calculate that if OAS and GIS benefits continue to be funded by tax revenues, by the year 2050, employed persons may face a surcharge on combined federal and provincial income tax of between 30 and 40 percent!

Any country has just four ways of dealing with the escalating cost of public pensions: (1) increasing revenues, through increased contribution levels, special taxes, or transferring general revenue to pension funds; (2) decreasing benefits by tightening eligibility requirements, reducing incentives for early retirement, revising the indexation formula, or raising the retirement age; (3) shifting the burden of financing pensions to individuals, through altering the tax treatment of RRSPs, or to the private pension system, by changing regulations governing it; and (4) lowering the dependency ratio by increasing labour force participation among older workers by means of reduced pension benefits, incentives for remaining in the labour force, the elimination of mandatory retirement, or the reduction of discrimination in the hiring and paying of older workers. While Canada has begun to address the issue by raising revenues and proposing to shift a greater responsibility for pension provision to individuals and private plans, benefits continue to expand, and no effort has yet been made to encourage older workers to remain in the labour force if they so choose, aside from anti-age discrimination provisions in the Canadian Charter of Rights and Freedoms.

It is by no means inevitable that older Canadian workers will continue to choose to retire at or before age 65. Both government pension policies and corporate personnel policies have encouraged early retirement in recent years by offering pension entitlements at ever earlier ages. Beginning in 1987, workers could choose to begin receiving Canada Pension benefits as early as age 60; in the corporate sector, and even in the public sector, retirement incentive programs have been proliferating. Although no systematic data exist for Canada, a recent survey of 400 companies in the United States revealed that almost 41 percent of companies with 1,000 or more employees had implemented such programs

(Yankelovich, Skelly and White, Inc., 1985). As the smaller age cohorts born in the 1970s reach working age and labour shortages develop, individual firms may begin to develop policies encouraging older workers to remain in their jobs, just as governments will be motivated to reduce the rate of early retirement to reduce deficits and prevent higher taxation levels for the working population. The prospects of altering retirement patterns are discussed in the next section.

Retirement and the Labour Force

Canada's labour force has been in an unprecedented state of flux over the past two decades, growing at a rate faster than that of any Western industrialized nation, despite the reduction in labour force participation among older workers. This phenomenal rate of growth has been largely fueled by the entry of the baby-boom generation to the labour force and dramatically increasing rates of participation on the part of women, which have largely offset the effects of increasing levels of early retirement. However, as Foot (1987b) observes, the baby-boom generation has now been completely absorbed into the labour force, and the smaller birth cohorts following it will provide increasingly smaller numbers of new workers. Although women continue to enter the labour force in increasing numbers, older women appear to be retiring earlier, so that this source of labour force growth is unlikely to be sustained in the long run. The consequence of all these factors is that the labour force participation rate of older workers is likely to have an increasing effect on the overall growth of the labour force.

The labour supplied by persons over age 55 will grow in importance, and indeed may be required to sustain the continued growth of the economy. Perhaps a foreshadowing of these developments can be observed in advertisements by companies such as McDonald's restaurants for older employees, as the pool of teenagers upon which they customarily draw is declining. A grandfatherly figure in a McDonald's uniform, a participant in McDonald's "McMasters" program, is portrayed having an enjoyable time slinging hamburgers alongside a group of young persons. As the baby-bust generation ages, firms will increasingly find themselves designing policies to retain their older workers, who are likely to be healthier and have a longer life expectancy than at present. This is a scenario that many managers would currently find implausible, as their major problem at the moment is to redesign their organizations to accommodate the blocked careers of middle-aged baby-boomers who find that the pyramidal shape at the top of the organization does not provide a sufficient number of middle and upper management positions to satisfy their aspirations (see Denton and Spencer, 1982), the so-called "plateauing" effect. Yet the current glut of middle-management candidates will surely be followed by a shortage as the baby-bust cohorts move through their careers.

But are older workers prepared to postpone retirement, even with the prospect of financial incentive dangled before them? There is evidence that in the past two decades, as retirement and the role of retiree have become increasingly acceptable, even valued, in our society, the work ethic has weakened and leisure values have begun to take precedence. However, a recent study by Rosen and Jerdee (1985) suggests that at least among managerial, professional, and technical workers, financial incentives might induce older persons, even those past age 65, to postpone retirement. Nearly half the respondents indicated that they would postpone retirement if the U.S. Social Security system were changed to abolish the earnings penalty on recipients aged 65 to 72 or to accord added benefits for years worked past age 65. Rosen and Jerdee also found that changes in organizational policies, including career assistance programs for older workers, flexible work assignment plans, modified pension and benefit plans, and the encouragement of organizational norms supporting alternative retirement ages elicited widespread support.

Earlier in this chapter we cited evidence that many Canadian workers are routed into retirement prematurely and involuntarily by losing their jobs and simply being unable to find another due to the obsolescence of their skills or just the reluctance of employers to hire an older person. That they persist in their job searches, in some cases for several years, suggests that there is a group of older workers who, given the opportunity, would remain on the job. Also indicating that a substantial portion of older persons are interested in remaining in the labour force is the large number of those who are formally retired but continue to either hold part-time jobs or who start their own businesses. The existing research does not make it clear whether these are in fact "voluntary" workers or whether they must work for the extra income, but it is obvious that the work ethic does not necessarily diminish with age. The shift in Canada's economy from extraction and manufacturing to services noted in Chapter 3 also augurs well for expanded labour force participation among older workers, since jobs in service industries tend to be less physically demanding and success in performing them is more likely to be related to the experience that older workers have in abundance.

CONCLUSIONS

This chapter has been devoted to arguing that the decision to retire made by individuals is influenced not only by other individual-level characteristics, but also by the social structure in which the individual is enmeshed. Characteristics of the labour market, the occupation and economic sector in which an individual works, as well as employment status and the unemployment rate encountered in the local labour market, and ascribed characteristics of the individual, particularly ethnicity and gender, contribute to the matrix within which the retirement decision is made. Indeed, the phrase "retirement decision" may have too voluntaristic a cast, given the powerful influence of supraindividual forces on the probability of retirement. Can the older, discouraged worker who declares herself retired be said to have made a retirement decision? Voluntary retirement decisions are usually made by upper white-collar workers who are protected by private pension plans and who have been benefiting from the tax advantages of an RRSP. Workers who lack such protection are usually buffeted by the social forces described here and retire when circumstances dictate.

As for the social structural consequences of retirement, we have chosen to focus our attention only on those that have clear links to the institution of retirement itself, income and poverty, pension plans, and the contours of the labour market. Although these were discussed separately, the difficulty of separating the issues they raise should have been apparent. The enhancement of public pension benefits has been largely responsible for the decline in poverty rates among elderly persons; the manipulation of pension benefits by governments is an important factor in determining rising rates of early retirement; the lack of opportunities in the labour force for older workers contributes to their acceptance of pension benefits in place of unemployment insurance or welfare payments. Retirement is an institution that continues to evolve in Canadian society, and many of the consequences of that evolution are difficult to envision from our current vantage point, particularly given the dramatic aging the Canadian population has experienced and will continue to experience for decades to come. Ironically, from a social structural point of view, it is the size of birth cohorts that has had the most profound impact on retirement and its consequences for Canadian society as a whole. We have yet to fully appreciate the full implications of that impact.

CHAPTER 7

THE FUTURE OF RETIREMENT IN CANADA: POLICY IMPLICATIONS AND RESEARCH NEEDS

Although there was some speculation about the future of retirement in Chapter 6, the evidence reviewed there refers mainly to the past. One lesson the past teaches us is that retirement is not a static institution, fixed in amber for all time. It has undergone extensive change during the twentieth century, both in Canada and in other countries. The Canadian situation is now fraught with uncertainty. Forces encouraging a further reduction in the retirement age include recent changes in the Canada Pension Plan allowing benefits to be paid as early as age 60, which attracted over 140,000 Canadians into early retirement during 1987 alone, as well as the proliferation of early retirement incentive programs in both the public and private sectors. Suggesting that at least some Canadians would prefer to remain in the labour force after the arbitrary age of 65, several successful challenges to mandatory retirement policies based on provisions of the Canadian Charter of Rights and Freedoms and provincial human rights legislation have been mounted, particularly in the public sector. One task of this chapter will be to explore possible future scenarios for retirement in Canada by describing recently proposed changes in federal pension and taxation legislation. Secondly, the implications of existing retirement research for both public policy and professional practice will be assessed. Finally, based on both the likely future of retirement and the needs of policy makers and practitioners, an agenda will be provided for research on retirement in Canada, a "wish list" of research priorities to understand the institution of retirement as it evolves into the twenty-first century.

PENSION POLICY AND THE FUTURE OF RETIREMENT

Regardless of which party has controlled the Government of Canada, pension reform has constituted an important concern. However, in the 1980s Canadians have seen that the character of the approach of the government to this issue depends to a large extent on the party in power. Under the Liberal government of the early 1980s, a Report of the Parliamentary Task Force on Pension Reform (Canada, 1983) was issued, which based its recommendations on the principles that a reasonable minimum income should be guaranteed to elderly Canadians, there should be fairness in the opportunities and arrangements available to Canadians to provide for their retirement, and pre-retirement living standards should be maintained in retirement. While the Task Force did recommend a number of changes that addressed the problem of poverty among older women, particularly those that survive their husbands, and recommended some changes in taxation policy that would make the rules governing private pensions fairer, the recommendations served essentially to maintain the existing three-tiered income security system for the elderly. Though it emphasized that the Canada Pension Plan must be placed on a sounder financial footing, there was never any hint that the principles of universality or full indexation to the cost of living be changed.

Before the Task Force recommendations could be translated into legislation, a Progressive Conservative government was elected in 1984, bringing with it a new approach to retirement income policy. The new government suggested early on, in discussion papers and budget documents, that it would seek to limit the universality of the Old Age Security program and move to at least partially de-index its benefits as cost saving measures. An outcry from both the opposition parties and the public quickly forced the government to drop these plans. The government's pension reform proposals revealed in both the White Paper on Tax Reform of June, 1987 and the draft legislation and regulations released by Minister of Finance Michael Wilson in 1988 cover five areas: changes to the Pension Benefits Standards Act governing private pension plans, changes to the Canada Pension Plan increasing both premiums and benefits, changes to registered retirement income funds, the creation of a spousal allowance, and changes to income tax regulations governing pensions and RRSPs.

The principles underlying the Progressive Conservative government's proposals seem to be to maintain a safety net for low-income Canadians, while shifting the burden for retirement saving onto middle- and upper-income groups, particularly in the form of RRSPs. Should the legislation be adopted, the rules governing RRSPs will be changed to allow persons not covered by a private pension plan eventually to contribute as much as $15,500 per year, giving them access to pensions equivalent to 70 percent of pre-retirement earnings, to a maximum of $60,000, which is some two and one-half times the current average industrial wage. Less obvious in these reform measures is an effort to keep the enormous amount of capital represented by retirement savings and pensions in private hands.

On the surface, the Liberal and Progressive Conservative governments' approaches to pension policy seem quite distinct, with the Liberals emphasizing universality and public control of funds and the Progressive Conservatives supporting individual efforts at retirement saving and private control of the capital generated. But from the point of view of the implications of these policies for the future of retirement in Canada, the important thing about both approaches is that they will likely reinforce the trend toward ever earlier retirement so firmly entrenched in Canada. While claiming to provide workers with an increasing number of options, they sustain the climate in which older workers feel almost morally obliged to make way for the young. Features of the Progressive Conservative reform proposals, such as the more generous tax treatment of RRSPs, are likely to encourage early retirement among groups, such as small business persons, who previously had worked much longer. The next section provides a more general discussion of the interpenetration of public policy and the institution of retirement, as well as some implications of the retirement research for practitioners.

IMPLICATIONS FOR PUBLIC POLICY AND THE PRACTITIONER

One of the most important implications of the retirement research for public policy (mainly pension policy) is the realization that policy has been both a response to retirement and the impetus for early retirement. In Chapter 2, it was argued that pension policy was developed to alleviate the impoverished circumstances of retired workers, while in Chapter 3 it was suggested that pension policy was utilized as a tool to encourage early retirement. Under what circumstances policy is a cause or an effect of retirement behaviour or, for that matter, has no effect, as was seen in the elimination of the earnings test in 1975, is a serious matter. For example, it is a fortuitous coincidence that early retirement policies coincide with the preference of most Canadians for early retirement, whatever the sources of that preference. When the predicted labour shortages occur in the next century, will changes in public policy be effective in changing older workers' preference for early retirement? The shifting role of public pensions in the retirement equation has not been thoroughly researched, making policy predictions somewhat risky.

While we are reluctant to make predictions about public policy, the research on retirement does inform some of the major policy issues currently being debated by Canadians. Specifically, the costs of eliminating mandatory retirement would seem to be minimal and somewhat transitory. The data indicate that abolishing mandatory retirement is not likely to create a groundswell of older workers, simply because most Canadians do not want to continue working past age 65. If they wish to continue working, it is likely to be part-time work that extends only a few years beyond age 65. The elimination of mandatory retirement might also set the stage for changing worker attitudes in a favourable direction toward work past the normal retirement age, which could have long-term benefits if there is to be a serious labour shortage in the foreseeable future. At the individual level, the elimination of mandatory retirement would have the potential of alleviating dissatisfaction with retirement, which is most acutely felt by those who are forced to retire involuntarily.

Tinkering with pension policy alone is probably not the most efficient way to solve the retirement problems faced by Canadian women and ethnic minorities. The research suggests strongly that the inequities women face in retirement are rooted in the sexual division of labour, both in the labour market and in the household, as was indicated in Chapter 6. Without changing inequitable pay scales for women, changes in public pension policy will be little more than palliative. The research on retirement and ethnicity reported in Chapter 6 underscores clearly the necessity of integrating immigration policy with public pension policy, particularly for the benefit of new Canadians from developing countries.

While often only implied, implications for the practitioner are found in every chapter. Although the individualistic conceptions of retirement described in Chapter 1 are attractive, they do not take into account the structural constraints faced by many retirees. Both Chapters 3 and 6 illustrate how individual retirement behaviour is circumscribed by political, social, and economic structures. To consider the individual in isolation without taking account of these constraints can lead to one-sided assessments that are in danger of holding the retiree responsible for conditions he or she ultimately cannot control. In short, political, economic and social structures can just as legitimately be the target for intervention as can the individual. The history of retirement outlined in Chapter 2 and the influence of pension policy documented in Chapter 3 highlight the potential practitioners have for affecting the evolution of the retirement system in Canada.

Chapters 4 and 5 provide indicators of who, in fact, might be at risk for problems in retirement - those who are forced to retire involuntarily, especially if they suffer poor health and have little income, those who are forced to work past the normal retirement age out of economic need, those for whom retirement constitutes a crisis, and those who experience other life changes at the time of retirement. Essentially, previous life style is probably the best indicator of how people will fare in their retirement, as underscored by the concept of status maintenance.

Chapter 6 should alert the practitioner to the differences in retirement experiences according to gender, ethnicity, type of occupation and sectoral location. The unique needs of women, blue-collar workers, immigrants from developing countries, and workers in the periphery of the economy demand special consideration that is frequently not found in prepackaged retirement programs.

FUTURE RESEARCH: AN AGENDA

The review of the societal, individual, and social structural issues surrounding retirement undertaken here frequently uncovered serious lacunae in the Canadian research. In part, this is because Canadian researchers in this area have not had available to them the kind of national, longitudinal data that have long been available in the United States placing researchers in the United States at the forefront in retirement research. The availability of such high-quality longitudinal data in the United States as that provided by the Retirement History Study conducted by the U.S. Social Security Administration, the National Longitudinal Surveys conducted by Ohio State University's Center for Human Resources Research, the Panel Study of Income Dynamics conducted by the Institute for Social Research at the University of Michigan, and the Duke Work and Retirement Study and Second Longitudinal Study conducted by Duke University's Center for the Study of Aging and Human Development (see Palmore et al., 1985, for descriptions of these data sets) have made the process of retirement in the United States perhaps the best understood in the world.

This is not to say that other sorts of data are not valuable in shedding light on the processes influencing retirement. Many interesting theoretical questions can be addressed only by means of small-scale, special-purpose qualitative or quantitative studies. Existing labour force data gathered by Statistics Canada can often be adapted to the study of retirement, particularly if it is available in machine-readable, unit record form, as in the case of the census Public Use Sample Tapes or the Monthly Labour Force Surveys. However, local studies, with their typically small sample sizes, do not permit generalization to the nation as a whole. Nor do they permit the researcher to explore the question of whether or not the retirement process may differ by region, ethnicity, or mother tongue, as some evidence reviewed in previous chapters indicates it does. Nevertheless, their role in theory building should not be underestimated, particularly in areas such as women's retirement where existing theory is inadequate.

Statistics Canada's national surveys are not designed to study retirement, and do not include occupational and industry data for prior jobs among persons not in the labour force at the time of the survey, which includes most retirees. Perhaps even more important, these surveys are cross-sectional instead of longitudinal, providing, in a well-worn metaphor, a series of snapshots of Canadian society at regular intervals instead of the motion picture required to capture social processes. Retirement, in particular, is the kind of process that requires that individuals be followed through their occupational careers and beyond if we are to fully understand it. What this implies is that a so-called panel research design must be applied in gathering data if the process of retirement is to be adequately captured. Although not specifically designed to study retirement, such a panel study of Canadians is being proposed for funding to the Social Sciences and Humanities Research Council by a group of sociologists. If appropriate items can be included in this data base, it might be an invaluable resource for studying the shifting dynamics of retirement in Canada.

From what we have said so far, one might be left with the impression that the problem with retirement research in Canada is merely a problem of the scarcity of appropriate data. It should be apparent from the literature reviews presented in previous chapters that the problem is also both theoretical and methodological. The vast preponderance of retirement research conducted in Canada has been from the individualistic, functionalist point of view, seldom recognizing the constraints placed on individual retirement decisions by social, political, and economic structures. We recognize that some aspects of the retirement process, particularly its consequences for individuals and families, are best understood within an individualist, perhaps social psychological, framework; however, the balance that favours this theoretical approach must be redressed if we are to achieve a rounded understanding of the institution of retirement in Canada. Methodologically, much Canadian research, particularly that utilizing published government data, has portrayed the retirement process quite simplistically, using cross-tabulations or comparisons of means. As complex as it is, the retirement process to be understood must be modelled using multivariate methods that have been widely available to social scientists for decades. In particular, powerful methods specifically designed to make sense of longitudinal data, such as log-linear models, time-series analysis, and event history analysis, are readily accessible to retirement researchers interested in more realistically modelling the process at the individual, group, or societal levels.

The review of the retirement research undertaken here also points out some specific issues that should be addressed in future Canadian research. Although the individual has been the focal point for retirement researchers for the last 40 years, a number of questions about the individual retirement experience remain unanswered. By now it should be obvious that the timing of retirement is an important issue. Further investigations of those persons who are forced to retire early, particularly because of poor health, are needed if retirement preparation is to be useful. Why so many people retire on time at age 65 is an enigma, given the apparent options now available to Canadians to retire at almost any age. Whereas pension eligibility may be the causative factor, it is still puzzling that the majority of Canadians believe that mandatory retirement at age 65 is an acceptable idea. Those workers, especially women and the self-employed, who work past the normal age of retirement require special attention, since the available research alludes to financial difficulty as being the motivating factor for work.

The retirement experience *per se* has not been well documented. It would be very helpful to uncover what it is about the retirement transition that precipitates a crisis for some individuals, despite the fact that their numbers may be small. The effectiveness of pre-retirement planning has been poorly researched and demands a better quality of investigation if it is to be in tune with the needs of retiring Canadians. Although the existing evidence suggests that retirement does not have serious consequences for most Canadians, it is clear that little is known about the impact of retirement on mental health and income, particularly indirect income from sources such as home ownership. Finally, the research on retirement satisfaction bodes well for most Canadians. However, almost all of the variables purported to enhance retirement satisfaction have not been tested in the Canadian context. In particular, the effects of income, social relationships, leisure activities, the marital unit and occupation on satisfaction require further clarification.

Research on the effects of social, economic, and political structures on retirement is really only in its infancy in Canada. Although we know that retirement patterns vary across sectors of the economy crudely defined, a next important step in this line of research is to specify exactly what it is about the nature of work in core and periphery firms that produces these differences. Similarly, we now know that certain features of occupations influence retirement, but it is important to discover the specific mechanisms that produce that influence, a particularly important task if in the future a labour shortage arises that requires that older workers be called upon to delay retirement. In keeping with both the dynamic character of the retirement institution and the rapid pace of social change that Canadian society has been experiencing, future research must take into consideration the effects on retirement rates of such factors as Canada's continued shift toward a service economy, technological change, the rising educational levels or workers, and the increasing proportion of the labour force in professional occupations. As the composition of the labour force changes, the aggregate outcome of millions of individual retirement decisions is likely to shift as well.

Another line of research that must be pursued in Canada concerns the extent to which retirement is precipitated by the treatment of older workers both in the workplace and in the labour market. We saw in Chapter 6 that there is evidence that some Canadian workers retire after being displaced from their jobs simply because other employment is not available to them. How widespread is this phenomenon? Does some form of discrimination against older workers operate in the workplace that "encourages" them to retire, as appears to be the case in the United States (Wanner and McDonald, 1983)? Indeed, a whole area of retirement research that could illuminate these questions, as well as many others on the specific mechanisms of retirement, involves the study of older workers and the organizational setting. Only rarely are organizational variables represented in retirement research, but the work organization represents the stage upon which the retirement drama is played out. How do corporate cultures regarding the treatment of older workers contribute to early retirement? How are older workers rewarded within organizations? When few prospects remain for further promotion, what steps do organizations take to maintain the interest and motivation of older workers? How are private pension plans used to manipulate labour supply within organizations? At present, no Canadian research has been directed to questions of this kind, questions that get at the heart of the retirement process.

CONCLUSIONS

The main message of this monograph must be that retirement is an exceedingly complex, multi-faceted phenomenon that has thus far eluded full understanding on the part of the community of scholars devoted to studying it. As an individual experience, a social institution, a political issue, and an economic formation the faces of retirement are many. Not only are the factors affecting retirement at each of these levels numerous, but the levels themselves are often interpenetrating, exacerbating the complexity of the phenomenon. We certainly do not mean to imply that no progress has been made in understanding retirement, for it has. In particular the structural explanations that have been brought into play over the past several years have served to emphasize the constraints on retirement behaviour, and the cross-cultural research on retirement patterns has broadened the focus of even research concentrated within countries. Retirement at the individual level, while always conceptually viewed as a temporal process, has only recently been studied longitudinally.

Inexplicably, the issues surrounding retirement and the public pension system have not received attention commensurate with their importance to the lives of individual Canadians. Federal Finance Minister Michael Wilson, commenting on his government's pension reform policies, was recently quoted as saying, "I don't know why this hasn't received a greater amount of interest. To me it's one of the most far-reaching things we've done" (Calgary *Herald*, 1988). Our hope is that the conclusions of the research outlined here begin to inform the public debate in Canada on the future of retirement, persuading politicians, corporate managers, labour leaders, and citizens alike that retirement is not just an issue for the old, but one that has far-reaching consequences for Canadians of all ages.

BIBLIOGRAPHY

Achenbaum, A. W.
  1978 *Old Age in a New Land*. Baltimore, MD.: Johns Hopkins University Press.
Adams, O. B., and L. A. Lefebre
  1980 *La Retraite et la Mortalité: Examen de la Mortalité Chez un Groupe de Retraite's Canadiens*. Ottawa: Statistique Canada.
Akyeampong, E. B.
  1987 "Older Workers in the Canadian Labour Market." In *The Labour Force* (November), Statistics Canada. (Catalogue 71-001.) Ottawa: Minister of Supply and Services.
Ames, H. B.
  1987 "The City Below the Hill." In *Social History of Canada Series*. Toronto: University of Toronto Press. Reprint 1972.
Anderson, K., R. L. Clark, and T. Johnson
  1980 "Retirement in Dual-Career Families." In *Retirement Policy in an Aging Society*, edited by R. L. Clark, Durham, N.C.: Duke University Press.
Atchley, R.C.
  1971 "Retirement and Work Orientation." *Gerontologist* 11: 29-32.
  1972 *The Social Forces in Later Life: An Introduction to Social Gerontology*. Belmont, Cal.: Wadsworth.
  1976a *The Sociology of Retirement*. Cambridge, Mass.: Schenkman
  1976b "Selected Social and Psychological Differences Between Men and Women in Later Life." *Journal of Gerontology* 31: 204-11.
  1980 "What Happened to Retirement Planning in the 1970s?" In *Aging and Retirement*, edited by N. G. McCluskey and E. F. Borgatta. Beverly Hills, Cal.: Sage.
  1981 *The Process of Retirement. Comparing Women and Men*. Miami, Ohio: Scripps Foundation Gerontology Center, Miami University.
  1982 "Retirement As a Social Institution." *Annual Review of Sociology* 8: 263-87.
Atchley, R. C., and S. J. Miller
  1983 "Types of Elderly Couples." In *Family Relationships in Later Life*, edited by T. H. Brubaker. Beverly Hills, Cal.: Sage.
Averitt, R. T.
  1968 *The Dual Economy: The Dynamics of American Industry Structure*. New York: Norton.

Baillargeon, R.
  1982 "Determinants of Early Retirement." *Canada's Mental Health* 303: 20-22.
Barfield, R. E. and J. N. Morgan
  1969 *Early Retirement: The Decision and the Experience.* Ann Arbor, Mich.: University of Michigan, Institute for Social Research.
  1970 *Early Retirement: The Decision and the Experience and a Second Look.* Ann Arbor, Mich.: University of Michigan, Institute for Social Research.
Baron, M. L., G.F. Strieb, and E. A. Suchman
  1952 "Research on the Social Disorganization of Retirement." *American Sociological Review* 17: 479-532.
Beck, S. H.
  1982 "Adjustment to and Satisfaction with Retirement." *Journal of Gerontology* 37: 616-24.
Beck, S. H., and J. W. Page
  1986 "Involvement in Activities and the Psychological Well-Being of Retired Men." Unpublished paper.
Behling, J. H., K. M. Kilty, and S. A. Foster
  1983 "Scarce Resources for Retirement Planning: A Dilemma for Professional Women." *Journal of Gerontological Social Work* 5: 49-60.
Bell, B. D.
  1975 "The Limitations of Crisis Theory as an Explanatory Mechanism in Social Gerontology." *International Journal of Aging and Human Development* 6: 153-68.
  1976 "Role Set Orientations and Life Satisfaction: A New Look at an Old Theory." In *Time, Roles and Self Help in Old Age*, edited by J. Gubrium. New York: Human Services Press.
Bell, D.
  1973 *The Coming of Post-industrial Society.* New York: Basic Books.
Beveridge, W. E.
  1980 "Retirement and Life Significance: A Study of the Adjustment to Retirement of a Sample of Men at Management Level." *Human Relations* 33: 69-78.
Bixby, L. E.
  1976 "Retirement Patterns in the United States: Research and Policy Interaction." *Social Security Bulletin* 39: 3-19.
Bixby, L. E., and E. E. Rings
  1969 "Work Experience of Men Changing Retirement Benefits, 1966." *Social Security Bulletin* 32: 3-14.
Blank, A. M., and P. J. Ritchie
  1983 "Lack of Satisfaction in Post-retirement Years." *Psychological Reports* 53: 1223-26.

Blau, Z. S.
1973 *Old Age in a Changing Society*. New York: Franklin Watts.
Blishen, B. R., and H. A. McRoberts
1976 "A Revised Socio-economic Index for Occupations in Canada." *Canadian Review of Sociology and Anthropology* 4: 41-53.
Block, M. R.
1982 "Professional Women: Work Patterns as a Correlate of Retirement Satisfaction." In *Women's Retirement*, edited by M. Szinovacz. Beverly Hills, Cal.: Sage.
1984 "Retirement Preparation: Needs of Women." In *Retirement Preparation*, edited by H. Dennis. Toronto: Lexington.
Boaz, R. F.
1987a "Work as a Response to Low and Decreasing Real Income During Retirement." *Research on Aging* 9: 428-40.
1987b "Early Withdrawal from the Labour Force: A Response Only to Pension Pull or Also to Labour Market Push? *Research on Aging* 9: 530-47.
Bond, J. R.
1982 "Volunteerism and Life Satisfaction Among Older Adults." *Canadian Counselor* 16: 168-72.
Bond, S. L., and J. R. Bond
1980 "The Impact of Pre-retirement Programs." *Canadian Counselor* 14: 68-71.
Boskin, M. J.
1977 "Social Security and Retirement Decisions." *Economic Inquiry* 15: 1-25.
Bosse, R., and D. J. Ekerdt
1981 "Change in Self-perception of Leisure Activities With Retirement." *Gerontologist* 21: 650-54.
Bould, S.
1980 "Unemployment As a Factor in Early Retirement Decisions." *American Journal of Economics and Sociology* 39: 123-36.
Bowen, W. G., and T. A. Finegan
1969 *The Economics of Labour Force Participation*. Princeton: University Press.
Boyd, M.
1985 "Revising the Stereotype: Variations in Female Labour Force Interruptions." Paper presented at the annual meeting of the Canadian Sociology and Anthropology Association, Montreal.
Brown, J. C.
1975 "Retirement: A Penalty or a Promise?" *Canadian Welfare* 51: 5-9.

Brown, J. C., and A. Martin Matthews
   1981 "Changes in Economic Well-being at Retirement." Paper presented at the annual meeting of the Canadian Association on Gerontology, Toronto, November.
Brubaker, T. H., and C. B. Hennon
   1982 "Responsibility for Household Tasks: Comparing Dual-Earner and Dual-Retired Marriages." In *Women's Retirement* edited by M. Szinovacz. Beverly Hills, Cal.: Sage.
Bryden, K.
   1974 *Old Age Pensions and Policy Making in Canada.* Montreal: McGill-Queen's University Press.
Burkhauser, R. V., K. C. Holden, and D. Feaster
   1988 "Incidence, Timing, and Events Associated With Poverty: A Dynamic View of Poverty in Retirement." *Journal of Gerontology* 43: 46-52.
Calasanti, T.
   1981 *"Is Retirement Research Atheoretical?"* Paper presented at the annual meeting of the Gerontological Society of America, Toronto, November.
Calgary *Herald*
   1988 "Pension Reform: Sweeping Rule Changes Affecting Every Working Canadian Await Approval." July 23: C6.
Campbell, A.
   1976 "Subjective Measures of Well-being." *American Psychologist* 31: 117-24.
Campione, W. A.
   1987 "The Married Woman's Retirement Decision: A Methodological Comparison." *Journal of Gerontology* 42: 381-86.
Canada
   1982 *Canadian Government Report on Aging.* Ottawa: Minister of Supply and Services.
   1983 *Report of the Parliamentary Task Force on Pension Reform.* Ottawa: Minister of Supply and Services.
Canadian Institute of Public Opinion
   1984 February 2. *Half Plan Retirement Before Age Sixty-five.* The Gallop Poll of Canada.
   1986 January 20. *Growing Number Approve of Forced Retirement at 65.* The Gallop Poll of Canada.
Casey B.
   1984 "Recent Trends in Retirement Policy and Practice in Europe and the USA: An Overview of Programmes Directed to the Exclusion of Older Workers and a Suggestion for an Alternative Strategy." In Symposium on *Aging and Technological Advances,* edited by P.K. Robinson, J. Livingston, and J. E. Birren. North Atlantic Treaty Organization, Scientific Affairs Division.

Casey, B., and G. Bruche
1983 *Work or Retirement?* Hampshire, Eng.: Gower.
Cavan, R., E. W. Burgess, R. J. Havighurst, and H. Goldhamer
1949 *Personal Adjustment to Old Age.* Chicago, Ill.: Science Research Associates.
Census of Canada
1851 *Census Returns 1851 Canada East.* Ottawa: Public Archives of Canada.
1976 *Labour Force Activity, Vol. 5.* Ottawa: Minister of Supply and Services.
Chappell, N.
1983 "Informal Support Networks Among the Elderly." *Research on Aging* 5: 77-99.
Chappell, N., L. A. Strain, and A. A. Blandford
1986 *Aging and Health Care: A Social Perspective.* Toronto: Holt, Rinehart and Winston.
Charles, D. C.
1971 "Effect of Participation in a Pre-retirement Program." *Gerontologist* 11: 24-28.
Chatfield, W. F.
1977 "Economic and Sociological Factors Influencing Life Satisfaction of the Aged." *Journal of Gerontology* 32: 593-99.
Chen, M. Y. T., and T. G. Regan
1985 *Work in the Changing Canadian Society.* Toronto: Butterworths.
Ciffin, S., and J. Martin
1976 *Retirement in Canada: Summary Report.* Staff Working Paper SWP-7604. Ottawa: Health and Welfare Canada.
1977 *Retirement in Canada: When and Why People Retire.* Staff Working Paper SWP-7804. Ottawa: Health and Welfare Canada.
Ciffin, S., J. Martin, and C. Talbot
1977 *Retirement in Canada,* Vol. 2, *Social and Economic Concerns.* Ottawa: Health and Welfare Canada.
Clark, R. C., and T. Johnson
1981 *Retirement in the Dual-Earner Family.* Research Paper No. 10-P-90543-4-02. Washington, D.C.: U.S. Government Printing Office.
Clark, R. C., T. Johnson, and A. A. McDermed
1980 "Allocation of Time and Resources by Married Couples Approaching Retirement." *Social Security Bulletin* 43: 3-17.
Cohen, M., S. Rea, and R. Lerman
1970 *A Micro Model of Supply.* Bureau of Labour Statistics, Staff Paper No. 4.
Cohn, R.M.
1982 "Economic Development and Status Change of the Aged." *American Journal of Sociology* 87: 1150-61.

Collette, J.
  1984 "Sex Differences in Life Satisfaction: Australian Data." *Journal of Gerontology* 39: 243-45.
Conference Board in Canada
  1983 *The Canadian Economy, 1961-1981 Data.* Ottawa: Conference Board in Canada.
Connidis, I.
  1982 "Women and Retirement. The Effect of Multiple Careers on Retirement Adjustment." *Canadian Journal on Aging* 1: 17-27.
  1987 "Life in Older Age: The View From the Top." In *Aging in Canada: Social Perspectives* (2nd Ed.), edited by V. W. Marshall. Markham, Ont.: Fitzhenry and Whiteside.
Covey, H.
  1981 "A Reconceptualization of Continuity Theory: Some Preliminary Thoughts." *Gerontologist* 21: 628-33.
Coward, L. E.
  1959 "Pension and Welfare Plans in Canada: History and Trends." *Society of Actuaries, Transactions* 10: 174-201.
Cowgill, D. O.
  1974 "Aging and Modernization: A Revision of the Theory." In *Late Life: Communities and Environmental Policy*, edited by J. F. Gubrium. Springfield, Ill.: Charles C. Thomas.
Crawford, L., and J. Matlow
  1972 "Some Attitudes Towards Retirement Among Middle-Aged Employees." *Relations Industrielles* 27: 616-32.
Cross, M. S. (ed.)
  1974 *The Working Man in the 19th Century.* Toronto: Oxford University Press.
Cross, M. S., and S. Gregory (eds.)
  1982 *Pre-industrial Canada, 1760-1849.* Toronto: McClelland and Stewart.
Cross, M. S., and G. S. Kealey
  1982 *Readings in Canadian Social History*, Vol. 1, *New France to the Conquest*, 1760. Toronto: McClelland and Stewart.
  1983 *Readings in Canadian Social History*, Vol. 4, *The Consolidation of Capitalism, 1896-1929.* Toronto: McClelland and Stewart.
Curtis, J. E., and P. G. White
  1984 "Age and Sport Participation With Age or Increased Specialization With Age." In *Sport and the Sociological Imagination*, edited by N. Theberge, and P. Donnelly. Fort Worth, Tex.: Texas Christian University Press.
Debates of the Senate of the Dominion of Canada
  1926-27 March 16, pp. 95-100. Ottawa: F. A. Acland.
  1916-17 March 23, pp. 130-161. Ottawa F. A. Acland.

Denton, F. T., and S. Ostry
   1967 *Historical Estimates of the Canadian Labour Force.* Ottawa: Statistics Canada.
Denton, F. T., and B. G. Spencer
   1982 "Population Aging, Labour Force Change and Promotion Prospects." *Quantitative Studies in Economics and Population,* Report No. 30. Hamilton, Ont.: McMaster University.
Depner, C. E., and B. Ingersoll
   1982 "Employment Status and Social Support: The Experience of the Mature Woman." In *Women's Retirement,* edited by M. Szinovacz. Beverly Hills, Cal.: Sage.
Dobson, C., and P. C. Morrow
   1984 "Effects of Career Orientation on Retirement Attitudes and Retirement Planning." *Journal of Vocational Behaviour* 24: 73-83.
Doering, M., S. R. Rhodes, and M. Schuster.
   1983 *The Aging Worker.* Beverly Hills, Cal.: Sage.
Donahue, W., H. L. Orbach, and O. Pollack
   1960 "Retirement: The Emerging Social Pattern." In *Handbook of Social Gerontology: Social Aspects of Aging,* edited by C. Tibbitts. Chicago: University of Chicago Press.
Dorfman, L. T., J. Kohout, and D. A. Heckert
   1985 "Retirement Satisfaction in the Rural Society." *Research on Aging* 7: 577-99.
Dowd, J. J.
   1975 "Aging As Exchange: A Preface to Theory." *Journal of Gerontology* 30: 584-94.
   1980 "Exchange Rates and Old People." *Journal of Gerontology* 35: 596-602.
Dowd, J. J., and V. L. Bengtson
   1978 "Aging in Minority Populations: An Examination of the Double-Jeopardy Hypothesis." *Journal of Gerontology* 33: 427-36.
Driedger, L., and N. L. Chappell
   1987 *Aging and Ethnicity: Toward an Interface.* Toronto: Butterworths.
Dunlop, D. P.
   1980 *Mandatory Retirement Policy: A Human Rights Dilemma?* Ottawa: Conference Board in Canada.
Economic Council of Canada
   1979 *One in Three: Pensions for Canadians to 2030.* Ottawa: Minister of Supply and Services.
Eisdorfer, C.
   1972 "Adaptation to Loss of Work." In *Retirement,* edited by F. M. Carp. New York: Behavioral Publications.
Ekerdt, D. J.
   1987 "Why the Notion Persists That Retirement Harms Health." *Gerontologist* 27: 454-57.

Ekerdt, D. J., L. Baden, R. Bosse, and E. Dibbs
1983 "The Effect of Retirement on Physical Health." *American Journal of Public Health* 73: 779-83.
Ekerdt, D. J., and R. Bosse
1982 "Change in Self-reported Health With Retirement." *International Journal of Aging* 15: 213-23.
Ekerdt, D. J., R. Bosse, and C. Goldie
1983 "The Effect of Retirement on Somatic Complaints." *Journal of Psychosomatic Research* 27: 61-67.
Ekerdt, D. J., R. Bosse, and J. S. LoCastro
1983 "Claims That Retirement Improves Health." *Journal of Gerontology* 38: 231-36.
Elder, G. H., Jr.
1974 "Age Differentiation and the Late Life Course." In *Annual Review of Sociology,* Vol. 1, edited by A. Keles et al. Palo Alto: Annual Reviews Inc.
Emerson, A. R.
1959 "The First Year of Retirement." *Occupational Psychology* 33: 197-208.
Entwisle, B., and C. K. Winegarden
1984 "Fertility and Pension Programs in LDCs: A Model of Mutual Reinforcement." *Economic Development and Cultural Change* 32: 331-54.
Epstein, L. A.
1966 "Early Retirement and Work Life Experience." *Social Security Bulletin* 29: 3-10.
Epstein, L. A., and J. Murray
1967 *The Aged Population of the U.S.* Washington, D.C.: Government Printing Office.
1977 *The Aged Population of the U.S.: The 1963 Social Security Survey of the Aged.* Research Report No. 19. Washington, D.C.: Social Security Administration.
Eran, M., and D. Jacobson
1976 "Expectancy Theory Prediction of the Preference to Remain Employed or to Retire." *Journal of Gerontology* 31: 605-10.
Estes, C. L.
1979 *The Aging Enterprise.* San Francisco: Jossey-Bass.
1983 "Social Security: The Social Construction of a Crisis." *Milbank Memorial Fund Quarterly* 61: 445-61.
Estes, C. L., L. E. Gerard, and J. H. Swan
1982 "Dominant and Competing Paradigms in Gerontology: Toward a Policy of Aging." *Aging and Society* 4: 151-64.

Estes, C. L., J. H. Swan, and L. E. Gerard
1984 "Dominant and Competing Paradigms in Gerontology: Towards a Political Economy of Aging." In *Readings in the Political Economy of Aging*, edited by M. Minkler and C.L. Estes. Farmingdale, N.Y.: Baywood.
Ewers, J. C.
1967 *Indian Life on the Upper Missouri*. Norman Okla.: University of Oklahoma Press.
Farakhan, A., B. Lubin, and W. A. O'Connor
1984 "Life Satisfaction and Depression Among Retired Black Persons." *Psychological Reports* 55: 452-54.
Fields, G. S. , and D. J. Mitchell
1984 *Retirement, Pensions and Social Security*. Cambridge, Mass.: MIT Press. Fillenbaum, G. G.
1971 "The Working Retired." *Journal of Gerontology* 26: 82-89.
Financial Post
1949 "Will Retirement Kill You?, June 25: 15.
1957 "Retirement Can Kill You If Leisure Comes Too Fast." July 6: 30.
1963 "How Tired Executives Fight Back At Boredom." Aug. 31: 19.
1984 "Reassessing Benefits of Early Retirement as Recovery Fades." Aug. 11: 16.
Fischer, D. H.
1978 *Growing Old in America*. New York: Oxford University Press.
Fishbein, M.
1963 *Readings in Attitude Theory and Measurement*. New York: John Wiley and Sons.
Fly, J. W., G. R. Reinhart, and R. Hornby
1981 "Leisure Activity and Adjustment in Retirement." *Sociological Spectrum* 1: 135-44.
Foner, A., and K. Schwab.
1981 *Aging and Retirement*. Monterey, Cal.: Brooks/Cole.
Foot, D. K.
1987a "Population Aging and Government Deficits in Canada." Discussion paper on the Demographic Review. Ottawa: Institute for Research on Public Policy.
1987b "Population Aging and the Canadian Labour Force." Discussion paper on the Demographic Review. Ottawa: Institute for Research on Public Policy.
Fox, J. H.
1977 "Effects on Retirement and Former Work Life on Women's Adaptation in Old Age." *Journal of Gerontology* 32: 196-202.
Freuchen, P.
1961 *Peter Freuchen's Book of the Eskimos*. Cleveland: World.

Friedmann, E. A., and R. J. Havighurst
  1954 *The Meaning of Work and Retirement.* Chicago: University of Chicago Press.
Friedmann, E., and H. L. Orbach.
  1974 "Adjustment to Retirement." In *American Handbook of Psychiatry,* edited by S. Arieti. New York: Basic Books.
Gagan, D.
  1978 "Land, Population and Social Change: The Critical Years in Rural Canada West." *The Canadian Historical Review* 59: 293-318.
  1981 *Hopeful Travellers: Families, Land and Social Change in Mid-Western Peel County, Canada West.* Toronto: University of Toronto Press.
George, L. K.
  1980 *Role Transitions in Later Life.* Monterey, Cal.: Brooks/ Cole.
  1981 "Subjective Well-being: Conceptual and Methodological Issues." In *Annual Review of Gerontology and Geriatrics,* Vol. 2, edited by C. Eisdorfer. New York: Springer.
George, L. K., G. G. Fillenbaum, and F. Palmore
  1984 "Sex Differences in the Antecedents and Consequences of Retirement." *Journal of Gerontology* 39: 364-71.
George, L. K., and G. L. Maddox
  1977 "Subjective Adaptation to Loss of the Work Role: A Longitudinal Study." *Journal of Gerontology* 32: 456-62.
Gerber, L. M.
  1983 "Ethnicity Still Matters: Socio-demographic Profiles of the Ethnic Elderly in Ontario." *Canadian Ethnic Studies* 15: 60-80.
Gigy, L. L.
  1985-86 "Preretirement and Retired Women's Attitudes Toward Retirement." *International Journal of Aging and Human Development* 22: 31-44.
Giordano, J. A., and N. H. Giordano
  1983 "A Classification of Preretirement Programs: In Search of a New Model." *Journal of Educational Gerontology* 9: 123-37.
Glasmer, E. D.
  1981 "The Impact of Preretirement Programs on the Retirement Experience." *Journal of Gerontology* 36: 244-50.
Glasmer, F. D., and G. F. Dejong
  1975 "The Efficacy of Preretirement Preparation Programs for Industrial Workers." *Journal of Gerontology* 3: 595-600.
Globe, The
  1905a "Man's End Is At Forty." Feb. 24: 1.
  1905b "Link Took Chloroform." Mar. 2: 7.

Globe and Mail

1985 "PM Faces Politician's Nightmare over Canadian Pension Furor." June 20: 8. "Politics of Indexing." June 22. "Tories Retreat on De-indexing Pension: Rise in Gas Corporate Taxes to Make-up Loss."June 28: 1, 5.

"Restructuring Social Plans the Key to Deficit Reduction." Sept. 3: B11.

"Commission Urges Replacing Programs With One Payment." Sept. 6: 1.

"CPP Premium to Double: $24 in 1987 Is First Step." Dec. 14: A1.

Golan, N.

1978 *Treatment in Crisis Situations. Treatment Approaches in the Human Services.* New York: Free Press.

Goudy, W., E. Powers, and P. Keith

1975 "Work and Retirement: A Test of Attitudinal Relationships." *Journal of Gerontology* 30: 193-98.

Goudy, W., E. Powers, P. Keith, and D. A. Reger

1980 "Changes in Attitudes Toward Retirement: Evidence From a Panel Study of Older Males." *Journal of Gerontology* 35: 942-48.

Graebner, W.

1980 *A History of Retirement.* New Haven: Yale University Press.

Gratton, B., and M. R. Haug

1983 "Decision and Adaptation: Research on Female Retirement." *Research on Aging* 5: 59-76.

Grinnell, G. B.

1921 *Blackfoot Lodge Tales.* New York: Charles Scribner and Sons.

Guemple, L.

1980 "Growing Old in Inuit Society." In *Aging in Canada*, edited by V. W. Marshall. Don Mills, Ont.: Fitzhenry and Whiteside.

Guest, D.

1985 *The Emergence of Social Security in Canada.* (2nd ed.) Vancouver: University of British Columbia Press.

Guillemard, A. M.

1977 "The Call to Activity Amongst the Old: Rehabilitation or Regimentation." In *Canadian Gerontological Collection I*, edited by B. T. Wigdor. Canadian Association on Gerontology.

1980 *La Vieillesse et l'Etat.* Paris: Presses Universitaires de France.

1983 "The Making of Old Age Policy in France: Points of Debate, Issues at Stake, Underlying Social Relations." In *Old Age and the Welfare State*, edited by A. M. Guillemard. Beverly Hills, Cal.: Sage.

Gunderson, M., and J. Pesando

1980 "Eliminating Mandatory Retirement: Economics and Human Rights." *Canadian Public Policy* 6: 352-60.

Gurland, B. J.
   1975 "The Comparative Frequency of Depression in Various Adult Age Groups." *Journal of Gerontology* 31: 3.
Gustman, A. L., and T. L. Steimer
   1984 "Partial Retirement and the Analysis of Retirement Behaviour." *Industrial and Labour Relations* 37: 403-15.
Gutman, G. M. (ed.)
   1981 *Canada's Changing Age Structure: Implications for the Future.* Burnaby, B.C.: Simon Fraser University Publications.
Gutmann, D.
   1972 "Ego-Psychological and Developmental Approaches to the 'Retirement Crisis' in Men." In *Retirement,* edited by F. M. Carp. New York: Behavioral Publications.
Haber, C.
   1978 "Mandatory Retirement in 19th Century America: The Conceptual Basis for a New Work Cycle." *Journal of Social History* 12: 77-96.
Halifax Chronicle Herald
   1985 "Alcan Making Early Retirement Offer." Mar. 30: 16.
Hamilton, C., and J. Whalley
   1984 "Reforming Public Pensions in Canada: Issues and Options." In *Pensions Today and Tomorrow: Background Studies,* edited by D. W. Conklin, J. H. Bennett, and T. J. Courchene. Toronto: Ontario Economic Council.
Hardy, M.A.
   1982a "Social Policy and Determinants of Retirement: A Longitudinal Analysis of Old White Males, 1969-1975." *Social Forces* 60: 1103-22.
   1982b "Job Characteristics and Health: Differential Impact on Benefit Entitlement." *Research on Aging* 4: 457-78.
Hardy, M. A., and E. K. Pavalko
   1986 "The Internal Structure of Self-reported Health Measures Among Older Male Workers and Retirees." *Journal of Health and Social Behavior.* 27: 346-57.
Harpaz, I.
   1983 *Meaning of Working: Its Nature and Consequences. A Final Report to the U.S.-Israel Binational Science Foundation.* Hafia: University of Hafia.
   1985 "Meaning of Working Profiles of Various Occupational Groups." *Journal of Vocational Behavior* 26: 25-40.
Harpaz, I., and Y. Kremer
   1981 "Determinants of Continued and Discontinued Participation in Pre-retirement Training: An Israeli Case Study." *Journal of Occupational Psychology* 54: 213-20.
Havens, B., and N. L. Chappell
   1983 "Triple Jeopardy: Age, Sex and Ethnicity." *Canadian Ethnic Studies* 15: 119-32.

Haynes, S. G., A. J. McMichael, and H. A. Tyroler
1977 "The Relationship of Normal, Involuntary Retirement to Early Mortality Among U.S. Rubber Workers." *Social Science and Medicine* 11: 105-14.

Hayward, M. D.
1986 "The Influence of Occupational Characteristics on Men's Early Retirement." *Social Forces* 64: 1032-45.

Hayward, M. D., and M. A. Hardy
1985 "Early Retirement Processes Among Older Men: Occupational Differences." *Research on Aging* 7: 491-515.

Health and Welfare Canada
1977a "Canadian Approaches to Social Security." *International Security Review* 36: 233-56

1977b *Retirement in Canada: Summary Report.* Ottawa: Minister of Health and Welfare.

1982a *Canadian Government Report on Aging.* Ottawa: Minister of Supply and Services.

1982b *Suicide Among the Aged in Canada.* Ottawa: Policy and Information Branch.

1983 *Fact Book on Aging in Canada.* Ottawa; Minister of Supply and Services.

1986 *Canada Pension Plan Actuarial Report.* Ottawa: Minister of Supply and Services.

Hendricks, J., and C. E. McAllister
1983 "A Structural Model of Retirement: Toward a Theoretical Reformulation." *Gerontologist* 23: 295.

Henretta, J. C., and R. T. Campbell
1976 "Status Attainment and Status Maintenance: A Study of Stratification in Old Age." *American Sociological Review* 41: 981-92.

Henretta, J. C., and A. M. O'Rand
1983 "Joint Retirement in the Dual Worker Family." *Social Forces* 62: 504-20.

Herzog, John P.
1982 "Aging, Pensions and Demographic Change." In *Canada's Changing Age Structure: Implications for the Future*, edited by G. M. Gutman. Burnaby, B.C.: Simon Fraser University Publications.

Hinds, S. W.
1963 "The Personal and Socio-medical Aspects of Retirement." *Royal Society of Health Journal* 83: 281.

Hoffman, A.
1985 *Residents in Ontario: Age Differences.* Toronto: Minister for Senior Citizens Affairs, Seniors Secretariat.

Hooker, K., and D. G. Ventis
1984 "Work-Ethic, Daily Activities, and Retirement Satisfaction." *Journal of Gerontology* 39: 478-84.

Horley, J.
  1984 "Life Satisfaction, Happiness, and Morale: Two Problems With the Use of Subjective Well-being Indicators." *Gerontologist* 24: 124-27.

Hornstein, G. A., and S. Wapner
  1985 "Modes of Experiencing and Adapting to Retirement." *International Journal of Aging and Human Development* 21: 291-315.

House of Commons Debate
  1907-8 Feb. 3. *House of Commons Debates of the Dominion of Canada. Fourth Session - Tenth Parliament.* Ottawa: S. E. Lawson.
  1921 Feb. 14. *House of Commons Debates of the Dominion of Canada. Fifth Session - Thirteenth Parliament.* Ottawa: F. A. Ackland King's Printer.

House of Commons Journals
  1944-45 *Fifth Session of the Nineteenth Parliament of Canada.* Ottawa: Emond Cloutier King's Printer.

House of Industry
  1886 "Charity in Toronto." In *The Working Man in the 19th Century,* edited by M. S. Cross (1982). Toronto: Oxford Unviersity Press.

Howard, J. H., and J. Marshall
  1983 "Retirement Adaptation: What Research Says About Doing It Successfully." *Business Quarterly* (Summer) 48: 29-39.

Hunter, A. A., and M. C. Manley
  1986 "On the Task Content of Work." *Canadian Review of Sociology and Anthropology* 23: 47-71.

Hunter, W. W.
  1968 *Preretirement Education for Hourly Rated Employees.* Ann Arbor: Division of Gerontology, University of Michigan.

Hwalek, M., I. Firestone, and W. Hoffman
  1982 "The Role Social Pressures Play in Early Retirement Propensities."*Aging and Work* 5: 157-67.

Irelan, L.
  1972 "Retirement History Study: Introduction." *Social Security Bulletin.* Washington, D.C.: Department of Health, Education and Welfare.

Irelan, L. M., and D. B. Bell
  1972 "Understanding Subjectively Defined Retirement: A Pilot Analysis." *Gerontologist* 12: 354-56.

Jackson, J. J.
  1980 *Minorities and Aging.* Belmont, Cal.: Wadsworth.

Jacobson, D.
  1972 "Fatigue-Producing Factors in Industrial Work and Pre-retirement Attitudes." *Occupational Psychology* 46: 193-200.

Jacobson, D., and W. Eran
  1980 "Expectancy Theory Components and Non-expectancy Moderators as Predictors of Physician's Preference for Retirement." *Journal of Occupational Psychology* 53: 11-26.

Jaslow, P.
1976 "Employment, Retirement and Morale Among Older Women." *Journal of Gerontology* 31: 212-18.
Johnson, J., and G. B. Strother
1962 "Job Expectation and Retirement Planning." *Journal of Gerontology* 17: 418-23.
Kafer, N. F. , and D. Davies
1984 "Vulnerability of Self and Interpersonal Strategies: A Study of the Aged." *Journal of Psychology* 116: 203-26.
Kaim-Caudle, P. R.
1973 *Comparative Social Policy and Social Security: A Ten Year Study.* London: Martin Robertson and Co.
Kalbach, W. E., and W. W. McVey
1979 *The Demographic Bases of Canadian Society.* Toronto: McGraw-Hill Ryerson.
Kaminski-da Rossa, V.
1984 "A Workshop That Optimizes the Older Worker's Productivity." *Personnel* 47-56.
Kaplan, H. R., and C. Tausky
1974 "The Meaning of Work Among the Hard-Core Unemployed." *Pacific Sociological Review* 17: 185-98.
Kapsalis, C.
1979 "Pensions and the Work Decision." Paper presented at the Annual Meeting of the Canadian Economic Association, Toronto.
Kasschau, D. L.
1974 "Re-evaluating the Need for Retirement Preparation Programs." *Industrial Gerontology* 1: 42-59.
Katz, M. B.
1975 *The People of Hamilton, Canada West.* Cambridge, Mass.: Harvard University Press.
Kaye, L. W., and A. Monk
1984 "Sex Role Traditions and Retirement From Academe." *Gerontologist* 24: 420-26.
Kealey, G. S.
1980 *Toronto Workers Respond to Industrial Capitalism, 1867-1892.* Toronto: University of Toronto Press.
Keating, N., and P. Cole
1980 "What Do I Do With Him 24 Hours a Day? Changes in the Housewife Role After Retirement." *Gerontologist* 20: 80-89.
Keating, N. and M. Doherty
1986 *Retirement and Farm Transfer.* Project No. 84-0442, Agricultural Research Council of Alberta.
Keating, N., and B. Jeffrey
1983 "Work Careers of Ever Married and Never Married Retired Women." *Gerontologist* 23: 416-21.

Keith, P. M.
1982 "Working Women Versus Homemakers: Retirement Resources and Correlates of Well-being." In *Women's Retirement*, edited by M. Szinovacz. Beverly Hills, Cal.: Sage.
Keith, P. M., K. Hill, W. T. Goudy, and E. A. Powers
1984 "Confidants and Well-being: A Note on Male Friendships in Old Age." *Gerontologist* 24: 318-20.
Kenny, J., and B. Portis
1982 "Preretirement Planning Programs." *CTM The Human Element* 14: 32-35.
Kerckoff, A.C.
1966 "Husband-Wife Expectations and Reactions to Retirement." In *Social Aspects of Aging*, edited by I. Simpson and J. C. McKinney. Durham: Duke University Press.
Kerr, C., J. T. Dunlop, F. H. Harbinson, and C. Myers
1960 *Industrialism and Industrial Man*. Cambridge, Mass.: Harvard University Press.
Kilty, K. M., and J. H. Behling
1985 "Predicting the Retirement Intentions and Attitudes of Professional Workers." *Journal of Gerontology* 40: 219-27.
Kimmel, D. C., K. F. Price, and J. W. Walker
1978 "Retirement Choice and Retirement Satisfaction." *Journal of Gerontology* 33: 575-85.
Kinsley, B., and F. Graves
1983 *The Time of Our Lives*. Ottawa: Employment and Immigration Canada.
Korpi, W.
1983 *The Democratic Class Struggle*. London: Routledge and Kegan Paul.
Kremer, Y.
1985 "Predictors of Retirement Satisfaction: A Path Model." *International Journal of Aging and Human Development* 20: 113-21.
Kremer, Y., and I. Harpaz.
1982a "Attitudes Toward Pre-retirement Counselling: A Path Model." *Journal of Occupational Behavior* 3: 205-13.
1982b "Leisure Patterns Among Retired Workers: Spillover or Compensatory Trends?" *Journal of Vocational Behavior* 21: 183-95.
Kroeger, N.
1982 "Preretirement Preparation: Sex Differences in Access, Sources and Use." In *Women's Retirement*, edited by M. Szinovacz. Beverly Hills, Cal.: Sage.
Labour Commission
1889 *Royal Commission on the Relations of Labour and Capital in Canada, Report*. Ottawa: Queen's Printer.

Labour Gazette
1903 "The Superannuation and Pension Fund of the Canadian Pacific Railway Company" 3: 552-54.
1957 *"Compulsory Retirement Said Cruel, Wasteful"* 57: 933.

Larson, R.
1978 "Thirty Years of Research on the Subjective Well-being of Older Americans." *Journal of Gerontology* 33: 109-25.

Laycock, J.E.
1952 "The Canadian System of Old Age Pensions." Unpublished Doctoral dissertation, University of Chicago.

Lemon, B. S., V. L. Bengston, and J. A. Peterson
1972 "An Exploration of the Activity Theory of Aging: Activity Types and Life Satisfaction Among In-Movers to a Retirement Community." *Journal of Gerontology* 27: 511-23.

Lesage, J.
1950 "What Canadians Suggested." *Canadian Business* (Nov.): 18-24.

Levy, S. M.
1980-81 "The Adjustment of the Older Women: Effects of Chronic Ill Health and Attitudes Toward Retirement." *International Journal of Aging and Human Development* 12: 93-98.

Liang, J., and T. J. Fairchild
1979 "Relative Deprivation and Preception of Financial Adequacy Among the Aged." *Journal of Gerontology* 34: 746-59.

Liang, J., E. Kahana, and E. Doherty
1980 "Financial Well-being Among the Aged: A Further Elaboration." *Journal of Gerontology* 35: 409-20.

Lipton, M. A.
1976 "Age Differentiation in Depression: Biomedical Aspects." *Journal of Gerontology* 31: 3.

Livson, F.
1962 "Adjustment to Retirement." In *Aging and Personality*, edited by S. Reichard et al. New York: John Wiley.

Loether, H. J.
1964 "The Meaning of Work and Retirement." In *Blue Collar World*, edited by A. B. Shostak and W. Gomberg. Englewood Cliffs, N.J.: Prentice-Hall

Lowenthal, M. F., and P. Berkman
1967 *Aging and Mental Disorder in San Francisco.* San Francisco: Jossey-Bass.

Lowenthal, M. F., and C. Haven
1968 "Interaction and Adaptation: Intimacy as a Critical Variable." In *Middle Age and Aging*, edited by B. Neugarten. University of Chicago: Chicago Press.

Lupri, E., and J. Frideres
1981 "The Quality of Marriage and the Passage of Time: Marital Satisfaction Over the Family Life Cycle." *Canadian Journal of Sociology* 6: 283-305.

Lynch, J. H., D. M. McKenzie, S. K. Bettis, T. Straugh, and F. Scott
1979 "Three Educational Methodologies in Pre-retirement Planning Programs: A Study of Relative Effectiveness." In *A Research Study of Retirement Preparation Programs.* University of Oregon Center for Gerontology.

Macbride, A.
1976 "Retirement as a Life Crisis: Myth or Reality?" *Canadian Psychiatric Association Journal* 21: 547-56.

Macdonald Royal Commission
1985 *Canada, Royal Commission on the Economic Union and Development Prospects for Canada.* D. Macdonald, Chairman. Report, Part I. Ottawa: Minister of Supply and Services.

MacLean, M. J.
1983 "Differences Between Adjustment and Enjoyment of Retirement." *Canadian Journal on Aging* 2: 3-8.

Macleans
1961 "A Case For Retiring But at 50, A Case: For Retiring Not At 50, A Case: For Retiring (Not Quitting) At 50." Nov. 18: 71.
1980 "Refusing the Golden Handshake." Aug. 18: 44, -45.

Manheim, B., and A. Cohen
1978 "Multivariate Analysis of Factors Affecting Work Centrality of Occupational Categories." *Human Relations* 31: 525-33.

Markides, K., and H. Martin
1979 "A Casual Model of Life Satisfaction Among the Elderly." *Journal of Gerontology* 34: 86-93.

Marsh. L.
1943 *Report on Social Security for Canada XXI, 56.* Ottawa: King's Printer.

Marshall, V. W.
1980a "State of the Art Lecture: Sociology of Aging." In *Canadian Association on Gerontology. Collection III,* edited by J. Crawford. Canadian Association on Gerontology.
1980b *Last Chapters: A Sociology of Aging and Dying.* Monterey, Cal.: Brooks/Cole.
1981 "Social Characteristics of the Future Aged." In *Housing for an Aging Population,* edited by B. Wigdor and L. Fond. Toronto: University of Toronto Press.
1987 *Aging in Canada: Social Perspectives.* (2nd ed.) Markham, Ont.: Fitzhenry and Whiteside.

Marshall, V., and J. Tindale

1978-79 "Notes for a Radical Gerontology." *International Journal of Aging and Human Development* 9: 163-75.

Martin Matthews, A.

1987 "Widowhood as an Expected Life Event." In *Aging in Canada. Social Perspectives*, edited by V. W. Marshall. (2nd ed.) Markham, Ont.: Fitzhenry and Whiteside.

Martin Matthews, A., and K. H. Brown

1981 "1981 Economic and Social Welfare of the Recently Retired: Factors Which Contribute to the Perception of the Crisis." Paper presented at the 12th International Congress of Gerontology, Hamburg, West Germany.

1987 "Retirement as a Critical Life Event: The Differential Experience of Women and Men." *Research on Aging* 9: 548-71.

Martin Matthews, A., K. H. Brown, C. K. Davis, and M. A. Denton

1982 "A Crisis Assessment Technique for the Evaluation of Life Events: Transition to Retirement as an Example." *Canadian Journal on Aging* 1: 28-39.

Martin Matthews, A., and J. A. Tindale

1987 "Retirement in Canada." In *Retirement in Industrialized Societies*, edited by K. S. Markides and C. L. Cooper. Toronto: John Wiley and Sons.

Martin Matthews, A., J. A. Tindale, and J. E. Norris

1984 "The Facts on Aging Quiz: A Canadian Validation and Cross Cultural Comparison." *Canadian Journal on Aging* 3: 165-74.

Martin, J., and A. Doran

1966 "Evidence Concerning the Relationship Between Health and Retirement." *Sociological Review* 14: 329-43.

McConnel, C. E., and F. Deljavan

1983 "Consumption Patterns of the Retired Household." *Journal of Gerontology* 38: 480-90.

McDaniel, S. A.

1986 *Canada's Aging Population*. Toronto, Butterworths.

McDonald, P. L.

1983 "Retirement: A Socioeconomic Analysis." Unpublished Doctoral dissertation, Department of Sociology, University of Calgary.

McDonald, P. L., and R. A. Wanner

1982 "Work Past Age 65 in Canada: A Socioeconomic Analysis." *Aging and Work* 5: 169-80.

1984 "Socioeconomic Determinants of Early Retirement in Canada." *Canadian Journal on Aging* 3: 105-16.

1986 "Retirement and the Structure of Occupations." Paper presented at the Annual Meeting of the Canadian Association on Gerontology, Quebec City.

1987 "Retirement in a Dual Economy: The Canadian Case." In *Aging in Canada*, edited by V. W. Marshall. (2nd ed.) Markham, Ont.: Fitzhenry and Whiteside.

McGoldrick, A.
1983 "Company Early Retirement Schemes and Private Pension Scheme Options: Scope for Leisure and New Lifestyles." *Leisure Studies* 2: 187-202.

McMahon, L. J.
1981 "Pre-retirement Programs in Alberta." Unpublished paper.

McPherson, B. D.
1980 "Retirement From Professional Sport: The Process and Problems of Occupational and Psychological Adjustment." *Sociological Symposium* 30: 126-43.
1983 *Aging as a Social Process*. Toronto: Butterworths.

McPherson, B. D. and N. Guppy
1979 "Pre-retirement Life-style and the Degree of Planning for Retirement." *Journal of Gerontology* 34: 254-63.

McPherson, B. D. and C. Kozlik
1980 "Canadian Leisure Patterns by Age: Disengagement, Continuity or Ageism?" In *Aging in Canada: Social Perspectives*, edited by V. W. Marshall. Don Mills, Ont.: Fitzhenry and Whiteside.
1987 "Age Patterns in Leisure Participation: The Canadian Case." In *Aging in Canada: Social Perspectives*, edited by V. W. Marshall. (2nd ed.) Markham, Ont.: Fitzhenry and Whiteside.

Meissner, M., E. W. Humphreys, S. M. Meis, and W. J. Scheu
1975 "No Exit for Wives: Sexual Divison of Labour and the Cumulation of Household Demands." *Canadian Review of Sociology and Anthropology* 12: 424-39.

Messer, E.F.
1969 "Thirty-eight Years Is a Plenty." In *Trends in Early Retirement*, edited by W. Donahue et al. Ann Arbor, Mich.: University of Michigan Press.

Méthot, S.
1987 "Employment Patterns of Elderly Canadians." *Canadian Social Trends* Autumn: 7-11.

Miller, M.
1979 *Suicide After Sixty: The Final Alternative*. New York: Springer.

Miller, S. J.
1965 "The Social Dilemma of the Aging Leisure Participant." In *Older People and Their Social World*, edited by A. M. Rose and W. A. Peterson. Philadelphia, Penn.: F. A. Davis Co.

Minkler, M.
1981 "Research on the Health Effects of Retirement: An Uncertain Legacy. " *Journal of Health and Social Behavior* 22: 117-30.

1984 "Introduction" In *Readings in the Political Economy of Aging,* edited by M. Minkler and C. Estes. Farmingdale, N.Y.: Baywood.

Monahan, D. J., and V. L. Greene
1987 "Predictors of Early Retirement Among University Faculty." *Gerontologist* 27: 46-52.

Montreal Gazette
1983 "Raise Pension Age, Insurer Says." Feb. 9: D1.

Morgan, L. A.
1980 "Work in Widowhood: A Viable Option?" *Gerontologist* 20: 581-87.

Morrow, P. C.
1980 "Retirement Preparation: A Preventive Approach to Counseling the Elderly." *Counseling and Values* 24: 236-46.
1982 "Human Resource Planning and the Older Worker: Developing a Retirement Intentions Model." *Journal of Occupational Behavior* 3: 253-61.

Morse, N. C., and R. C. Weiss
1955 "The Function and Meaning of Work and the Job." *American Sociological Review* 20: 191-98.

Mutran, E., and D. Reitzes
1981 "Retirement, Identity and Well-being: Realignment of the Role Relationships." *Journal of Gerontology* 36: 733-40.

Myles, J. F.
1981 "Income Inequality and Status Maintenance: Concepts, Methods, and Measures." *Research on Aging* 3: 123-41.
1982 "Social Implications of Canada's Changing Age Structure." In *Canada's Changing Age Structure: Implications for the Future,* edited by G. M. Gutman. Burnaby, B.C.: SFU Publications.
1983 "Conflict, Crisis, and the Future of Old Age Security." *Milbank Memorial Fund Quarterly* 61: 462-72.
1984a *Old Age in the Welfare State: The Political Economy of Public Pensions.* Toronto: Little, Brown.
1984b "Conflict, Crisis, and the Future of Old Age Security." In *Readings in the Political Economy of Aging,* edited by M. Minkler and C. L. Estes. Farmingdale, N.Y.: Baywood.

National Council of Welfare
1984 *Sixty-five and Older.* Ottawa: Minister of Supply and Services.
1988 *Poverty Profile, 1988.* Ottawa: Minister of Supply and Services.

Nelsen, N. E., and E. E. Nelsen
1972 "Passing in the Age Stratification System." Paper presented at the Annual Meeting of the American Sociological Association, New Orleans.

Newman, E. S., S. R. Sherman, and C. Higgins
1982 "Retirement Expectations and Plans: A Comparison of Professional Men and Women." In *Women's Retirement,* edited by M. Szinovacz. Beverly Hills, Cal.: Sage.

Nusberg, C.
1986 "Early Retirement Ubiquitous in Western Nations." *Aging International* 13: 26-32.

O'Brien, G. E.
1981a "Leisure Attributes and Retirement Satisfaction." *Journal of Applied Psychology* 66: 371-84.
1981b "Locus of Control, Previous Occupation and Satisfaction With Retirement." *Australian Journal of Psychology* 33: 305-18.

O'Brien, G. E., and P. Dowling
1981 "Age and Job Satisfaction." *Australian Psychologist* 16: 49-61.

Olson, L. K.
1982 *The Political Economy of Aging: The State, Private Power and Social Welfare.* New York: Columbia University Press.

O'Rand, A. M., and J. C. Henretta
1982a "Delayed Career Entry, Industrial Pension Structure, and Early Retirement in a Cohort of Unmarried Women." *American Sociological Review* 47: 365-73.
1982b "Midlife Work History and Retirement Income." In *Women's Retirement,* edited by M. Szinovacz. Beverly Hills, Cal.: Sage.

O'Rand, A. M., and R. Landerman
1984 "Women's and Men's Retirement Income Status: Early Family Role Effects." *Research on Aging* 6: 25-44.

O'Rourke, J. R., and H. L. Friedman
1972 "An Inter-Union Pre-retirement Training Program: Results and Commentary." *Industrial Gerontology* Spring: 49-62.

Ouellet, F.
1982 "The Rural Economic Crisis in Lower Canada." In *Pre-Industrial Canada,* 1760-1849, edited by M. S. Cross and G. S. Kealey. Toronto: McClelland and Stewart.

Palmore, E.
1964 "Retirement Patterns Among Aged Men." *Social Security Bulletin* 27: 3-10.
1965 "Differences in the Retirement Patterns of Men and Women." *Gerontologist* 5: 4-8.
1967 "Employment and Retirement." In *The Aged Population of the United States,* edited by L. Epstein. Washington, D.C.: U.S. Government Printing Office.
1982 "Preparation for Retirement: The Impact of Preretirement Programs on Retirement and Leisure." In *Life After Work,* edited by N. J. Osgood. New York: Praeger.

Palmore E., B. M. Burchett, G. G. Fillenbaum, L. K. George, and L. M. Wallman
1985 *Retirement: Causes and Consequences.* New York: Springer.

Palmore, E., B. A. Fillenbaum, and L. K. George
   1984 "Consequences of Retirement." *Journal of Gerontology* 39: 109-16.
Palmore, E., L. K. George, and G. G. Fillenbaum
   1982 "Predictors of Retirement." *Journal of Gerontology* 37: 733-42.
Pampel, F. C., and S. Park
   1986 "Cross-national Patterns and Determinants of Female Retirement."
   American Journal of Sociology 91: 932-55.
Pampel, F. C., and J. A. Weiss
   1983 "Economic Development, Pension Policies, and the Labour Force
   Participation of Aged Males: A Cross-national, Longitudinal
   Approach." *American Journal of Sociology* 89: 350-72.
Pampel, F. C., and J. B. Williamson
   1985 "Age Structure, Politics, and Cross-national Patterns of Public
   Pension Expenditure." *American Sociological Review* 50: 782-99.
Parker, D. F., and L. E. Dyer
   1976 "Expectancy Theory as a Within-Person Behavioral Choice Model:
   An Empirical Test of Some Conceptual and Methodological
   Refinements." *Organizational Behavior and Human Performance* 17:
   97-117.
Parker, S.
   1982 *Work and Retirement*. London: Allen and Unwin.
Parnes, H. S., B. M. Fleisher, R. D. Milgus, and R. S. Splitz
   1970 *The Preretirement Years: A Longitudinal Study of the Labor Market
   Experience of Men*, Vol. I. Washington, D.C.: U.S. Department of
   Labor.
Parnes, H. S., M.G. Gagen, and R. H. King
   1981 "Job Loss Among Long-Service Workers." In *Work and Retirement:
   A Longitudinal Study of Men*, edited by H. S. Parnes et al.
   Cambridge, Mass.: MIT Press.
Parnes, H. S., and G. Nestel
   1971 *Retirement Expectations of Middle-Aged Men*. Columbus, Ohio:
   U.S. Department of Labor.
   1975 "Early Retirement." In *The Preretirement Years: Five Years into
   the Work Lives of the Labour Market Experience of Men*, Vol. I, edited
   by H. S. Parnes et al. Washington, D.C.: Department of Labor
   Manpower Research and Development.
   1981 "The Retirement Experience." In *Work And Retirement: A
   Longitudinal Study of Men*, edited by H. S. Parnes et al. Cambridge,
   Mass.: MIT Press.
Penning, M. J.
   1983 "Multiple Jeopardy: Age, Sex, and Ethnic Variations." *Canadian
   Ethnic Studies* 15: 81-105.

Pentland, H. C.
  1981 *Labour and Capital in Canada*, 1650-1860. Toronto: James Loremont.
Peppers, L.
  1976 "Patterns of Leisure and Adjustment to Retirement." *Gerontologist* 16: 441-46.
Peterson, D. A.
  1972 "Financial Adequacy in Retirement: Perception of Older Americans." *Gerontologist* 12: 378-83.
Peterson, J. A.
  1984 "Preretirement Counselling." In *Retirement Preparation*, edited by H. Dennis. Toronto: Lexington.
Phillipson, C.
  1982 *Capitalism and the Construction of Old Age.* London: Macmillan.
Philpot, H. J.
  1871 *Guide Book to the Canadian Dominion Containing Information for the Emmigrant, the Tourist, the Sportsman, and the Small Capitalist.* London.
Picot, G., and T. Wannell
  1987 "Job Loss and Labour Market Adjustment in the Canadian Economy." In *The Labour Force* (Mar.), Statistics Canada. (Catalogue 71-001.) Ottawa: Minister of Supply and Services.
Pilkey, C. G.
  1984 "Public versus Private Pensions." In *Pensions Today and Tomorrow: Background Studies*, edited by D. W. Conklin, J. H. Bennett, and T. J. Courchene. Toronto: Ontario Economic Council.
Pollman, A. W., and A. C. Johnson
  1971 "Early Retirement: A Comparison of Poor Health to Other Retirement Factors." *Journal of Gerontology* 26: 41-45.
  1974 "Resistance to Change, Early Retirement Factors." *Journal of Gerontology* 1: 33-41.
Portnoi, V. A.
  1981 "The Natural History of Retirement: Mainly Good News." *Journal of the American Medical Association* 245: 1752-54.
Poser, E. G., and M. L. Engels
  1983 "Self-efficacy Assessment and Peer Group Assistance in a Preretirement Intervention." *Educational Gerontology* 9: 159-69.
Powers, E.A., P. M. Keith, and W. J. Goudy
  1980 "A Panel Study of Nonmetropolitan Older Workers." *Aging and Work* 3: 163-74.
Price, K. F., J. W. Walker, and D. C. Kimmel
  1979 "Retirement Timing and Retirement Satisfaction." *Aging and Work* 2: 235-45.

Price-Bonham, S., and C. K. Johnson
  1982 "Attitudes Toward Retirement: A Comparison of Professional and Nonprofessional Married Women." In *Women's Retirement,* edited by M. Szinovacz. Beverly Hills, Cal.: Sage.
Prothero, J., and L. R. Beach
  1984 "Retirement Decisions: Expectations, Intention, and Action." *Journal of Applied Social Psychology* 14: 162-74.
Quinn, J. F.
  1977 "Microeconomic Determinants of Early Retirement: A Cross-sectional View of White Married Men." *Journal of Human Resources* 12: 329-46.
Raffel, J.
  1980 "Combating Employee Resistance to Retirement Planning Seminars." *Personnel Journal* Oct.: 845-46.
Reich, M. H.
  1977 "Group Preretirement Education Programs: Whither the Proliferation?" *Industrial Gerontology* 4: 29-43.
Reichard, S., F. Livson, and P. G. Peterson
  1962 *Aging and Personality.* New York: John Wiley
Reid, D. W., G. Haas, and D. Hawkings
  1977 "Locus of Desired Control and Positive Self-concept of the Elderly." *Journal of Gerontology* 32: 441-50.
Reno, V.
  1971 "Why Men Stop Working at or Before Age 65: Findings From the Survey of New Beneficiaries." *Social Security Bulletin* 34: 3-17.
Richardson, Virginia
  1988 "Crisis Intervention and Retirement." Paper presented at the National Association of Social Workers, Philadelphia, Penn.
Riddick, C. C.
  1985 "Life Satisfaction for Older Female Homemakers, Retirees, and Workers." *Research on Aging* 7: 383-95.
Riddick, C. C., and S. N. Daniel
  1984 "The Relative Contribution of Leisure Activities and Other Factors Related to the Mental Health of Older Women." *Journal of Leisure Research,* 16: 136-48.
Riley, M. W., and A. Foner
  1968 *Aging and Society,* Vol. 1. New York: Russell Sage Foundation.
Riley, M. W., M. Johnson, and A. Foner
  1972 "Elements in a Model of Age Stratification." In *Aging and Society,* Vol. 3, *A Sociology of Age Stratification,* edited by M. W. Riley, M. Johnson, and F. Foner. New York: Russell Sage Foundation.
Roadburg, Alan
  1985 *Aging: Retirement, Leisure and Work in Canada.* Toronto: Methuen.

Rodwell, L.
1965 "Saskatchewan Homestead Records." In *The Workingman in the Nineteenth Century*, edited by M. S. Cross. Toronto Oxford University Press.

Rosen, B., and T. H. Jerdee
1985 *Older Employees: New Roles for Valid Resources*. Homewood, Ill.: Dow Jones-Irwin.

Rosenberg, G. S.
1970 *The Worker Grows Old*. San Francisco: Jossey-Bass.

Rosencranz, H. A., C. T. Pihland, and T. E. McNevin
1968 *Social Participation of Older People in a Small Town*. Columbia, Missouri: Department of Sociology, University of Missouri.

Rosma, G., P. Bondy, and M. Blehman
1985 "Modeling Retiree Life Satisfaction Levels: The Role of Recreational, Life Cycle and Socio-environmental Elements." *Journal of Leisure Research* 17: 29-39.

Rudd, D. S.
1984 "The Coverage Question in the Pension Debate." In *Pensions Today and Tomorrow: Background Studies*, edited by D. W. Conklin, J. H. Bennett, and T. J. Courchene. Toronto: Ontario Economic Council.

Ryser, C., and A. Sheldon
1969 "Retirement and Health." *Journal of the American Geriatric Society* 17: 180-90.

Salek, S. D., and J. L. Otis
1963 "Sources of Job Satisfaction and Their Effect on Attitudes Towards Retirement." *Journal of Industrial Psychology* 1: 101-6.

Sauer, W. J., and R. Warland
1982 "Morale and Life Satisfaction." In *Research Instruments in Social Gerontology*, Vol. 1, *Clinical and Social Psychology*, edited by D. J. Manzen and W. A. Peterson. Minneapolis: University of Minneapolis Press.

Saunders, R. E.
1897 "What Was the Family Compact?" *Ontario History* 49 (1957): 73-78.

Schmitt, N., B. W. Coyle, J. Rauschenberger, and J. K. White
1979 "Comparison of Early Retirees and Non-retirees." *Personnel Psychology* 32: 327-40.

Schmitt, N., and J. T. McCune
1981 "The Relationship Between Job Attitudes and the Decision to Retire." *Academy of Management Journal* 24: 795-802.

Schwab, K.
1976 "Early Labour Force Withdrawal of Men: Participants and Non-participants Aged 58-63." In *Almost 65: Baseline Data From the Retirement History Study*, U.S. Dept. of Health Education and Welfare, Social Security Administration, Office of Research and Statistics, Washington, D.C.: U.S. Government Printing Office.

Seccombe, K., and G. R. Lee
1986 "Gender Differences in Retirement Satisfaction and Its Antecedents."*Research on Aging* 8: 426-40.
Seidon, R. H.
1980 "Mellowing With Age: Factors Influencing the Non-white Suicide Rate." Paper presented at the 13th Annual Meeting, American Association of Suicidology.
Seltzer, M. M., and R. C. Atchley
1971 "The Impact of Structural Integration into the Profession on Work Commitment, Potential for Disengagement and Leisure Preferences Among Social Workers." *Sociological Focus* 5: 9-17.
Shanas, E.
1972 "Adjustment to Retirement: Substitution or Accommodation?" In *Retirement*, edited by F. M. Carp. New York: Behavioral Publications.
Shapiro, E., and N. P. Roos
1982 "Retired and Employed Elderly Pensioners: Their Utilization of Health Care Services." *Gerontologist* 22: 187-93.
Sharon, N., and E. Argov
1983 "Post-retirement Orientation to Work and Successful Placement." *Aging and Work* 6: 261-76.
Shaw, L. B.
1984 "Retirement Plans of Middle-Aged Married Women." *Gerontologist* 24: 154-59.
Sheppard, H. L.
1976 "Work and Retirement." In *Handbook of Aging and the Social Sciences*, edited by R. H. Binstock and E. Shanas. New York: Van Nostrand Reinhold.
Shouksmith, G.
1983 "Change in Attitude to Retirement Following A Short Pre-retirement Planning Seminar." *Journal of Psychology* 114: 3-7.
Simon, B.
1987 *Never Married Women*. Philadelphia: Temple University Press.
Simpson, I. H.
1975 "Review Symposium on *Work in America*." *Sociology of Work and Occupations* 2: 182-87.
Simpson, I. H., K. W. Back, and J. C. McKinney
1966 "Work and Retirement." In *Social Aspects of Aging*, edited by I. H. Simpson and J. C. McKinney. Durham, N.C.: Duke University Press.
Simpson, R. L., and I. H. Simpson
1962 "Social Origins, Occupational Advice, Occupational Values, and Work Careers." *Social Forces* 40: 264-71.
Skoglund, J.
1979 "Work and Retirement." *Aging and Work* 2: 103-12.

1980 "Attitudes Toward Work and Retirement in Sweden: A Multigroup Multivariate Analysis." *International Journal of Aging and Human Development* 11: 147-62.

Smith, T. W.

1979 "Happiness, Time Trends, Seasonal Variations, Inter-survey Differences, and Other Mysteries." *Social Psychology Quarterly* 42: 18-30.

Smyth, E. S., and M. Holder

1981 *"Ready or Not: Planning for Creative Retirement, an Evaluation."* Paper presented at the annual meeting of the Canadian Association on Gerontology, Toronto.

Snell, L., and K. H. Brown

1986 *Financial Strategies of the Recently Retired.* Paper No. 86-2. Guelph: University of Guelph, Gerontology Research Center.

Snider, E. L.

1980 "Explaining Life Satisfaction: It's the Elderly's Attitudes That Count." *Social Science Quarterly* 61: 253-63.

Snyder, E.

1980 *"A Reflection on Commitment and Patterns of Disengagement from Recreational Activity."* Paper presented at the North American Society for the Sociology of Sport, Denver, Colorado.

Social Service Council of Canada

1914 *Social Service Congress.* Toronto: Social Service Council of Canada.

Special Senate Committee on Retirement Age Policies

1979 *The Report of the Special Senate Committee on Retirement Age Policies.: Retirement Without Tears.* Hull, Que.: Minister of Supply and Services

Spence, D. L.

1966 "Patterns of Retirement in San Francisco." In *The Retirement Process*, edited by F. M. Carp. Publication No. 1778, U.S. Department of Health and Welfare, Institute of Child Health and Human Development. Washington, D.C.: Public Health Service.

Spilerman, S.

1977 "Careers, Labour Market Structure, and Socioeconomic Achievement." *American Journal of Sociology* 83: 551-93.

Statistics Canada

1982a *The Declining Labour Force Participation Rate of Men Age 55 and Over: An Examination of Possible Causes.* Labour Force Research Paper No. 24. Ottawa: Minister of Supply and Services.

1982b *Pension Plans in Canada 1980.* (Catalogue No. 74-401.) Ottawa: Minister of Supply and Services.

1982c *Historical Statistics of Canada.* edited by F. H. Leacy. (2nd ed.) Ottawa: Minister of Supply and Services.

1984 *Social Security: National Programs,* Vol. 3, *Canada and Quebec Pension Plans 1984.* (Catalogue No. 86-506.) Ottawa: Minister of Supply and Services.

1985a *Canada Yearbook 1985.* Ottawa: Minister of Supply and Services.

1985b *Women in Canada: A Statistical Report.* Ottawa: Minister of Supply and Services.

1987 *The Labour Force.* (Nov.) Ottawa: Minister of Supply and Services.

Stone, L., and M. Maclean

1979 *Future Income Prospects for Canada's Senior Citizens.* Montreal: Institution for Research on Public Policy.

Stone, R., and M. Minkler

1984 "The Sociopolitical Context of Women's Retirement." In *Readings in the Political Economy of Aging,* edited by M. Minkler and C. L. Estes. Farmingham, N.Y.: Baywood.

Stones, M. J., and A. Kozma

1980 "The Components of Happiness: Implications for Retirement Counseling." *Canadian Counselor* 4: 93-96.

Strain, L., and N. Chappell

1982 "Confidants, Do They Make A Difference in Quality of Life?" *Research on Aging* 4: 479-502.

Streib, G. F., and C. J. Schneider

1971 *Retirement in American Society: Impact and Process.* Ithaca: Cornell University Press.

Stull, D. E.

1988 "A Dyadic Approach to Predicting Well-being in Later Life." *Research on Aging* 10: 81-101.

Stull, D. E., and R. L. Hatch

1984 "Unravelling the Effects of Multiple Life Changes." *Research on Aging* 6: 560-71.

Sussman, M. B.

1972 "An Analytic Model for the Sociological Study of Retirement." In *Retirement,* edited by F. M. Carp. New York: Behavioral Publications.

Synge, J.

1980 "Work and Family Support Patterns of the Aged in the Early Twentieth Century." In *Aging in Canada,* edited by V. W. Marshall. Don Mills, Ont.: Fitzhenry and Whiteside.

Szinovacz, M.

1982 *Women's Retirement: Policy Implications of Recent Research.* Beverly Hills, Cal.: Sage. Tausky, C.

1960 "Meaning of Work Among Blue Collar Men." *Pacific Sociological Review* 12: 49-55.

Taylor, F.

1947 *Scientific Management.* New York: Harper.

Third Career Research Society

1976 *Retirement In Alberta.* Edmonton, Alta.: Alberta Department of Advanced Education and Manpower.

Thomas, L. G.
1975 *The Prairie West to 1905: A Canadian Sourcebook.* Toronto: Oxford University Press.
1979 "Fur Traders in Retirement." *Beaver* 310: 14-21.

Thompson, W. E., and G. F. Streib
1958 "Structural Determinants: Health and Economic Deprivation in Retirement." *Journal of Social Issues* 14:18.

Tolbert, C. M.
1982 "Industrial Segmentation and Men's Career Mobility." *American Sociological Review* 47: 457-77.

Townsend, P.
1981 "The Structured Dependency of the Elderly: Creation of Social Policy in the 20th Century." *Aging and Society* 1: 5-28.

Tracy, M. B.
1979 "Trends in Retirement." *International Social Security Review* 32: 131-59.
1982 "Removing the Earnings Test of Old Age Benefits in Canada: The Impact on Labour Supply of Men Ages 65-69." *Aging and Work* 5: 181-90.

Triandis, H. C.
1971 *Attitudes and Attitude Change.* New York: John Wiley.

Tuckman, J., and I. Lorge
1953 "Attitudes Toward Old People." *Journal of Social Psychology* 37: 249-60.

Tyhurst, J. S., L. Salk, and M. Kennedy
1966 "Mortality, Morbidity, and Retirement." *American Journal of Public Health* 47: 1434-44.

Vancouver *Sun*
1979 "Pensions Seen Behind Mandatory Retirement Fight." Nov. 29: A14.
1980 "Retirement Piggy Bank Running Out." June 26: A18.
1983 "Pension Revision at Expense of Seniors Won't Do." Feb. 10: F5.
1985 "The Best Will Leap at Retirement Offer." May 11: A9.

Vecchio, R. P.
1980 "The Function and Meaning of Work and the Job: Morse and Weiss (1955) Revisited." *Academy of Management Journal* 23: 361-67.

Vroom, V. H.
1964 *Work and Motivation.* New York: John Wiley.

Walker, A.
1981 "Towards a Political Economy of Old Age." *Aging and Society* 1: 73-94.

1983 "Social Policy and Elderly People in Great Britain: The Construction of Dependent Social and Economic Status in Old Age." In *Old Age in the Welfare State*, edited by A. M. Guillemard. Beverly Hills, Cal.: Sage.

1985 "Policies for Sharing the Job Shortage: Reducing or Redistributing Unemployment." In *The Future of Welfare*, edited by R. Klein, B. Blackwell, and M. Higgins. Oxford: Blackwell.

Walker, J. W., D. C. Kimmel, and K. F. Price

1980-81 "Retirement Style and Retirement Satisfaction: Retirees Aren't all Alike." *International Journal of Aging and Human Development* 12: 267-81.

Walker, J., and K. J. Price

1974 "The Impact of Investing, Early Retirement, Rising Cost of Living and Factors on Projected Retirement Patterns: A Manpower Planning Model." *Industrial Gerontology* 1: 35-48.

Wallace, E.

1950 "The Origin of the Social Welfare State in Canada, 1867-1900." *Canadian Journal of Economics and Political Science* 16: 386.

Wan, T. T. H., and B.G. Odell

1983 "Major Role Losses and Social Participation of Older Males." *Research on Aging* 5: 173-96.

Wan, T. T. H., B. G. Odell, and D. T. Lewis

1982 *Promoting the Well Being of the Elderly. A Community Diagnosis.* New York: Haworth Press.

Wanner, R. A., and L. S. Lewis

1983 "Economic Segmentation and the Course of the Occupational Career." *Work and Occupations* 10: 307-24.

Wanner, R. A., and P. L. McDonald

1983 "Ageism in the Labor Market: Estimating Earnings Discrimination Against Older Workers." *Journal of Gerontology* 38: 738-44.

1986 "The Vertical Mosaic in Later Life: Ethnicity and Retirement in Canada." *Journal of Gerontology* 41: 662-71.

1987 "Retirement, Public Pension Policy, and Industrial Development: A Time-series Analysis." Paper presented at the annual meeting of the Canadian Sociology and Anthropology Association, Hamilton, Ont.

Watson, W. H.

1982 *Aging and Social Behavior: An Introduction to Social Gerontology.* Monterey, Cal.: Wadsworth.

Wilensky, H. L.

1975 *The Welfare State and Equality: Structural and Ideological Roots of Public Expenditures.* Berkley, Cal.: University of California Press.

Winnipeg *Free Press*

1983 " UIC Benefits Used to Lure Retirements." Feb. 14: 1,4.

1985 "Inco Offers Incentives for Early Retirement." Feb. 13: 2.
"Golden Handshake' Offered Bureaucrats." May 9: 17.
"Help Lacking on Financing Retirement." June 21: 28.

Wolinsky, F. D.
1983 "Health Care Policy and the Elderly: Short Term Cures and Long Term Catastrophes." Paper presented at the annual meeting of the Society for the Study of Social Problems, Detroit, Mich.

Wolozin, H.
1985 "Corporate Power in an Aging Economy: Labor Force Policy." *Journal of Economic Issues* 19: 475-86.

Wood, S.
1980 "Managerial Reactions to Job Redundancy Through Early Retirements." *Sociological Review* 28: 783-807.

Yankelovich, Skelly and White, Inc.
1985 *Workers Over 50: Old Myths, New Realities.* Washington, D.C.: American Association of Retired Persons.

INDEX

59248

McDonald, P. Lynn
    Retirement in Canada